Rethinking Development
Strategies in Africa

Africa in Development

Volume 5

Series Editor: Jeggan C. Senghor
Institute of Commonwealth Studies
University of London

Johnson W. Makoba

Rethinking Development Strategies in Africa

The Triple Partnership
as an Alternative Approach
– The Case of Uganda

PETER LANG

Oxford · Bern · Berlin · Bruxelles · Frankfurt am Main · New York · Wien

Bibliographic information published by Die Deutsche Nationalbibliothek.
Die Deutsche Nationalbibliothek lists this publication in the Deutsche
Nationalbibliografie; detailed bibliographic data is available on the
Internet at http://dnb.d-nb.de.

A catalogue record for this book is available from the British Library.

Library of Congress Cataloging-in-Publication Data:

Makoba, Johnson W.
   Rethinking development strategies in Africa : the triple partnership
as an alternative approach : the case of Uganda / Johnson W. Makoba.
      p. cm. -- (Africa in development ; 5)
   Includes bibliographical references and index.
   ISBN 978-3-03911-948-6 (alk. paper)
   1. Economic development--Africa. 2. Economic development--Uganda. 3.
Non-governmental organizations--Africa. 4. Non-governmental
organizations--Uganda. 5. Microfinance--Africa. 6.
Microfinance--Uganda. I. Title. II. Series: Africa in development ; v.
5.
   HC800.M349 2011
   338.96--dc23
                                    2011032320

ISSN 1662-1212
ISBN 978-3-03911-948-6

© Peter Lang AG, International Academic Publishers, Bern 2011
Hochfeldstrasse 32, CH-3012 Bern, Switzerland
info@peterlang.com, www.peterlang.com, www.peterlang.net

Printed in Germany

To my wife, Karen, and daughters,
Laura Namataka and Emma Ludesi,
for their love and understanding.

Contents

Acknowledgments

This book is the culmination of my research efforts and evolving thought process over the past three decades centring round the challenges and prospects for development in Africa. The study builds on my previous work on state and market strategies of development and celebrates a proposed triple partnership for development in Africa. This calls for the state, the non-governmental sector and donor agencies to collaborate in the development process.

I wish to express my thanks and gratitude to Dr Jeggan Senghor, Editor of the *Africa in Development Series* issued by Peter Lang International Academic Publishers, for his support, encouragement and helpful comments on the draft manuscript. I am also grateful to Professor Tim Shaw, Director of the Institute for International Relations, the University of West Indies (UWI), who read the completed manuscript, provided insightful comments and suggestions, and recommended it for publication. I salute Professor Goran Hyden of the University of Florida for his inspirational insights on the Autonomous Development Fund Model for improving the impact and effectiveness of aid in Africa. I am also grateful to Lucy Melville, the Publications Director and her team in Oxford, England, for the technical aspects of production.

I am thankful to all my colleagues in the Sociology Department at the University of Nevada, Reno, who have persistently encouraged me to write a book on development strategies in Africa, focusing on how non-governmental organizations and microfinance can best work. They have often heard me talk about these things and the theme has been prominent in my course on Third World Development. Because of their encouragement and support I was able to use my sabbatical leave in 2008 to embark on this book project. Now it is a reality.

My special thanks go to Jennifer Lowman, a graduate student in the Interdisciplinary Social Psychology doctoral programme at the University of Nevada, Reno, who served as my research assistant for five months. Her hard work, dedication and professionalism improved the quality of the research materials I used to write this volume. I am also grateful to Kathie Stanfield, my Administrative Assistant, for typing revisions to the final manuscript draft and assisting with the indexing. Jon Ashby copyedited the final draft of the manuscript and provided me with valuable advice on the presentation of the text. I wish, too, to thank Dr Jonathan Kelley for reading the initial rough draft of the manuscript and making useful comments on style and presentation.

Last, but not least, my heartfelt thanks to my wife, Karen, and daughters, Laura and Emma, to whom this book is dedicated – for their love, patience and understanding over the time I was doing the research and writing the manuscript. I am especially grateful to Karen for typing and retyping various drafts of the manuscript with great enthusiasm and a high degree of professionalism.

I am solely responsible for the views expressed and the conclusions reached in this book.

July 2011
Reno, Nevada, USA

Acronyms and Abbreviations

AAF-SAP	African Alternative Framework to Structural Adjustment Programs
AAS	Advisory Agricultural Services [provided by the National Agricultural Advisory Services]
ACIR	Africa Capacity Indicators Report
ADF	Autonomous Development Fund
AFCAP	Africa Community Access Programme
AFDB	African Development Bank
Afri Cap Fund	Africa Capital Microfinance Fund
AGI	Africa Governance Initiative
AGOA	[The US] African Growth and Opportunity Act
AIMS Project	Assessing the Impact of Microenterprise Services [USAID]
AMFIU	The Association of Microfinance Institutions in Uganda
APRM	African Peer Review Mechanism under the New Partnership for Africa's Development [NEPAD]
ARAs	Autonomous Revenue Authorities [in Sub-Saharan Africa]
ASA	Activists for Social Alternatives [microfinance in India]
ASA	Association for Social Advancement [Bangladesh]
AU	African Union
BRAC	Bangladesh Rural Advancement Committee
BRICS	Brazil, Russia, India, China and South Africa
BRI	Bank Rakyat Indonesia
CAADP	Comprehensive Africa Agricultural Development Programme

CARD	Center for Agriculture and Rural Development in the Philippines [an NGO and bank]
CBK	Cooperative Bank of Kenya
CBOs	Community-based organizations
CBTs	Community-based trainers in Uganda [established by CARE]
CBZ	Commercial Bank of Zimbabwe
CEM	[Uganda] Country Economic Memorandum
CEPR	Center for Economic and Policy Research [Washington DC]
CERUDEB	Centenary Rural Development Bank [Uganda]
CGAP	Consultative Group to Assist the Poor [World Bank Unit]
CMF	Center for Microenterprise Finance [Uganda; funded under the USAID-PRESTO Project]
CMH	Commission on Macroeconomics and Health [World Health Organization]
COD	Cash on Delivery
COWI	Consultancy Within Engineering
CPI	Corruption Perception Index [used by Transparency International]
CRBs	Cooperative Rural Banks [Sri Lanka]
CRECER	Credito con Educacion Rural [Bolivia]
DANIDA	Danish International Development Agency
DBS	Direct Budget Support
DBZ	Development Bank of Zambia
DFID	[British] Department for International Development
DREPs	District Resource Endowment Profile Survey [carried out in Uganda, 1999]
EBA	[European Union] Everything But Arms
ECA	[United Nations] Economic Commission for Africa

EITI   Extractive Industries Transparency Initiative

ERP   Economic Recovery Program [launched in Uganda in May 1987]

EU   European Union

EXIM   [Chinese government] Export-Import Bank

FDI   Foreign Direct Investment

FFH   Freedom From Hunger

FINCA Uganda   Foundation for International Community Assistance

FOCCAS   Foundation for Credit and Community Assistance [Uganda]

FSDU   Financial Sector Deepening Project in Uganda [British Department for International Development]

G8   The top eight (8) industrialized countries of the world

GDP   Gross Domestic Product

GNI   Gross National Income

GNP   Gross National Product

GOU   Government of Uganda

GSP   [The US] Generalized System of Preferences

HIPCs   Highly Indebted Poor Countries

IAMFI   International Association of Microfinance Investors

ICC   International Criminal Court

ICF   Investment Climate Facility

IFAD   International Fund for Agricultural Development

IFC   International Finance Corporation

IMF   International Monetary Fund

IPO   Initial Public Offering [of shares to the public]

IPOD   Inter-Party Forum for Dialogue [Uganda]

KIA   Kenya Institute for Administration

K-REP   Kenya Rural Enterprises Project Bank [a leading commercial bank targeting the microfinance sector]

MAAIF   The Ministry of Agriculture, Animal Industry and Fisheries[Uganda]

MABS   Microenterprise Access to Banking Services [the Philippines; funded by USAID]

MCA   [The United States] Millennium Challenge Account

MDGs   [United Nations] Millennium Development Goals

MDIs   Deposit-taking Microfinance Institutions [established in Uganda in 2003]

MFA   [Norwegian] Ministry of Foreign Affairs

MFDP   Ministry of Finance and Development Planning [Botswana]

METI   Ministry of Economy, Trade and Industry [Japan; created in 2001 to replace MITI]

MFIs   Microfinance Institutions

MIP   Microenterprise Innovation Project [USAID]

MITI   Ministry of International Trade and Industry [Japan; created in 1946]

MIVs   Microfinance Investment Vehicles

MOFPED   Ministry of Finance, Planning and Economic Development [Uganda]

MOP   Microfinance Outreach Plan

MPs   Members of Parliament [Uganda]

MSC   Microfinance Support Center [Uganda]

MSEs   Microfinance and Small Enterprises

MTCS   Medium Term Competitiveness Strategy [Uganda]

NAADS   National Agricultural Advisory Services

NDP   National Development Plan [Uganda, 2010–15]

NEPAD   New Partnership for Africa's Development

NGOs   Non-governmental Organizations

NPM   New Public Management Approach

NPOs   Non-Profit Organizations

NRA   National Resistance Army

NRM   National Resistance Movement [Uganda]

ODA   Overseas Development Aid

OECD   Organization for Economic Cooperation and Development

OI   Opportunity International

OIBM   Opportunity International Bank of Malawi

PAF   Poverty Action Fund

PAP   Poverty Alleviation Program

PAPSCA   Program for Alleviation of Poverty and the Social Costs of Adjustment

PAT   Poverty Assessment Tool

PEAP   Poverty Eradication Action Plan [Uganda]

PEPFAR   [US] President's Emergency Plan for AIDS Relief Program

PFA   Prosperity for All Program [Uganda]

PMA   Plan for Modernization of Agriculture [Uganda]

PPP   Public-Private-Partnership [business model developed by the Uganda Investment Authority]

PRDP   Peace and Reconciliation Development Plan [for Northern Uganda]

PRESTO Project   Private Enterprise Support and Development Organizational [USAID]

PRIDE Uganda   Promotion of Rural Initiatives and Development Enterprises [Uganda Limited]

PRSC   Poverty Reduction Support Credit

PRSP   Poverty Reduction Strategy Paper

PSD/CB   Private Sector Development Capacity Building [financed by World Bank]

PSDSG	Private Sector Donor Sub-Group [created in Uganda]
PVO	Private Voluntary Organization
RFIs	Regulated Financial Institutions
RFS	Rural Farmer's Scheme [Uganda]
RFSS	The Rural Financial Services Strategy [Uganda]
RMSP	Rural Microfinance Support Project
ROSCAS	Rotating Savings and Credit Associations
Rural SPEED	Rural Savings Promotion and Enhancement of Enterprise Development [USAID Program, launched in Uganda in 2004]
SACCOS	Savings and Credit Cooperatives
SAPs	Structural Adjustment Programs
SD	Sustainable Development
SEEP	Small Enterprise Education and Promotion
Shs	Uganda Shillings
SL	Sustainable Livelihoods
SLF	Sustainable Livelihoods Framework
SPAs	Social Performance Assessments
SSA	Sub-Saharan Africa
SWAPs	Sector-Wide Approaches [for funding by donors]
TCDTF	Tanzania Cultural Development Trust Fund
TI	Transparency International
UCA	Uganda Cooperative Alliance
UCB	[Defunct] Uganda Commercial Bank
UCSCU	Uganda Cooperative Savings and Credit Union
UCSD	Uganda Coalition for Sustainable Development
UIA	Uganda Investment Authority

UMI	Uganda Management Institute
UML	Uganda Microfinance Limited
UNCDF	United Nations Capital Development Fund
UNDP	United Nations Development Program
UPE	Universal Primary Education in Uganda
UPPAP	The Uganda Participatory Poverty Assessment Project
URA	Uganda Revenue Authority
USAID	United States Agency for International Development
UWFT	Uganda Women Finance Trust
VSLAs	Village Savings and Loan Associations
WHO	World Health Organization
WTO	World Trade Organization
YES	Youth Entrepreneurship Scheme [Uganda]

CHAPTER ONE

Development Strategies in Africa: An Assessment

> What Africa requires is clear. It needs better governance and the building of the capacity of African States to deliver. It needs peace. It needs political and economic stability to create a climate for growth – and growth in which poor people can participate.
> — Commission for Africa Report, 2005: 65

> Africa's development and the welfare of its people depend above all upon the political commitment and the capability of its leaders ... and ... an international environment that is fair and supportive of their efforts. Currently, it has neither.
> — Africa Progress Report, 2010: 56

1.0 Introduction

Nearly three billion people in the world today live in abject poverty, most of them in developing countries, especially in Sub-Saharan Africa. The international community has made poverty reduction one of its top priorities, as exemplified in the United Nations Millennium Development Goals (MDGs), which, inter alia, aim to halve extreme poverty by the year 2015. Until recently, development aid has been seen as the primary tool to reduce poverty and promote development. However, this has proved inadequate both in reducing poverty and inequality, and in promoting sustainable economic development. As a result, the international community and governments in developing countries have embraced development-oriented nongovernmental organizations and microfinance as new agents for promoting *bottom-up* economic development and poverty alleviation.

In this study, we argue that the state, nongovernmental organizations and even the private sector, each working on its own and separately, cannot bring about the desired development in Africa. More importantly, the study contends that state and market failure in Africa call for a new paradigm that enables the state, the nongovernmental sector and donors, as well as the private sector, to collaborate in the development process. We discuss this strategy within the conceptual framework of a triple partnership which focuses on three major actors, namely the state, the nongovernmental sector and donor agencies. The establishment of a proposed Autonomous Development Fund model is seen as a new vehicle to promote and strengthen three-way collaboration among the three dominant actors in the development process.

Development-oriented nongovernmental organizations (NGOs) and microfinance institutions (MFIs) are regarded as the *third sector* and are located between the state and market (in terms of institutional space); they are seen as fostering the well-being of the poor and other marginalized segments of society. However, despite the growing popularity and importance of NGOs and MFIs there is a need for a tripartite approach that engages all three dominant actors in the development process – especially in Sub-Saharan Africa. The proposed Autonomous Development Fund (ADF) model would greatly complement these major actors by seeking to achieve the twin goals of greater aid effectiveness and increased accountability in African countries determined to pursue sustainable development.

In this introductory chapter, we examine three interrelated themes concerning the development process in Africa. First, we consider development in broad and inclusive terms and seek to link development to a human-centred approach. Second, we make a critical examination of the two dominant models of development – the state and the market – with a view to proposing a new model that includes development-oriented nongovernmental organizations (NGOs) and microfinance institutions (MFIs). Third, we analyse the role played by aid, trade, direct foreign investment and diaspora remittances in Africa's development.

Development is concerned with economic growth, poverty reduction and empowering people (Harper and Leicht, 2007). It entails improving people's economic, social and psychological status as well as increasing their capacity for participation in decision-making and in the development process (McMichael, 2008). Both market and state models of development in Africa are not only weak but tend to be *top-down*, and to discourage popular participation in development; they alienate or marginalize people, and often offer no real choices in solving the problems faced by the poor.

1.1 Development and People's Well-being

Development tends to be linked to economic growth rates and be measured in terms of Gross Domestic Product (GDP) and income per capita. This is due to the overwhelming influence exerted by economists (McMichael, 2008 and 2010; Hyden, 2007). But when considered in terms of economic growth rates or Gross Domestic Product (GDP), a country may be doing well in macro-economic terms, while its people, especially the poor and marginalized groups, may be suffering. As noted in the Africa Progress Report: 'Africa's growth needs to be measured not just in GDP figures but also by the degree to which it brings social benefits for all its people' (Africa Progress Report, 2010: 9 and Africa Progress Report, 2011: 8). Hence, high growth rates or GDP do not necessarily equate to improved well-being (Gertner, 2010). As will be seen in Chapter Two, Uganda's consistently high economic growth rates have not translated into substantial transformation in people's well-being.

The Human Development Index devised by the United Nations Development Programme (UNDP) may have problems, but it represents a vast advance over single indicators such as per capita income. The Index is a broader and more inclusive measure of the impact of development. Its basic composite index consists of achievements in three core dimensions of human development: (1) long and healthy life; (2) knowledge and education; and (3) material standard of living. In this sense, development is perceived as 'better material security, literacy, health and life expectancy [as well as] ... freedom, self-determination, and better life' (Harper and Leicht, 2007: 293). Development should be the goal, while economic growth and poverty reduction should be regarded as the means to achieve that goal. Unfortunately, current Poverty Reduction Strategy Papers (PRSP) – the cornerstones of African development policies – appear to view poverty reduction rather than development as the goal. Sustainable development entails 'growth with relative equity, so that the fruits of development are widely shared' (Harper and Leicht, 2007: 294).

An African Governance Index (also known as the Ibrahim Index) has been developed by the Mo Ibrahim Foundation, and works in a similar way to the Human Development Index. It is a regional index for Africa, and considers governance from the point of view of the citizen, measuring what economic, social and political goods and services citizens receive from both governments and non-state providers (www.Moibrahimfoundation. org/en/section/). Its basic composite is based on eighty-nine indicators grouped into four main categories: (1) safety and rule of law; (2) partici-pation and human rights; (3) sustainable economic opportunity; and (4) human development. It is suggested that an equivalent of the Ibrahim Prize for African Leadership could be awarded to recognize leaders and ministers who have a lasting impact in achieving these goals. The recent World Development Report emphasizes especially the need to eradicate corruption (World Development Report, 2011: 288).

Kimenyi (2010: 2) points out that the main objective of economic development in Africa should be 'lifting millions [of people] out of poverty and raising the overall human development.' According to the Commis-sion for Africa Report (2005: 30), development in Africa means achieving 'well-being, happiness and membership in a community'. Even 'the Inter-national Monetary Fund and World Bank, once ardent proponents of the neo-classical model, have come to the realization that development that does not improve the lives of poor people will only provoke resistance and crisis' (Rapley, 2007: 206). However, critics insist that the World Bank's support of targeted aid to the poor has less to do with poverty reduction and more to do with political stability.

A recent Ugandan NGO forum report correctly observed that what matters in human development is 'much more than the production of goods and services, or the rise and fall of national incomes'. It is about 'creating an environment in which people can develop their full potential, lead productive and creative lives in line with their needs and interests' (NGO Civil Society Organization Perspective, 2009: 11). There is a growing realization that development comes from what people achieve when they fulfil themselves in this way: it is the cumulative product of their endeavours (Hyden, 2008: 10). Hence, people are (or should be) at the very centre of the development process and development is (or should be) about people's well-being. The 2004 World Development Report supports this view, stressing particularly the potential of those currently living in poverty and how they should themselves have a voice in policy-making and in improving services. The dialogue would provide incentives for service-providers to improve their act (http://www.ebooks.ebookmall.com/). As Durning points out (1988: 1):

> real development is the process whereby individuals and societies build the capacity to meet their own needs and improve the quality of their own lives. Physically, it means finding solutions to the basic necessities of nutritious food, clean water, adequate clothing and shelter, and access to basic healthcare. Socially, it means developing the institutions that can promote the public good and restrain individual excess [or self-interest]. Individually, it means self-respect, for without personal dignity, economic progress is a charade.

In other words, development needs to be based on a respect for people's well-being, and well-being itself depends on feelings of self-worth and fulfilment, attitudes that need to be enhanced (Uphoff et al., 1998: 197).

In addition to having access to basic services such as education, healthcare and clean water, each individual or group should participate in community decisions and enjoy human, economic and political freedoms. In this sense, development has a dual impact – improving people's well-being and empowering them as well. Sen (a Nobel Laureate in Economics) in his work on *Development as Freedom*, 'interprets development as a process of expanding the real freedoms that people enjoy. [Achieving] freedom hinges upon the other determinants such as freedom for participation in public discussion, political and civic rights, provision for educational and health facilities, elimination of poverty, tyranny, social deprivation, intolerance and unrestrained power of the repressive states' (Pattnaik, 2008: 3).

According to Sen, improving human capabilities or agency improves both well-being (and thus development) and political as well as economic freedoms in society (Yee, 2003). Focusing on improving what Sen calls the drivers of growth, such as education and basic health, in turn, improves human capabilities (which he considers broader and more important than 'human capital' per se). Considered this way, the goal of development seems to be to 'enlarge the range of people's choices to make development more democratic and participatory' (McMichael, 2000: 3).

The human-centred approach proposed in this study – one that goes beyond the state and market models – considers development in terms of people's well-being and empowerment. The *bottom-up* approach used by most development-oriented NGOs and MFIs seeks to improve their clients' well-being and empowerment. According to Kristof and Wu Dunn (2009: 219), the 'bottom-up approach in development has repeatedly shown its superiority in bringing about economic and social change'. In sharp contrast, the state-led approach tends to be *top-down* and seeks to control and dominate people. In the same way, 'the hoped for *trickle down effect* [of the market has] generally failed to emerge' (Schmidt, 2008: 4). NGOs and MFIs are increasingly perceived as constituting a potential alternative approach to states and markets or as essential actors working in collaboration with them. NGOs and MFIs seek to achieve development while reducing poverty and inequality. Unlike states or markets, they are uniquely suited for the dual process of transforming and empowering marginalized segments of the population in African and other developing countries. The twin goals of improving the people's well-being and empowerment can more readily be achieved through a strategy that is people-centred. Such a strategy also tends to be democratic and participatory. And, as we discuss in Chapters Three and Four, microfinance empowers women, by giving them access to financial services and by supporting their participation in economic activity and decision-making at both the household and community levels.

1.2 The State and Market Strategies of Development in Africa Revisited

Two contrasting views from the state-market debate that dominated the 1980s continue to exert some influence today. First, market-oriented or neoclassical economists view the state or government as irrelevant and often see it as an obstacle to the development process. Hence, they advocate the reduction or elimination of state involvement in economic activity. Neoclassical economists consider economic growth to be a result of the efficient allocation of resources by market forces or the *invisible hand* (Makoba, 1998). In contrast, structural development theorists stress the importance of the state or government in guiding, regulating or intervening in the economy. Such proponents of state involvement in the economy argue that it is necessary to attain the goals of growth and equity.

Regardless of their political or ideological orientation, all countries in Africa accepted the almost exclusive role of the state in the development of their economies in the 1960s and 1970s (Shivji, 2005). At the time, there was a strong belief that state control of the economy would lead to rapid economic development as African countries had to 'run' whilst others 'walk[ed]', as the late President Nyerere of Tanzania put it (Smith, 1972). Furthermore, there was widespread reliance on an import substitution industrialization strategy (using parastatals) which was seen as an important tool to transform predominantly subsistence agricultural economies into industrial ones (Makoba, 1998). However for over two decades, African countries failed to deliver basic services such as healthcare, education or clean water and were unable to reduce poverty (Bolton, 2008).

The state was engaged in planning, managing and executing various projects and programmes, either directly through government ministries, or indirectly via a myriad of public enterprises. Overall, the development plans and policies of economic and managerial control undertaken through public enterprises failed to deliver the anticipated economic development. Development planning failed for three main reasons. First, the plans set unrealistic targets for both the public and private sectors to achieve within the plan period. The private sector was rarely consulted and the potential of the public sector was often overstated. Second, within the implementing government ministries, departments or agencies, there was a lack of both discipline and commitment to ensure that the priorities and targets agreed upon in the plan were effectively executed. Third, and perhaps most importantly, there was a *policy gap* or *policy deficit* between (on the one hand) policy design and analysis undertaken by technocrats on the basis of economic assumptions, and (on the other) policy decisions made at executive or cabinet level based on political considerations (Hyden, 2008; Bates, 1988). As a result, various development projects and programmes failed 'because design had ignored politics or politicians had ignored their responsibility to make calculations of costs associated with keeping activity going ... after the conclusion of donor support' (Hyden, 2008: 128).

Policies of economic and managerial control instituted in the late 1960s and mid 1970s failed due to several factors, including widespread corruption, economic mismanagement, patronage and lack of transparency or accountability, insufficient capital and lack of human and institutional implementation capacity. Critics of the African state argue that it has failed to promote economic development by being organizationally weak, predatory (rather than development-oriented), and engaged in patronage or rent-seeking behaviour. Both states and institutions in Africa are weak (this is the reason why donors call for both capacity building and institutional development). In spite of this untenable situation, reformers or technocrats on the continent (with the exceptions of South Africa, Botswana and Mauritius) have been largely marginalized, while political leaders who are mainly swayed by political considerations tend to play a more pivotal role in decisions involving development. Yet evidence seems to suggest that states with a high degree of administrative capacity concentrated in the executive branch with support from technocrats tend to have the desired implementation capacity (Rapley, 2007). Hyden (2008: 69) observes that the African state 'is not only weak as an organizational instrument, but it is also open to undue influences by political patrons representing [different ethnic] communities whose interests cannot be ignored.' Such ethnic or community interests tend to undermine the state or its institutions, rendering both counterproductive to national development. However, as discussed later, the social capital approach used by NGOs and MFIs that relies on trust and social ties, can channel ethnic and community-based interests or values (at least at the client or customer level) in a positive way.

Other critics insist that the African state has failed to deliver expected development results because it is predatory rather than developmental in nature. The African state is not a developmental state in the same sense as the Southeast Asian state, because it has problems such as: lack of autonomy from society or external control; ministers who rarely comply with formal rules or laws that constitute public authority; and public officials who take state resources for personal or private use. According to Hyden (2008: 70), 'the state in Africa is like a blind man sensing his way around and responding to constraints and opportunities set by others [both internal and external forces] rather than an instrument of development charting and sustaining new ways forward.' A strong developmental state model, such as the one that served the Southeast Asian countries so well, must be firmly interventionist with the authority, resources and capacity (both human and institutional) to guide or direct both the private and public sectors to achieve the desired economic development. Unfortunately, most African states are corrupt, inept and mismanaged; a few (such as Somalia) are failed states, and others (like Zimbabwe) are fragile or near collapse.

According to Meredith (2005: 687), 'at the core of the African crisis is the failure of African leaders to provide effective government. Few [African] countries have experienced wise or competent leadership.' Economic mismanagement, corruption and lack of accountability appear to have contributed significantly to the severe economic crisis experienced by African countries in the mid 1980s. For example, 'a report prepared for the African Union in 2002 estimated that corruption cost Africa $148 billion annually – more than a quarter of the continent's entire gross domestic product. [In addition], the World Bank has estimated that 40 per cent of Africa's private wealth is held offshore' (Meredith, 2005: 687). It is also reported that 'by the mid 1980s most Africans were poor or poorer than they had been at the time of independence, crippled by debt, mismanagement and a collapse of tax revenues. African governments could no longer afford to maintain proper public services or meet the basic needs of their citizens' (Meredith, 2005: 368).

In a recent interview, Sidya Touré, a former Prime Minister in Guinea (Conakry) is quoted as saying: 'We've got a standard of living that is lower than before independence ... In every town, there is no electricity, no water, nothing. The peasants are practising subsistence agriculture' (Nossiter, 2010: 4, 8). And in a statement lamenting a world full of contradictions and deep crises, the Second Synod of African Bishops noted bluntly: 'Africa is the most hit by the global economic crises. Rich in human and natural resources, many of our people [sic] are still left to wallow in poverty and misery, wars, and conflicts, crisis and chaos. These are very rarely caused by natural disasters. They are largely due to human decisions and activities by people who have no regard for the common good and this often through a tragic complicity and criminal conspiracy of local leaders and foreign interests' (2009: section 5). The same statement adds: 'whatever maybe the responsibility of foreign interests, there is always the shameful and tragic collusion of the local leaders; politicians who betray and sell out their nations, dirty business people who collude with rapacious multinationals, African arms dealers and traffickers who thrive on small arms that cause great havoc on human lives, and local agents of some international organizations who get paid for peddling toxic ideologies that they don't believe in' (2009: section 36).

The failure of the state-led strategy to deliver basic services and economic development provided an opportunity and justification for the World Bank and the International Monetary Fund (IMF) to impose neoliberal policies under the Structural Adjustment Programs (SAPs) in the 1980s. In the 1960s and 1970s Western economists had advocated that the state should serve as the engine of economic growth; but in the 1980s they saw the state as the cause of economic crisis and called for market-driven policies.[1] However, as we discuss below, the policies imposed by the World Bank and IMF contributed to a steep decline in Africa's economy during the 1980s – to the extent that this era soon became known as 'the lost decade' (Harper and Leicht, 2007; Meredith, 2005).

---

1   See Hyden (2008: 129–30); also Makoba (1998: 17–24) in which I discuss the political and ideological reasons for this paradigm shift in the 1980s.

The Structural Adjustment Program (SAP) promoted by the World Bank and the IMF set forth a series of economic reforms designed to raise agricultural commodity prices, remove subsidies, devalue local currencies, remove tariff barriers, privatize state enterprises, decontrol prices, reduce budget deficits and public borrowing, and lift restrictions on foreign investment. The central focus of these reforms was to remove the state from direct involvement in the economy.

The intent of the SAPs, based on the (erroneous) assumption that 'one size fits all', was to take state influence out of the market and assume that economic incentives alone would distribute resources where they were needed' (Hyden, 2008: 128). However, this approach, used by donors for decades has proved ineffective in achieving economic development or poverty reduction (Brown, 2009: 449). According to McMichael (2010: 235), this type of neoliberal development has become increasingly exclusionary. For example, the policy reforms of the 1980s not only contributed to state retreat, but significantly failed to benefit peasant producers and African economies in general. The reduced role of the state in the economy meant doing more with less, thereby undermining the developmental role and legitimacy the African state could have had. According to Rapley (2007: 223), evidence shows that poorer countries, especially those in Sub-Saharan Africa, 'need an expanded role for the state, beyond the confines permitted by neoclassical theory'. As a result of neoliberal policies, peasants were both marginalized and neglected. Hence, the expected transformation of the agricultural sector into a modern commercial or industrial sector did not materialize. To this day, 'peasants remain uncaptured in the sense that they have failed to respond to the new policies' (Hyden, 2008: 140). As we discuss in Chapter Two, the Poverty Reduction Strategy Paper (PRSP) and the SAPs in Uganda have failed to transform the agricultural sector or substantially reduce rural poverty and inequality. The failure of these reforms led to the Economic Commission for Africa's (ECA's) publication of the African Alternative Framework to Structural Adjustment Programs (AAF-SAP), which among other things, called for adjustment with transformation and the adoption of a pragmatic approach between the public and private sectors (ECA, 1989: iii). Rather than rely on a condition-based strategy that marginalizes the state and the people, the AAF-SAP envisaged an environment for sustainable development in which African states play a central role and the people are motivated and empowered to participate in economic development (Mehta, 2002: 64).

Overall, the neoliberal policies of the 1980s and 1990s have not only failed, but in some cases have caused more harm than good (Makoba, 2010 and Rapley, 2007). Arrighi et al. (2007: 330) show how, with these policies, there has been a sharp deterioration in the economic performance of African countries: the median rate of per capita income there has fallen from 2.5 per cent in 1960–79, to zero in 1980–98. Martin (2002: 38) confirms these disappointing (or nonexistent) growth rates, and a study by the Center for Economic and Policy Research (CEPR) based in Washington DC could only conclude that the twenty-year era of globalization and neoliberal policies from 1980 to 2000 'brought substantially less progress than was achieved in the previous twenty years' (Nyamugasira and Rowden, 2002: 8). Sachs (2005: 189) sums up the situation with the claim that SAPs 'had little scientific merit and produced even fewer results. By the start of the twenty-first century, Africa was poorer than during the late 1960s, when the IMF and World Bank had first arrived on the African scene, with disease, population growth, and environmental degradation spiralling out of control.' It is reported that:

> Half of Africa's 880 million people live on less than US$1 a day. Its entire economic output is no more than $420 billion, just 1.3 per cent of world GDP, less than that of a country like Mexico. Its share of world trade has declined to half of what it was in the 1980s, amounting to only 1.6 per cent; its share of global investment is less than 1 per cent. It is the only region where per capita investment and savings has declined since 1970. (Meredith, 2005: 682)[2]

---

2   See also Hyden (2008: 16). According to Hyden, 'as many as 40 per cent of Africans ... live on less than one US dollar a day, while as many as 75 per cent live on less than two US dollars a day. Africa's share of the poorest people in the world increased from 25 to 30 per cent during the 1990s'. Martin Meredith (2005: 681) observes that 'in reality, fifty years after the beginning of the independence era, Africa's prospects are bleaker than ever before. Already the world's poorest region, it is falling further and further behind all other regions.'

Africa therefore remains a marginal, unintegrated area in the global market (Hyden, 2008: 1). Even proponents of neoliberal policies such as the World Bank admit that 'while the poverty rate in South Asia fell from 52 per cent in 1981 to 31 per cent in 2002, the poverty rate actually increased in Sub-Saharan Africa from 42 per cent to 44 per cent and the number of people living in poverty nearly doubled' (World Bank, 2007: 18–19). Sachs (2005: 21) observes that 'poverty in Africa is rising in absolute numbers and as a share of the population, while in the Asian region it is falling in both absolute numbers and as a proportion of the population.' And it is estimated that 'three quarters of Africans live on less than US$2 per day. The vast majority live in rural areas and have negligible access to basic services' (Senghor, 2009: 11). Hence, compared to other regions of the world, Africa has suffered the greatest economic crisis since the 1980s. The plight of the African continent and its peoples since independence is an indictment of failed policies of both state and market to deliver economic development or improve people's conditions of living. It can be argued that neither the state nor the market has succeeded in developing the economies of the Sub-Saharan Africa countries – and there has certainly been no 'transformation' as once was promised (Hyden, 2008: 150). This is because there is no strong, dynamic state or private sector in most African countries; instead, we find weak political leadership and declining markets. As a result, the African situation presents a classic dilemma for proponents of both market-led and state-led economic growth alike (Makoba, 1998: 33). This is one reason why there is a need for a third approach to development – an approach through a 'triple partnership' involving the public, private, and nongovernmental sectors, supported by donors, all of whom could work together to achieve economic growth and reduce the poverty and inequality in African countries.

What has emerged since the 1980s 'is an even broader consensus that calls for governments to do what they do well and markets to do what they do well' (Rapley, 2007: 119). In a recent commencement speech at a US college, Sen explained how the two must back each other up: 'A well functioning market economy can make a huge contribution to the growth of incomes and living standards. In the absence of sensible regulations, the market can also yield a complete disaster. What we have to work for now is to seek an appropriate combination of activities of the market and the state' (quoted in Dillon, 2010: A22). Indeed, the intervention Western governments made in the financial market after the global meltdown it suffered in 2008 shows just how much controls from an effective state can be necessary (Cheru and Calais, 2010: 236).

What all this underscores is that it is unrealistic to analyse and seek to apply state and market strategies to the development process in terms of an either/or proposition. The Southeast Asian developmental state combined its authority, resources and capacity to guide both the public and private sectors to achieve unprecedented economic growth. In Africa, Botswana, a notable exception to the general norm, followed a comparable course. While most African industrial development policies in the 1980s were failing because of the SAPs, the Botswana state expanded its involvement in the industrial sector, thereby defying 'the thrust of the prevailing development orthodoxy, which claim[ed] that African states cannot enhance industrial development through interventionist strategy' (Owusu and Samatar, 1997: 17). An empirical study made by Owusu and Samatar (1997: 7) on Botswana's industrial policy shows that the 'policy has guided industrial development to: (1) diversify the country's economic base away from diamonds and cattle; (2) improve gender equality in industry; (3) increase citizen participation in the industrial project; and (4) improve regional, rural, and urban balance in the distribution of the country's industries.' In general, African states lack both autonomy and the capacity to undertake successful economic development. Hence, current efforts aimed at reforming the economy and improving governance 'should also be directed at increasing both state autonomy and the capacity to implement economic development' (Makoba, 1998: 38).

Since the 1980s, both neoclassical and structural development paradigms seem to have undergone *revisionism* or *rethinking*. This rethinking – which includes bringing back the state and redefining its role in economic activity – is largely due to the negative effects of structural adjustment, making the development debate more technocratic and less polarized (though still highly politicized). As a result of such revisionism within the neoliberal paradigm, the new focus is not on 'the notion of less state [or] more market; rather, the focus is on a *smarter* or *better state*' (Rapley, 2007:

4). In addition to 'smarter or better states', Africa needs strong institutions. The US. President, Barack Obama, noted in his 2009 speech in Accra, Ghana, that 'Africa needs strong institutions not strong (i.e. authoritarian) leaders.' Also, the neoliberals' concern with improving the state's administrative and technical capacity has contributed to demands for decentralization in order to bring the state closer to the people and to improve service delivery and accountability. This view of the state is not radically different from that of past development theorists who wanted a more decentralized approach to development, involving the people (Rapley, 2007: 6). Hence, the central question today is 'how [government] intervention can be made in a way that pursues national policy priorities in the most effective, least costly and most sustainable manner' (IFAD Rural Poverty Report 2011, 2010: 228).

Since the 1990s the World Bank has come to accept the need for a greater state role in economic development (Rapley, 2007: 136): it realizes now that even the success of market-driven policies requires effective state management. The state needs to be involved too in policies for targeting aid to the poor and protecting the environment, as has become increasingly clear. A way forward can only be achieved by 'changing the larger context in which the state and market co-exist and reinforce each other' (Callaghy, 1994: 215). As Sachs (2005: 327) stresses, 'all successful economies are mixed economies, relying on both the public sector and the private sector for economic development.'

However, despite an emerging consensus in development theory and practice favouring people-centred development, the neoliberal paradigm is still powerful, and it dominates at the global level (Hyden, 2008: 248). Above all, the implementation of development policies and priorities in Africa depends on political leadership – and this is currently driven more by the politics of patronage than by economic considerations or public interest.

1.3 The Need for a New Approach to Development in Africa

The failure of both state and market strategies to bring about economic development and poverty reduction in Africa calls for an alternative development strategy. New players such as NGOs and MFIs have already arisen. The retreat of state involvement in the development and delivery of basic services in the 1980s and 1990s caused nongovernmental organizations and microfinance institutions to emerge; they were needed to fill the *development vacuum* created. NGOs and MFIs are increasingly supplementing the retreating state in Africa (Harper and Leicht, 2007; Rapley, 2007). Surveying the poorest countries, especially those in Sub-Saharan Africa, Rapley has found that NGOs now play an even stronger role than states in directing development. There is a wide range of them, and they are indeed filling the 'vacuums created by state retrenchment' (Rapley, 2007: 177). Even critics of NGOs in Africa acknowledge that they are taking over the work of states which, following the imposition of SAPs, retreated from their responsibilities, creating gaps only the NGOs could fill (Shivji, 2007).

Sachs (2005: 24) very rightly points out that 'our generation's challenge is to help the poorest of the poor to escape the misery of extreme poverty so that they may begin their own ascent up the ladder of economic development. The end of poverty, in this sense, is not only the end of extreme suffering but also the beginning of economic progress and of the hope and security accompanying development'. For the extreme poor to survive and be part of the development process, they need financial services to invest in income-generating activities and have access to health and education services for their families. Development-oriented NGOs and MFIs are designed to provide the poor with opportunities to access financial and other services.

Microfinance institutions (MFIs) in particular, are better suited to bringing the poor into the economy and providing them with financial services such as credit, savings, and insurance. Lack of access to credit is seen as the most important obstacle to directing productive assistance to the poor. McKee (1989: 95) observes that 'credit is by far the most common *missing piece* identified ... Lack of access to credit is viewed as a significant obstacle. A central rationale for [MFI] programmes is that making capital available will itself unlock considerable self-employment, enterprise start-ups, and expansions.' Echoing the same sentiment, Panjautab-Drioadisuryo and Cloud (1999: 769) observe that 'credit is often the missing link for low-income families that try to make a living by operating small microenterprises.'

According to Moyo (2009: 132), 'beyond the direct capital injection [microfinance] puts into a borrower's pockets, it can also be a powerful development tool. Even small loans can boost business productivity gains and contribute to job creation and raise family living standards (better nutrition, better health and housing, more education).' In this way, MFIs can and do serve as the first step or rung for the poor to climb on the economic development ladder (Sachs, 2005; Sachs, 2002).

NGOs and MFIs seek to improve the well-being of the poor and empower them to participate in decision-making at household and community levels. Achieving the twin goals of improving people's well-being and empowering them is possible through a people-friendly, democratic and participatory strategy, the one often promoted by NGOs and MFIs. These bodies are located somewhere between the state and the market, thereby constituting a third approach to development.[3]

NGOs and MFIs cater primarily for the poor and other marginalized segments of the population such as women, children and disadvantaged groups like the disabled, youths with no prospects, and refugees. These are groups often excluded by both states and markets. Indeed, as one observer aptly noted, developmental NGOs are 'needed to cater for those groups whose place at the state or market table is not reserved' (Hyden, 1997: 27). 'NGOs play an essential role, by offering both material and spiritual support to people who are all too readily forgotten by mainstream society; and by acting as society's conscience vis-à-vis decision makers and politicians.' Often it is the NGOs that offer excluded people a place to become socially active, so they can become 'involved in activities which allow them

---

3   The third approach, also known as 'the third way', 'the civil society', or simply the 'middle sector', includes trade unions, associations and member-based organizations, cooperatives and religious-based charities. Here, our focus is on development-oriented NGOs and MFIs. In their developmental work, NGOs and MFIs are considered to be neither part of the public sector nor of the private – even though they often receive resources and support from either or both of these sectors, as well as from donors.

to perceive themselves as dignified and valuable human beings, an approach not always pursued by public social services' (Schwinner, 1999: 2).

The proposed new approach incorporates important aspects of social capital – that is, *solidarity* and *trust* within communities and targeted marginalized groups. Through NGOs and MFIs, the economic and developmental role of social capital in African society has been rediscovered. Social bonds, based on solidarity and trust, can and do play a critical role for individuals and groups trying to access financial services. Africa's strength lies in such social networks. They may be invisible to many outsiders and to insiders who do not look deeply enough into the structures; but the support provided through these complex social networks enables many low-income Africans to survive, and even thrive or prosper.

In a study of sources of investment capital for small industries in Nigeria, Segynola (1990: 262) 'found that 84 per cent of investment finance came from personal savings, relatives and friends'. According to a National Survey on Access to Financial Services in Uganda, 'more people borrow from friends, relatives, retailers and similar sources (54 per cent of borrowers) than from financial institutions (7 per cent) or informal financial groups (11 per cent)' (DFID/FDU Final Report, 2007: viii–ix). It is possible that President Museveni's call to replace social relationships dominated by tribal or sectarian ties in Uganda by exchange relations dominated by profit could be achieved gradually through microfinance (1997: 188–9). Also, the shared values and trust of social capital make it possible for NGOs and MFIs to lend credit to the poorest of the poor, who have no credit history or collateral. This is largely because NGOs and MFIs seek to harness and interface community values and needs in order to improve people's well-being. At the same time, MFIs relying on *joint liability* or *solidarity-group liability* are able to reduce financial risks and ensure high repayment rates. A highly successful scheme of this kind that caught the attention of the world was the 'Grameen Bank', conceived by the Bangladeshi economist, Muhammad Yunus. According to Moyo (2009: 126), the essential stroke of genius in this idea lay in 'converting ... trust into collateral'.[4]

---

4   Professor Muhammad Yunus was awarded the Nobel Peace Prize in December
     2006.

The social capital paradigm based on the Grameen Bank Model (which, over the years, has undergone various modifications and adaptations in developing countries) entails lending small sums, ranging in size from US$50 to US$300, to the poorest of the poor (mostly women). These are sunk into income-generating activities or micro-businesses. The developmental approach thus depends on 'the social capital that turns [money] and human skills into something productive on a sustainable basis' (Hyden, 1998: 10). MFIs using the approach are seen as the most promising tools in promoting economic development and reducing poverty in developing countries, and even in depressed areas of developed countries (Meyerson, 1997). Kristof and Wu Dunn (2009: 187) affirm that small markets and micro-lending now provide a powerful system, supporting people who try to help themselves: 'Microfinance has done more to bolster the status of women and to protect them from abuse, than any laws could accomplish.' By offering financial services to the poor, microfinance brings previously excluded groups and the *unbankable* poor into the economy, and includes them in a culture of borrowing and lending as well as in microenterprise development. An estimated '10 to 20 per cent of [rural] households in Sub-Saharan Africa derive more than three-quarters of their income from the non-farm economy' (IFAD Rural Poverty Report 2011, 2010: 185). Opportunities for the poor in the non-farm economy include microfinance services that provide 'either wage employment or self-employment, that can provide them with their main route out of poverty' (IFAD Rural Poverty Report 2011, 2010: 184). Hence, microfinance can provide the poor in developing countries with a foothold on at least the first step of the development ladder (Sachs, 2002).

Today, there are an estimated 10,000 organizations ranging from NGOs to registered banks which, together, offer over 1 billion US dollars' worth of microfinance loans each year to several million customers around the world. According to Moyo (2009: 132) the projection is that 'this amount will have to grow twenty-fold (to US$20 billion) over the next five years to meet projected demand'. Moyo also points out that, despite the phenomenal growth and expansion of microfinance, especially in Latin America, Asia and (to a certain extent) Sub-Saharan Africa, 'the industry has yet to reach 5 per cent of the customers among the world's poor' (Moyo, 2009: 132).[5]

In Africa, microfinance has not worked as well as in Asia or Latin America – 'because it is newer there, and the models have not been adjusted, or because populations are more rural and dispersed or because the underlying economies are growing more slowly and investment opportunities are fewer' (Kristof and Wu Dunn, 2009: 19). But in spite of slower growth the potential for microfinance is still great.

The effectiveness of microfinance relying on social capital embedded within Africa's culture would appear to challenge the 'economy of affection thesis' seriously. This is the thesis 'which claims that informal, community-based self-help solutions are not conducive to promoting economic development or a civil sphere in Africa' (Hyden, 2008: 159–60).[6] Against this, one can argue convincingly from the evidence that, with the help of non-governmental organizations and MFIs, Africans are increasingly rediscovering the economic and developmental role of social units, such as groups or communities (Makoba, 1977: 119). This is true at the level of clients or customers, though the impact of small social units may not extend to the level of management and governance. Above all, social capital in the form of trust, 'reduces transaction costs in the economy and thereby facilitates growth and development' (Rapley, 2007: 221).

The rapid growth of NGOs worldwide, leading to what has been described as 'a global associational revolution' (Salamon, 1994), clearly demonstrates their expanding role in the development process. The growth can be attributed to several interrelated factors. The first is the changing

5   There is considerable variance in estimates, however. Assessing the situation in 2007, Getu (2007: 173) wrote: 'there is a huge gap between demand and supply as only 130 million of the 600 million estimated potential global micro-entrepreneurs are currently being served'; and Hermes et al. (2007) estimated there were 3,122 MFIs serving nearly 113 million poor people. These figures suggest there is no agreement on how many poor people worldwide are being served by MFIs.

6   In his earlier work, Hyden (1998: 10) acknowledged that the norm of social capital, 'reinforced by social support, status, honour and other rewards, generates the social capital that generates development.' Hence, the way in which the ingredients of social capital are utilized or channelled is critical.

attitude of the international donor community towards development assistance. Such a shift in attitude has been brought about by the end of the Cold War between East and West (following the collapse of the former Soviet Union and the fall of the Berlin Wall), a decline in aid contributions from leading industrialized countries, and a new emphasis by donor agencies on targeting aid to the needy or poorest of the poor. The second reason for the growth and expansion of NGOs in developing countries and especially in Sub-Saharan Africa, has to do with the failure of both states and markets to deliver the economic development expected of them, or to provide adequate basic services such as healthcare and education. Hence, a wide range of NGOs has emerged to fill in the development vacuum created by retreating states and declining or undeveloped markets on the African continent.

In order to maximize the impact of development assistance in the post-Cold War era, the international donor community (including leading industrialized countries, the G7, and the World Bank and IMF), is channelling an increasing share of Official Development Assistance (ODA) through nongovernmental organizations and microfinance institutions. They are thought to do this through NGOs 'precisely because they believe that the ... [NGOs] are better at getting things done than government departments are' (Hyden, 1995: 44). Donors view such organizations as having the capacity, integrity and commitment to serve the poor and reduce poverty through self-help solutions that also empower people by involving them in their own development process. By contrast, African states that are perceived as largely corrupt and inept are seeing their role in the economy diminished and relegated to that of creating an enabling environment or a legal and policy framework in which the private sector and NGOs can operate more effectively.

The third reason for the growth of NGOs is that they are considered cost-effective and seem to make better service provision than the states they are replacing (Edwards and Hulme, 1996: 2; Debbington and Farrington, 1993: 202). In 1992, the World Bank estimated that some 15 per cent of all aid to developing countries was delivered through NGOs (Harper and Leicht, 2007: 313). International development agencies such as the World Bank, the United Nations, and USAID have called for more NGO involvement in programmes that have traditionally been implemented through the state or its weak institutions. Beyond calling for NGO participation in the development process, the same international development agencies are supporting or collaborating with NGOs in the implementation of various development and environmental projects in developing countries. The scope is global. The World Bank reported that in 1997 it supported or approved projects involving NGOs with a geographical distribution as follows: '84 per cent in South Asia, 61 per cent in Africa, and 60 per cent in Latin America and the Caribbean' (World Bank, Progress Report 1997: 49). In 2000, when the total amount of bilateral aid was US$9.4 billion, USAID is reported to have channelled about a third of nearly US$2 billions' worth of development assistance funds through NGOs for implementation (Chhotray and Hulme, 2009: 10). And between 2005 and 2009, an average of 10.5 per cent of overseas development aid went through NGOs in the same way (http://stats.oecd.org/).

As a result of increased donor funding, the share of ODA aid channelled through NGOs in developing countries rose to 35 per cent by the 1990s. In some African countries, NGOs 'now provide or implement more than a fifth of total aid flows' (Van de Walle, 1999: 345). The growth and expansion of NGOs and the level of funding in Africa is clearly reflected at the country level. It is reported, for example, that in Kenya, there are about 500 NGOs and in Uganda, the number of both foreign and indigenous registered NGOs is more than twice that number. Other countries in Sub-Saharan Africa have a large number of both local and foreign NGOs. As previously noted, the amount of funding they receive has grown over the years. According to Ndegwa (1996: 20), 'official aid to Kenyan NGOs amounts to about US$35 million a year, which is about 18 per cent of all official aid received by Kenya annually.' In Chapter Three, we explore the unprecedented growth of NGOs and MFIs in Africa, with a special focus on Uganda.

The fourth reason for their expansion is that NGOs are considered suitable intermediaries for promoting participatory grassroots development and self-reliance, especially among the poor and other marginalized segments of the population. Also, NGOs try to organize and involve poor and marginalized groups into their own development – hence, achieving the dual goals of improving well-being and empowering their customers.

The fifth and final reason for growth is that NGOs are perceived by donors as flexible vehicles for meeting a variety of human needs. And they also tend to be innovative –using mechanisms like the *minimalist, cost-effective approach* (popular with MFIs), *assisted self-reliance* and *participatory development.* Unlike states or markets, NGOs can adopt innovative, people-centred strategies like this because of their small-scale operations, their greater flexibility and capacity to mobilize resources from both private and public sectors; and also because they can motivate and organize people to solve their own problems. Additionally, within development-oriented NGOs, there are microfinance institutions that seek to improve people's well-being through income-generating activities and provision of access to basic services such as education and healthcare. MFIs seek to promote overall economic development and poverty reduction by 'bringing in new income from outside the country, preventing income from leaving the community, providing new employment opportunities and stimulating backward and forward linkages to other community enterprises' (Management Systems International Report, 1995: ii).

Despite their growing role and contribution to the development process, NGOs and MFIs should not be perceived as a panacea or 'magic bullet' for solving problems of development in Africa that have eluded states and markets for decades. Instead, we propose that NGOs, the public and private sectors, must combine their resources and work together in a triple partnership that seeks to bring about sustainable development to the continent and improved livelihoods for millions of Africans. Hyden has observed that:

> ... as part of the continent's ongoing 'Second Liberation', restoring the value of voluntarism to its rightful position in society is as important as any other aspect of this process. At the same time, voluntary agencies and NGOs must not be treated differently from private and public sectors. After all, each of them has its place in the more specific tasks of service provision as well as in the general challenges of national development. Thus, rather than placing all the eggs in one basket (e.g. the NGO sector), it is important to create the conditions under which all sectors and individual organizations within them, can compete on an even basis and stimulate each other to greater achievements. (Hyden, 1995: 49)

1.4 Role of Aid, Trade, Foreign Investment and Diaspora Remittances in Africa's Development

Although donors continue to channel aid through NGOs and MFIs, a large portion of ODA aid still goes directly to individual African countries. It is in the interest of both poor and rich countries that aid continues to flow to poor ones. In the age of globalization, 'poor countries cannot develop on their own, and rich countries will leave them to remain poor at great cost to themselves' (Rapley, 2007: 224). In his address to the Synod of African Bishops in September 1995, Pope John Paul II, called on rich countries to 'become clearly aware of their duty to support the efforts of the countries struggling to rise from their poverty and misery. In fact, it is in the interest of rich countries to choose the path of solidarity, for only in this way can lasting peace and harmony for humanity be ensured' (Pope John Paul II, 1995: section 114). For most Sub-Saharan African countries aid 'is still the largest source of external financing and is critical to the achievement of the development goals and the targets of the Millennium Declaration and other internationally agreed development targets' (Sachs, 2005: 217–18).

In 2005, different donors made a number of commitments regarding total aid volume and the need to front-load aid in order to expedite its implementation. At the Gleneagles Summit in 2005, members of the G8 pledged to 'double development assistance to Africa by 2010' (African Progress Report, 2010: 38). At the same summit, the rich nations committed to the goal of giving 0.7 per cent of their annual income (or GNP) as aid to Africa. In the same year, the Commission for Africa, chaired by Tony Blair, the former British prime minister, called for more development assistance. In particular, the Commission called 'for an additional US$25 billion per year in aid, to be implemented in 2010' (The Commission for Africa Report, 2005: 16). The EU also agreed, that year, to new targets for its Official Development Assistance and 'committed its members to increase ODA to 0.56 per cent of GNI by 2010 and 0.7 per cent by 2015' (EU Strategy for Africa, 2005: 36). Three years later, in 2008, the UN Steering Committee for Millennium Development Goals (MDG) estimated that Africa 'required some US$112.7 billion in annual public expenditure to meet the MDGs, and US$122.5 billion if disaster response and coastal protection measures are included' (Africa Progress Report, 2010: 58). At a recent Africa–EU Summit in Tripoli, Libya, the EU renewed its commitment to increase aid, reaffirming its pledge to reach the target of 0.7 per cent of gross national income by 2015. It projected giving a figure of more than 50 billion Euros in aid to Africa in the three years following the Summit (http://www.guardian.co.uk/global-development/poverty-matters/2010/dec03/europe-africa ...). In general, it is believed that much of this funding could be secured if Africa's development partners were to fulfil the pledges they made over more recent years, such as the financing ambitions outlined in the Copenhagen Accord, for 'US$30 billion for support to developing countries for the period 2010–2012 and US$100 billion a year by 2020' (Africa Progress Report, 2010: 58). In addition, if the twenty-two ODA partners provided the 0.7 per cent of their annual income, as they pledged in 2005, they would be in a position to meet or exceed the annual aid requirements for deserving developing countries, especially those in Sub-Saharan Africa.

In spite of the promises for increasing ODA aid to Africa, 'the G8 as a whole remains significantly off track with its aid commitments to Africa ...' (Africa Progress Report, 2010: 38). The global economic crisis that began in 2008 has led major Western European donors, such as Italy, to postpone or abandon their pledges. More importantly, most of the large donors, including the United States, the UK, Germany and France, are still far below their target of giving 0.7 per cent of their annual income as aid. As Sachs (2005: 217) reports, their share of financial aid as a proportion of rich-world GNP had actually gone down during the 1990s – from 0.3 per cent to 0.2. Some experts doubt whether there is any country or bloc that can ever provide adequate, on-target aid to Africa and other developing countries (Finan, 1992). Instead, such experts suggest that 'what interests the developing countries [including those in Africa] is whether and when [the G8) can achieve the United Nations target of 0.7 per cent of the gross national product in the form of official aid, what [the G8] can do to reduce their indebtedness, what import policy the [EU] will pursue ... what training ... experts receive ... and how the efforts of the industrial and developing countries can be better coordinated' (Finan, 1992: 133).

Under the Millennium Challenge Account (MCA), the United States sought to increase foreign assistance 'to countries that demonstrated the will and capacity to use the increased funding effectively' (Sachs, 2005: 218). During the 2002 Monterrey (Mexico) G8 Summit, President Bush promised US$10 billion over three fiscal years under the MCA fund, but this promise was not completely kept. There was not enough MCA funding for countries that were competitive and met the criteria, but more importantly, even with the promised MCA funds, US aid was still less than 0.2 per cent of GNP (a far cry from the target of 0.7). And President Bush's commitment in 2004 to scale US contributions to fight AIDS in Africa up to US$15 billion, with US$3 billion a year over five years has not been completely realized either. Although the US did not keep its promise to raise the level of funding to fight AIDs, the President's Emergency Plan for AIDS Relief Program (or PEPFAR), has 'since 2004 ... spent US$19 billion to help distribute anti-viral treatments to about 2.5 million Africans infected with HIV' (Tutu, 2010: A23). This represents one of the few success stories in US development aid during the Bush Administration. Recently, President Obama, speaking at the United Nations Development Conference in New York, is reported to have said: 'Instead of dictating development projects and goals to poor countries ... the United States [will] seek partnerships with local governments and organizations to give them a voice in setting their priorities.' He went on to say that the administration would focus on choosing development projects where it believed American involvement could produce sustainable economic growth. The US intended to team up with other governments and with rich philanthropic enterprises like the Bill and Melinda Gates Foundation (Sanger and Kramer, 2010: A11). Although the three-year pledges at a recent Global Fund to Fight AIDS, Tuberculosis and Malaria held in New York failed to raise the hoped-for $20 billion to pay for AIDS drugs for four million patients worldwide through 2013, the US pledge of US$4 billion (nearly 40 per cent more than its previous contribution) was more generous than that of most other countries (McNeil Jr., 2010: A10). AIDS activists who had hoped the US would contribute US$6 billion instead of US$4 billion were disappointed, arguing that the Obama administration's failure to show leadership on this issue 'took the other donors off the hook [as] everyone could aim low' (McNeil Jr., 2010: A10).

Within the donor, academic and development communities, there is a lot of scepticism about aid. Some critics believe aid has been ineffective or counter-productive; while others think it has been stolen or wasted. Moyo (2009), in her controversial book, *Dead Aid*, claims that development assistance over the last several decades has made Africans poorer and must be ended altogether. According to Moyo, 'the notion that aid can alleviate systemic poverty and has done so, is a myth. Millions in Africa are poorer today because of aid; misery and poverty have not ended but have increased. Aid has been, and continues to be, an unmitigated political, economic, and humanitarian disaster for most parts of the developing world' (Moyo, 2009: xix). Other critics of aid tend to blame both donors and African governments for undermining progress on the continent. External aid is viewed as increasing dependence on external sources of funding, while reducing government accountability to its citizens.

Although the flow of aid to Africa remains inadequate and is often condition-based, the aid seems to make African countries more dependent on external development assistance. About 50 per cent of national budgets rely on such sources of funding. Critics argue that as a result of such dependence, 'government officials, instead of looking to the domestic area for resources or solutions, address themselves to the international community. [And], governments in this situation become more accountable to foreign governments and international aid agencies than to their own citizens' (Hyden, 2008: 256).

However, despite this dependence and accountability to external donors, it seems both multilateral and bilateral influences are not as great on African governments as is often claimed. This is because African countries are members of international financial institutions such as the World Bank and IMF, and they tend, in effect, to deflect or ignore pressures and criticisms brought against them. In public, some African leaders use nationalistic rhetoric to mobilize their citizens against what they consider to be foreign interference or control in domestic issues. Such rhetoric sometimes works. The international community is less influential than it would like to think, not only when it comes to policy but also over issues of governance or democratization. It is reported, for example, that 'the reintroduction of a multi-party system in Uganda was stimulated primarily by internal conflicts between factions within the NRM exposed in the 2001 elections and much less by international pressure for democratization' (Makara et al., 2009: 199).

There are critics who claim that aid costs too much, because it increases debt and achieves too little when it comes to promoting economic growth and poverty reduction. 'While Africa's external debt still stands at more than US$200 billion, its share of GDP has fallen from above 100 per cent in 2000 to less than 50 per cent in 2008' (Africa Progress Report, 2010: 42). However, despite progress made through Highly Indebted Poor Countries initiatives (HIPC), the debt burden remains high, hindering development prospects for many African countries. Sub-Saharan African countries still pay out more on debt service – a repayment of US$1 for every US$2 received in aid – than they spend on healthcare. This is estimated at around 3 per cent of their annual income (Commission for Africa Report, 2005: 28). In addition, aid flows are not only small and unpredictable, but much of the aid goes to cover relief, technical support or debt cancellation. This leaves only a small portion of the aid for the development of projects and programmes. For example, in 2002, 'only US$12 billion out of the US$43 billion [in foreign aid] went to low-income countries in a form that could be deemed budgetary support; and thus helped support the package of basic needs interventions' (Sachs, 2005: 298).

Basing its conclusions on the evidence of effectiveness, the Commission for Africa Report claims 'it is simply untrue that aid to Africa has been wasted in more recent years' (2005: 28). This sentiment is echoed by a more recent Africa Progress Report which states:

> The last couple of years have seen increased efforts to improve aid effectiveness by overcoming donor fragmentation, promoting collaboration and complementarity, and aligning financing more clearly with country systems, strategies and policies. They have also seen new approaches to aid delivery and innovative concepts to maximize aid impact. (Africa Progress Report, 2010: 58)

More importantly, donors (with the exception of USAID) have shifted from project and programme funding to direct budget support (DBS), sector-wide funding arrangements (SWAPs) and Cash on Delivery (COD). As a result of the shift, donors are now more concerned with policy and governance issues rather than aid coordination. Furthermore, the new Cash on Delivery mechanism of giving aid is seen as attractive and innovative for African countries with weak accountability and transparency. The COD system proposes making 'a payment of a fixed amount of aid money to poor countries when they fulfil the pledges they entered into. It is innovative because it focuses on output instead of input, improves transparency and, more importantly, facilitates local ownership' (ACIR 2011: 188). But as Hyden (2008: 254) observes, 'these upstream issues do not require field experience; [rather] they call for analytical skills including computer modeling.' The move toward DBS, SWAPs, COD and other innovative public or civil service reforms, though positive, will not necessarily determine whether aid is effective or not. This is in part due to the continued prevalence of widespread corruption, patronage and inadequate state capacity to implement development priorities effectively. There is also concern that renewed donor interest in such innovative mechanisms for aid delivery may increase the development impact of aid without necessarily increasing its volume (Africa Progress Report, 2011: 47).

Good development practice requires consistent monitoring and evaluation and a careful comparison of goals and outcomes. However, as Sachs points out:

> Under current development practice, the IMF and World Bank have rarely taken on specific development objectives as the standards for judging country performance, and by extension, their own advice. Instead, countries are judged on the basis of policy inputs, not outputs. A government may be told to cut its budget deficit by 1 per cent of GDP. It is judged on whether or not it carries out that measure, not on whether the measure produces faster growth, or reduction of poverty, or a solution to the debt crisis. The result is a descent into formalistic debates on whether or not a particular policy has been carried out, not on whether the policy was the right one in the first place. (Sachs, 2005: 80)

The Commission for Africa (2005) recommends more external aid – massive aid on the scale of The Marshall Plan – to address the structural problems facing African economies. Furthermore, the European Council has agreed 'to double aid between 2004 and 2010 and allocate half of it to Africa' (EU Strategy for Africa, 2005: 6). Despite this, a prominent scholar who believes that aid neither makes the poor wealthy nor promotes society-wide transformation in developing countries, contends that 'improving quality of aid should come before increasing quantity' (Easterly, 2003: 29). On different lines, Hyden (2008) and Moyo (2009) call for less external aid and more local or domestic funding. However, given slow growth and low levels of tax revenue and savings, it is unlikely that African countries can achieve adequate local funding. This means African countries in the short and medium terms will continue to be dependent on inflows of aid.

At the level of the whole continent, the launching of the New Partnership for Africa's Development (NEPAD) in 2001, promised a new relationship between Africa and its development partners in addressing development challenges. Better governance and sustainable development are central to NEPAD's success. Member African countries have committed themselves to better governance and have voluntarily agreed to the African Peer Review Mechanism under NEPAD (EU Strategy for Africa, 2005: 4). Unfortunately, so far, most African countries have not submitted to the Peer Review Process and some, like Uganda, have undergone the process but have not yet released the results. In general, most 'African governments have always found ways of wiggling themselves out of such binds' (Hyden, 2008: 113).

NEPAD also challenges the governments and peoples of Africa to look at development as a process of empowerment and self-reliance. Hence, through NEPAD, 'Africans are appealing neither for further entrenchment of dependency through aid, nor for marginal concessions' (El Mansour Diop, 2001: 2). Instead, African leaders and their people want to determine their own destiny and call upon the international development community to complement their efforts. To this effect, several programmes and projects have been identified for implementation in collaboration with development partners. The Commission for Africa's call (2005: 17) 'for a partnership for development, based on mutual respect and solidarity or collaboration, and rooted in sound analysis of what works, fits perfectly with NEPAD's focus on collaborative efforts aimed at meeting Africa's development challenges'. And the EU Strategy for Africa (2005: 2) aims to promote the achievement of the UN Millennium Development Goals. Both initiatives are analogous to Sachs' notion of 'clinical economics which calls for a multifaceted approach to tackling development problems and forming partnerships or collaboration between the host African government and the international development community' (Sachs, 2005: 81). Ultimately, the effective implementation of NEPAD's programmes and policies will depend on the commitment and political will of the African Union (AU) and of individual African leaders.

The importance of aid, and the need for more of it from development partners will continue, but given its past record, it does not appear that aid alone can solve the development challenges African countries face (Rapley, 2007: 225). The notion that Africa needs *trade, not aid* for its development rings hollow and is inappropriate. In reality, poor countries like those in Sub-Saharan Africa need 'trade plus aid or both aid and trade' (Sachs, 2005: 281). Hence, it is not an either/or situation, as sometimes presented by proponents of trade and foreign investment (such as Moyo, 2009). In the age of globalization, Africa seems to be declining and falling behind other regions of the developing world, a situation partly due to its position in the global market; a position characterized by economic dependency (in terms of aid) and marginalization (in terms of trade and direct foreign investment).

Africa's share of global trade fell from 6 per cent in the 1980s to less than 2 per cent in 2002 (Hyden, 2008: 219; Commission for Africa Report, 2005: 27; EU Strategy for Africa, 2005: 4). Even though there was some improvement by 2008, when Africa accounted for 3.5 per cent of global exports and 2.9 per cent of imports (Senghor, 2009: 74) the share of global trade was still very low. This decline has been attributed to several factors including: trade barriers and subsidies imposed by rich nations; the composition or 'mix' of African exports; and internal trade barriers within the continent. For purely domestic political reasons, rich countries such as the United States, the members of the European Union and Japan, have created trade restrictions and barriers to keep agricultural products from developing countries out of their markets. In particular, agricultural subsidies provided to farmers in rich countries have a dual impact. According to Moyo:

> Western farmers get to sell their produce to a captive consumer at home above world market prices, and they can also afford to dump their excess production at lower prices abroad, thus undercutting the struggling African farmer, upon whose meagre livelihood the export income crucially depends. With the millions of tons of subsidized exports [from rich countries] flooding the market so cheaply, African farmers cannot possibly compete. (Moyo, 2009: 16)

African farmers cannot, then, compete with such cheap agricultural imports, while most African countries lose immensely in terms of export-earnings. For example, 'in May 2003, trade ministers from Benin, Burkina Faso,

Chad and Mali filed an official complaint against the US and the EU for violating World Trade Organization rules on the cotton trade, claiming that, together, their countries lost some US$1 billion a year as a result of the subsidies' (Moyo, 2009: 116).

Efforts by the US and EU to improve trade with African countries – via the US African Growth and Opportunity Act (AGOA) in 2000 and Europe's Everything But Arms (EBA) in 2001 – have had minimal impact. Although Africa is commodity-rich, the continent does not produce or export sufficiently diversified goods to trade on the global market. The composition or 'mix' of Africa's exports for over four decades has remained relatively unchanged (Easterly and Reshef, 2010). According to Senghor (2009: 74), 'primary products – fuel, agricultural commodities and minerals – make up more than 75 per cent of the exports of half of the [fifty-three] countries in Africa. Fuel is 60% of the continent's total exports.' In addition to lack of product diversification, the narrow range of goods eligible under AGOA and EBA, coupled with restrictions and the amounts permitted, 'dramatically minimizes those schemes' effectiveness' (Moyo, 2009: 118). It is also believed 'that African leaders have so far taken insufficient advantage of existing mechanisms to level the playing field, such as [with] the United States' African Growth and Opportunity Act (AGOA)' (Africa Progress Report, 2010: 56). As a result, only a small group of African countries and just a few sectors have been able to benefit much from AGOA (Bangura, 2009: 46–7; Nauman, 2009).

It is reported, furthermore, that the handful of countries AGOA has helped are mostly the oil-rich and larger economies. 'Nigeria, South Africa, Gabon and Lesotho account for more than 90 per cent of AGOA duty-free benefits; and of the total US$14 billion export value [in 2003], petroleum products accounted for 80 per cent with textiles and clothes accounting for US$1.2 billion' (Moyo, 2009: 118). In 2007, 'the real benefit of AGOA to some 40 countries in Africa, covered US$2.1 billion worth of exports, compared to US$1 billion or 95 per cent of oil exports' (Nauman, 2009: 1). AGOA, which is subject to annual congressional review, has 'flexible' rules of origin, but access depends on certification by the US president. Economic, strategic and political considerations are factored into any congressional review or presidential certification. Indeed, critics of AGOA claim that it is 'designed primarily not to benefit Africa, but to secure US business interests – even when this comes at the expense of the majority of African people' (http://www.citizen.org/April 28, 1999). It is the same with the trade programme called the Generalized System of Preferences (GSP) created in 1974, which is subject to presidential certification. On the other hand, the benefits and impact from Europe's Everything But Arms are considered to be more favourable than those promised under AGOA because EU markets are more open and accessible to exports from developing countries. A quantitative study comparing the effects of the EU and US trade policies on exports to developing countries concluded 'that the EU's trade policy for the poorest countries in the form of the EBA and the Cotonou Agreement, has increased exports to the EU relatively more compared to developing countries' exports to the US under predominantly the GSP and the AGOA' (DiRubbo and Canali, 2008: 5).

In spite of intended trade improvements for Africa under AGOA and EBA, Africa's terms of trade with the rest of the world under World Trade Organization (WTO) rules are not expected to improve at all. The creation of the WTO and the subordination of the Lomé Convention principles that allowed African countries access to European markets on the basis of 'North-South Solidarity' implies that trading will now be unequal and governed by rules biased in favour of rich and emerging countries like China. In addition, the WTO terms of trade 'are such that there are a few incentives, especially for agricultural producers, to embark upon improvements that would enable them and their countries to grow richer' (Hyden, 2008: 223). Hence, it should be imperative for African countries, with the help of donors, to ensure that benefits offered by the Doha Round on the Development Agenda are upheld as part of the final agreement on trade reforms. However, the Doha Round negotiations, which started a decade ago, appear to have stalled. *The New York Times*, for example, reports: 'while a tentative agreement was reached to grant preferential access to most of the exports of the least developed countries, it has been held hostage by a lack of agreement in broader negotiations between rich countries and big developing countries' (editorial, 2011: A24). At the moment, 'the positions of both the developed and developing countries seem to have hardened: the developing countries have argued that they have already made too many concessions in a previous trade round; the rich nations [insist] they will give nothing without getting something in return' (*The New York Times*, editorial, 2011: A24). Donor countries should support building Africa's capacity to trade and adjust to reforms in the global trading regime. In the final analysis, trade should not be considered in isolation from overall economic reforms; rather it should be integrated with other areas of economic reform.

Within the African continent, trade between the various nations is minimal. It is estimated that 'a mere 12 per cent of all African goods go to other African countries' (Commission for Africa Report, 2005: 53). According to Moyo (2009: 117), 'African countries impose on average a tariff of 34 per cent on agricultural products from other African nations, and 21 per cent on their own products.' High tariffs – together with institutional barriers such as excessive bureaucracy, cumbersome customs procedures, corruption and bribes – constrain intra-African trade. To increase trade between African nations, these barriers and institutional problems have to be resolved, and ultimately removed, with the creation of regional free trade areas.

In sharp contrast to Africa's share of global trade, Africa–China trade is booming. Bilateral trade between China and Africa multiplied fifty-fold between 1980 and 2005, quintupling in the years 2000–6, with a rise from US$10 billion to $55 billion. Michel and Beuret, who relay these figures, expected it to reach $100 billion by 2010 (Michel and Beuret, 2009: 3), a sum which Gadzala and Hanusch (2010) believe may have been surpassed already in the all-time high trading figures of 2009 (Gadzala and Hanusch, 2010: 2). China is now Africa's third most important trading partner, still coming behind the US and France, but ahead of the UK (Moyo, 2009: 120). Today, 'China alone accounts for over 11 per cent of Africa's external trade and is the region's largest source of imports' (Africa Progress Report, 2010: 12). Most of the trade increase appears to come from oil exports from Sudan, where Chinese companies have been active since 1995, and from Angola, where the Chinese made major energy investments in the years 2003–4 (DeLorenzo, 2007: 1). China 'desperately needs Africa's copious raw materials to fund its colossal growth – materials such as oil and minerals, wood, fish and agricultural produce' (Michel and Beuret, 2009: 7). In exchange for products such as oil and gas, China is 'willing to make long-term investments in infrastructure projects and industry where Western investors would want quick returns. China has a lasting vision for Africa, and its goals far exceed the limited scope of former colonial powers' (Michel and Beuret, 2009: 7). DeLorenzo (2007: 1–2) points out that, while any increase in trade with North America and Europe has resulted from preferential trade arrangements (like AGOA and EBA), the boom in Chinese trade is driven by *complementaries* between the two economies.

Although China's main focus has been on increasing trade and direct investment in Africa, it has also helped with development assistance (though not on the scale of Western countries). It is reported that in recent years, 'China has ... pledged to train 15,000 African professionals, build thirty hospitals and 100 rural schools, and increase the number of Chinese government scholarships to African students from 2,000 per year to 4,000 per year by 2009', and, furthermore, 'in 2002, China gave US$1 billion in development aid to African countries' (Moyo, 2009: 104). Chinese aid to Africa is expected to increase dramatically. It was set to overtake World Bank assistance in 2007, with US$8.1 billion reaching Africa compared with only US$2.3 billion from the Bank (ACIR, 2011: 187; DeLorenzo, 2007: 2). The promise is that the Chinese aid effort will double, and, unlike some of Africa's traditional development partners, the Chinese are likely to keep their promise (ACIR, 2011: 187). Experts with insider knowledge say that, through fear of competition within the development arena, the World Bank has established a Memorandum of Understanding (MOU) with China over cooperation on major infrastructural development in Africa. This is said to have happened in 2007, but details are still unknown. In general, Western aid to Africa is condition-based, while Chinese development aid is said to be increasingly linked to the commercial interests of the Chinese Export-Import Bank (EXIM). The increase in China's foreign direct investment to Africa has been impressive and appears to mirror the phenomenal rise in trade. It is reported that between 2000 and 2005, direct Chinese investment (FDI) in Africa totalled US$30 billion. By mid 2007, 'the FDI total had reached US$100 billion' (Moyo, 2009: 105). China's investment input into Africa includes direct government investment and investment from private Chinese enterprises encouraged or supported by the government. According to Michel and Beuret, China has:

a two-pronged partnership model, public and private, which aims to make China the number one player in Africa. Ambitious entrepreneurs break ground and invest, and at the same time, the Chinese government signs enormous infrastructure contracts with its eye on the exploration and extraction of precious natural resources. On the ground, it can count on a broad and organized Chinese diaspora support, which in return, is rewarded by Beijing. (Michel and Beuret, 2009: 36–7)

China's direct foreign investments are most visible at the country level. It is reported that in the first half of 2006, some 30 per cent of Chinese crude oil imports came from Africa (Moyo, 2009: 105). It is, therefore, not surprising that oil-producing countries like Angola, Nigeria and Sudan are the largest beneficiaries of Chinese investments – money is put into oil and infrastructure development. In 2004, Nigeria and Sudan 'received more than half of Africa's FDI – Nigeria over US$4 billion and Sudan almost US$2 billion, while the rest of Africa got around US$4 billion' (Moyo, 2009: 105). China has also invested heavily in other African countries and in non-oil sectors:

> [It] has invested billions in copper and cobalt, in the Democratic Republic of Congo and Zambia; in iron ore and platinum in South Africa; in timber in Gabon, Cameroon and Congo-Brazzaville. It has also acquired mines in Zambia, textile factories in Lesotho, railways in Uganda, timber in the Central African Republic and retail developments across nearly every city capital. (Moyo, 2009: 105)

It is because of these vast investments in almost every African country, that China's partnership with Africa has been described as a 'geopolitical earthquake or tsunami' (Michel and Beuret, 2009). And, despite its impressive appearance, China's investment in Africa still represents a small fraction of its total Foreign Direct Investment (FDI) stock. 'The Stock of Chinese FDI in Africa in 2005 was US$1.6 billion, which represented only 3 per cent of China's total FDI. Most Chinese investment was directed to Asia (53 per cent) and Latin America (37 per cent)' (DeLorenzo, 2007: 1).

In general, African political leaders view the China–Africa partnership as long-term and mutually beneficial to their countries. However, critics assert that the presence of thousands of Chinese workers and companies robs Africans of jobs and creates intense competition with Chinese entrepreneurs who are often supported by their government. Some critics allege that the trade with China is unequal and represents the dumping of cheap Chinese goods in Africa, thereby undermining local commerce and industry. Finally, there are other critics who charge that 'in the absence of deliberate and proactive African action, the outcome of China's ... involvement in Africa [may] turn out to be neocolonialism by invitation' (Cheru and Obi, 2010: 2). The U.S. Secretary of State Hillary Clinton in a recent speech to African leaders in Zambia warned them about the perils of creeping 'new colonialism' spearheaded by China and claimed that 'China's investment practices in Africa have not always been consistent with international norms of transparency and good governance' (http://www.voanews.com/). For most Africans, the Chinese connection offers a long-awaited opportunity for economic growth sought since independence in the 1960s. However, it is not clear whether or not China seeks to offer Africa a 'Chinese' developmental model that aims to counter the ghost of Western colonialism and replace the Washington consensus with a 'Beijing consensus' (a consensus focusing on economic partnership, abstaining from interference in the internal affairs of African countries, even authoritarian ones). What is clear is that China's bifurcated or mixed model at home parallels its FDI approach to Africa, which includes both government and private sector investment. And in most cases, private sector investment is government-funded or supported. According to experts, 'China runs a bifurcated economy: at one level, a robust and competitive private sector dominates in industries like factory-assembled exports, clothing and food. And at higher levels like finance, communications, transportation, mining and metals – the so-called commanding heights – the central government claims majority ownership and a measure of management control' (Wines, 2010: A6). Although China has undergone decades of economic reforms since the 1980s, Chinese leaders have 'never relaxed state control over some sectors considered strategically vital, including finance, defence, energy, telecommunications, railways and ports' (Wines, 2010: A6). As a result of its public-private partnership model, 'state-owned Chinese companies can depend on the Ministry of Commerce, which manages most Chinese aid programmes, to add sweeteners to bids for African government contracts or assets. [For example], a US$5 billion oil-backed concessional loan was a prominent feature of the massive energy deals struck in Angola in

2005–2006' (DeLorenzo, 2007: 1). Evidence gathered on China–Africa relations indicates that China's economic dominance affects economies in Sub-Saharan Africa 'differentially depending on their trade complementarity, industrial competitiveness, degree of export diversification and general economic resilience'. So far, the resource-rich and oil-exporting countries are 'the biggest winners' (African Economic Conference, 2009: 2).

For development in Africa to become a reality under the partnership with China, African leaders must be fully committed and strategically engaged with their Chinese counterparts. They must be prepared to negotiate from a stronger, more informed position than they are in currently (Cheru and Obi, 2010: 2). For example, they must set up negotiating conditions that win favourable terms for their own regions, 'just as China has done to Western companies that want to build factories in its special zones' (Michel and Beuret, 2009: 257). To achieve this, African leaders must summon up their political will and have the courage to put public interest (not self-interest) at the top of the development agenda. If they fail to seize this moment, it will mean that African countries will miss out on an unprecedented 'win-win' opportunity for economic growth.

While China's direct investment in Africa is growing at a phenomenal rate, direct foreign investment from rich countries has either stagnated or declined since the 1980s. Hyden observes that despite their riches in natural resources,

> African countries have not been very successful in wooing investors to the continent. Africa's share of foreign direct investment (FDI) in 1998 was only 5 per cent of all FDI going to developing regions. FDI as a percentage of Gross National Income (GNI) was less than 7 per cent. Twenty-nine states in Africa did not even manage to attract US$50 million in foreign investment. (Hyden, 2008: 17)

Although direct foreign investment in Africa rose from US$9.1 billion in 2000 to US$88 billion in 2008, the African share in global FDI stagnated, remaining at 3 per cent (Senghor, 2009: 80). The level of American FDI in Africa is very low. Currently, it accounts for less than 1 per cent of total American FDI. As Kimenyi (2010: 2) remarks, this 'does not reflect high levels of commitment to promote economic growth in Africa'. Barriers to investment include poor governance, inadequate infrastructure, skill shortages, small markets and ineffective public financial management systems (Senghor, 2009; Commission for Africa, 2005). However, despite these challenges, 'Africa's economic climate has improved and a more proactive approach is evident from many countries' (Senghor, 2009: 82): by 2008, they had collectively agreed to 715 bilateral investment treaties. It is argued that private-public donor partnerships will be important in improving the investment climate in Africa. The Commission for Africa recommends that:

> African governments must unleash the strong entrepreneurial spirit of Africa's people. To promote this, donor governments and the private sector should coordinate their efforts behind the proposed Investment Climate Facility (ICF) of the African Union's NEPAD program. This requires US$550 million from donors and the private sector over seven years to identify and overcome the obstacles of doing business. (Commission for Africa, 2005: 241)

Africa's traditional sources of finance, such as official development assistance and foreign direct investment, have generally proved to be 'inadequate and unpredictable' the World Bank pronounces (2011: xii). However, according to the same report, diaspora remittances over the past decade 'have increased strongly ... easing the foreign exchange constraint facing most [African] countries and becoming a reliable source of external finance' (World Bank, 2011: xii). A recent joint World Bank and African Development Bank Report (2011) states that 'remittance inflows to Africa [have] quadrupled in the twenty years since 1990, reaching nearly $40 billion (2.6 percent of GDP) in 2010. They are the continent's largest source of net foreign inflows after foreign direct investment' (World Bank, 2011: 47). A breakdown of the US$40 billion remittance inflows shows that Nigerians in the diaspora invested 57 per cent, Kenyans 55 per cent, those from Burkina Faso 36 per cent, Ugandans 20 per cent, and Senegalese 15 per cent (http://www.mwakilishi.com/). Such remittances are said to help in promoting economic growth and poverty reduction through 'increased investments in health, education and housing in Africa. Diasporans also provide capital, trade, knowledge, and technology transfers' (http:www.worldbank.org/). This situation potentially brings benefits for the country of origin, the migrant and the country of destination – all three (Brown, 2011: 20).

To profit from this, some African countries have established divisions or units within foreign ministries and embassies abroad to promote easy access to investment/development information, and to offer dual citizenship to facilitate travel and business transactions in the diasporans' countries of origin. Although the impact of these changes is not yet clear, 'flows to Sub-Saharan Africa are expected to grow [and] to reach US$24 billion in 2012' (World Bank, Migration and Development Brief #13, 2010: 8).

There are two important lessons to be drawn from high-growth emerging countries (BRICS) such as Brazil, Russia, India, China and South Africa. The first lesson is that the state needs to invest in critical infrastructure, target and support selected sectors and provide an enabling regulatory environment. In these countries, economic success has justly been attributed to 'the role played by the state in guiding the market, and the willingness of the state to intervene and experiment with [various] policies to revive the economy, compete in global markets and reduce poverty in the process' (Cheru and Obi, 2010: 3). The second lesson is that a 'growing willingness and ability to provide grants and concessional finance has increased the resources available to African states ... [and] most emerging partners are styling their commercial engagement in Africa as South-South cooperation, complementing it with increasingly comprehensive development initiatives including financial assistance, infrastructure provision, and training and education' (Africa Progress Report, 2011: 47).

Senghor (2009: 89) points out that 'trade and investment are vital to economic growth and the pursuit of long-term prosperity, but their direct impact on poverty is often slight.' On the other hand, targeted aid is critical for promoting sustainable development, or at the very least, providing the basis for increased trade and investment (both domestic and foreign). As Hansen and Twaddle (1998a: 19) observe: '[Aid] should be concentrated upon the task of removing bottlenecks as well as assisting employment creation measures, in accordance with ... wider development strategies ... worked out by government authorities.' The above analysis of the African development experience shows that aid, trade, foreign direct investment and remittances are critical for achieving robust growth and sustainable development.

The overriding assumption is that wider development strategies instituted by African governments should seek to mobilize and channel all domestic and international resources towards sustainable development in a methodical way. Economic growth and poverty reduction should be construed as the means, rather than the goal, for achieving economic development and improving people's well-being.

1.5 Structure of this Study

The next chapter looks at Uganda. It shows how, despite high rates of growth due to large infusions of aid over nearly two decades, there has been very little reduction in levels of poverty and inequality: improvement in the well-being of the majority of the population has not been significant. The Ugandan case is analogous to a 'growth without development' scenario (as opposed to 'growth with equity'). The situation has largely arisen because the NRM Government used donor support for policies that were neither pro-poor nor aimed at the transformation of the peasant-based rural agricultural sector, which supports four out of five households in the country. This is shown in the low investment-and-development budget allocation made to the agricultural sector. Additionally, various rural programmes and initiatives intended to promote growth have not only excluded the poor (especially subsistence farmers), but have been mismanaged due to political interference and widespread corruption.

Chapter Three examines the importance of NGOs and MFIs in seeking to achieve the twin goals of improving the well-being of the poor and promoting long-term economic development in the poorer African countries, again with a special focus on Uganda. Increasingly, NGOs and MFIs have been receiving large sums of development aid, aimed at achieving either the UN Millennium Development Goals (MDGs) or specific country goals of growth and poverty reduction. As a result, poverty reduction programmes in many Sub-Saharan African countries, including Uganda, tend to incorporate NGOs and MFIs in their national development processes. Within the nongovernmental sector, evidence indicates that microfinance interventions have the greatest potential to reduce poverty and to contribute to food security and empowerment of the poor, especially women.

In Uganda, NGOs and MFIs have been heavily involved in providing basic social services and solutions to poverty reduction. Although microfinance services reach an estimated 3 per cent of Ugandans, microfinance and small enterprises (MSEs) provide, between them, about 90 per cent of the total non-farm employment in the country. Roughly 70 per cent of microfinance borrowers and 65 per cent of active savers in Uganda are women. In spite of this, most rural women in Uganda remain unserved or under-served. Both donors and government have cut back their funding of MFIs in the country. In particular, when the NRM Government concluded that MFIs could not achieve either increased outreach or access to rural credit, it started diverting its funding to politically-driven savings and credit cooperatives (SACCOS). However, one vehicle for increasing credit to rural areas in Uganda that may have promise is the *linkage banking* being pioneered by Post Bank Uganda: there are mixed results so far.

Chapter Four reviews the literature on microfinance performance and impact assessment. The literature comes up with conflicting evidence about the impact of microfinance. This is due to three major difficulties: (1) the problem of what to measure and how to measure, often compounded by MFIs seeking a double 'bottom line' of financial and social goals; (2) the tendency to confuse performance indicators (such as outreach) and impact assessment indicators (such as income generation or empowerment); and (3) impact studies derived from embedded or integrated approaches that seek to link performance and impact assessment. In the past, donors and microfinance practitioners took differing approaches to impact assessment, because donors focused on institutional sustainability to justify funding rather than assisting management to learn and improve their operations. However, emerging practitioner-oriented impact assessment tools such as ImpAct or Progress Tracking, seek to improve service delivery – in other words, performance – *and* prove impact or track progress toward desired outcomes. Hence, they seek both to improve and prove the effectiveness of microfinance on poverty reduction and client empowerment. Additionally, the chapter discusses four levels of approach used to evaluate the impact of microfinance interventions: (1) the household approach; (2) the wider impacts perspective; (3) the benefits process approach; and (4) the livelihoods framework. While most impact studies confine themselves to the household approach, the wide impacts perspective focuses on meso- and macro-levels and broadens the scope of impacts to include both participants and non-participants. On the other hand, the Sustainable Livelihoods Framework and the Benefits Process Approach go beyond the economic impact of microfinance to consider social impact. Both consider the root causes of poverty and food insecurity as well as the direct and indirect impacts of microfinance on clients. The chapter argues that, while practitioners and experts tend to be divided over microfinance performance or potential impact, they agree about the ultimate goal of microfinance intervention, which is reducing poverty and empowering people.

Chapter Five provides an analysis of the ongoing controversial debate about the commercialization of microfinance and mission drift, and considers paths taken to commercialization in Latin America, Asia and Africa. The future of commercialization is also discussed. Commercialization implies using a market or business approach to achieve both sustainability and outreach; and, in recent years, it has provoked an intense and emotional debate within the microfinance community. The debate revolves around the potential for this process to trigger 'mission drift'. While the proponents of the commercialization thesis view it as the path to microfinance sustainability and outreach, opponents are primarily concerned about mission drift and the exploitation or abandonment of poor clients. Evidence indicates that the potential for mission drift is real, but at the moment it is not a threat to the commercialization thesis. The chapter also discusses claims by opponents of subsidies to MFIs who assert that subsidies reduce efficiency and prolong donor dependency, while proponents of subsidies argue that donor-supported large MFIs, like the Grameen Bank or BRAC in Bangladesh, have continued to increase outreach and achieve sustainability without commercialization. Hence, commercialization is seen as a necessary, but not a sufficient condition for sustainability and outreach.

Additionally, the chapter addresses two central questions concerning commercialization. The first question is whether it is a natural, even inevitable, process or whether it is is donor-driven. The second is whether or not MFIs are able to cover their costs while increasing outreach. The discussion of the first question draws on the experiences of commercialization in Latin America, Asia and Africa – experiences that show divergent trends. And the response to the second question uses the experiences of both commercial and non-commercial MFIs to indicate that both have achieved the twin goals of sustainability and outreach, but that this has taken several years.

Finally, the chapter argues that commercialization offers a rare opportunity to combine socially responsible investment with profitability (a combination experts in microfinance think of as the 'holy grail' of their discipline). However, private investors – unlike social investors – expect investments in commercial MFIs to generate high returns. As a result, some commercial MFIs, like Compartamos in Mexico, charge their poor clients high interest rates to fuel profitability for their investors. This is not only likely to blur the lines between usury and microfinance, as foreseen by Muhammad Yunus, but threatens the microfinance double 'bottom line'.

After considering the failure of both states and markets in Africa to achieve sustainable development, Chapter Six proposes a triple partnership based on an Autonomous Development Fund model (ADF) that engages the state, the nongovernmental sectors, and supporting donor agencies in the development process. The proposed approach would initially start in selected African countries committed to genuine economic reform and would complement, rather than supplement, ongoing government, NGO and donor development programmes and initiatives. Such a tripartite approach ensures that aid is neither controlled by donors nor falls into the hands of recipient governments. It seeks to achieve the twin goals of greater aid effectiveness and increased local control and accountability. The achievement of these goals would be possible as the model seeks to provide competent management and governance of the autonomous fund, develop strong internal controls and ensure accountability to a legitimate *external* entity (such as a country's parliament). Above all, the autonomous fund would be insulated from politics and government interference.

Chapter Six goes on to discuss some of the most important criticisms raised against the proposed model. It also considers recent and ongoing reforms of public institutions in Africa, including the creation of executive agencies serving as a *road map* or providing the *building blocks* for a developmental state and the eventual establishment of autonomous development funds. Chapter Six advocates discontinuation of the use of existing public and private financial institutions in Africa as intermediaries for ADF funds, as these institutions tend to be vulnerable to patronage politics and corruption – two major challenges autonomous funds seek to avoid. However, it is envisaged in the model that such pre-existing institutions and the executive agencies could compete for ADF funds on an equal basis. Finally, it is expected of the African state that it will continue public sector reforms as well as pursue a broad, collaborative development strategy focusing on subsistence agriculture, infrastructural development and the non-farm economy. Above all, NGOs and MFIs, like donors and governments, are required to rethink their strategies and roles under the new development paradigm.

Chapter Seven – the final chapter – provides a comprehensive overview and synthesis of the study and gives a summary and conclusions. Although development efforts in Africa have failed over the past three decades due to a variety of factors, the core of Africa's crisis is seen as the failure of its political leadership to provide good, effective governance and sound economic management. This, combined with great disappointment in neoliberal policies, has contributed to a new appreciation of how urgent it is to find a third approach – beyond market and state-led strategies – for the development process. The proposed tripartite model calls for governments, NGOs and donors to work in tandem to maximize the impact of development assistance. As the chapter points out, the success of the new partnership will depend on all the three major actors redefining their roles and relationships in the development process. More importantly, it will require a *smarter* developmental state and strong public institutions that are insulated from politics but operate within the legal framework. The proposed Autonomous Development Fund model is expected to improve the three-way collaboration of the main actors in Uganda and other African countries on the basis of mutual interest or shared developmental goals and priorities. It is also expected to increase professionalism and efficiency and to reduce corruption and patronage. To conclude, Chapter Seven suggests that the ADF model has the potential to provide the *retreating African state* with another chance to rediscover its relevance and return to the core of the development process.

CHAPTER TWO

Economic Reforms in Uganda since 1986

2.0 Introduction

The economic crisis that began in Sub-Saharan Africa in the early 1970s worsened in the 1980s, and Africa's economic performance during the 1980s was abysmal, with an average annual growth rate in GDP of less than one percentage point. During this period, Uganda faced a severe economic crisis, its economy teetering between decay and collapse (Hansen and Twaddle, 1998a). The economic crisis of the 1980s forced most African countries, including Uganda, to accept and swallow the bitter pill of Structural Adjustment Programs (SAPs) imposed by the World Bank and the International Monetary Fund (IMF). Between 1980 and 1988, thirty-three African countries had concluded Standby Arrangement Facilities, twelve had Extended Fund Facilities from the IMF and fifteen had Structural Adjustment Loans from the World Bank (ECA, 1989: 16). The National Resistance Movement government (NRM), which came to power in Uganda in 1986, resisted these economic reforms at first but, due to the severity of the economic crisis it had inherited, it soon relented and accepted them.

This chapter describes the economic policy and major reforms undertaken in Uganda since the mid 1980s. These policies were aimed at promoting economic recovery, development and poverty reduction and they were influenced by the neoliberal paradigm. However, as we discussed in the previous chapter, economic policies imposed on various African countries in the 1980s under the Washington Consensus failed to deliver the expected economic growth and benefits to the majority of the population. Overall, Structural Adjustment Programs (SAPs) diminished the role of the state in economic activity, and made the economic crisis in African countries worse.

Although Uganda has consistently enjoyed high rates of economic growth since the mid 1990s (doubling its GNP between 1992 and 2004), both income inequality and poverty have persisted or increased. This can be seen especially in the contrasts between rural and urban areas as well as between different regions in the country. There is much concern about this: increased growth, it is clear, does not necessarily lead to poverty reduction or the improved well-being of the majority of the poor – in Uganda, or, indeed, Africa (Mbele, 2007; UNDP, Management Development and Governance Report, 1997). A major study done by Deininger and Okidi (2003) has shown that, in spite of improved growth during the 1992–2000 period, poverty and inequality increased in rural areas as well as in certain regions, especially ones in northern Uganda (which had only recently emerged from nearly two decades of rebel-induced insecurity and political instability).

Another important study concludes that, despite Uganda's impressive growth rates in its macroeconomic performance and despite improvements in the social services sector, 'such redevelopment ... has not been uniformly experienced in terms of the country's different regions and classes, genders and generations' (Shaw and Mbabazi, 2004: 1). The same study goes on to suggest that 'Uganda now consists of at least two distinct yet interconnected "states" or "economies" ... the more prosperous central and southern areas of the country ... [and] the highly insecure and impoverished north' (Shaw and Mbabazi, 2004: 1). However, the poverty reduction interventions in the north under the Peace and Reconciliation Development Plan (PRDP) seem to be making some progress, though rather slowly (Ssewanyana et al., 2010). For example, it is reported that between 1992 and 2009 there was increased income inequality and a greater number of poor people concentrated in the northern and eastern regions of the country than in the central and western regions that have generally benefited from access to resources from the government, the private sector and non-governmental organizations. In addition, 'income inequality as measured by the Gini coefficient increased from 0.365 in 1992/93 to 0.408 in 2005/06. Growing income disparities are [also] evident between 2005/06 and 2009/10, when the Gini reached 0.426' (Ssewanyana et al, 2010: 11). Poverty and income disparities widened between rural and urban areas as well as between regions (AFDB/OECD,

2008: 602). Uganda's ranking in the UNDP Human Development Indicators in 2006 had even dropped a position to 145th (AFDB/OECD, 2008: 612). And in 2010, Uganda ranked number 24 out of 53 African countries on the Ibrahim Index of African governance, as mentioned in the previous chapter (http://www.moibrahimfoundation.org/en/section/).

2.1 NRM Government Policies from 1986 to 2010

The National Resistance Movement government led by President Yoweri Museveni took power on 25 January 1986 after a five-year guerrilla war. Under the NRM government, Uganda can increasingly be characterized as a hybrid or pseudo-democratic regime blending democratic and authoritarian tendencies (Ekman, 2009: 7–9). Although such regimes hold periodic multi-party elections, they tend to circumvent the opposition and reduce or control the interaction between citizens and opposition parties. Very often, the regime may manipulate or rig elections in order to stay in power. The government's recent use of excessive force against opposition leaders and protesters in the 'walk-to-work' movement, discussed later in this chapter, clearly reveals this authoritarian tendency.

The NRM government had a Ten-Point Programme for rehabilitating – or rescuing – the Ugandan economy, which was on the verge of collapse. Among the programme points, two focused on the structure of the Ugandan economy. The aims were: first, to follow a mixed economy model; and second, to seek to build an independent, integrated and self-sustaining national economy (Museveni, 1997: 217). However, after only three years, President Museveni abandoned the Ten-Point Programme and instead chose to implement the Structural Adjustment Programs (SAPs) imposed by the World Bank and the IMF (Kibikyo, 2008: 1). Critics of the government contend that Museveni and his compatriots 'sold out' to the Western neoliberal ideology of market-driven economic development. President Museveni (1997: 181) claims that his government 'did not adopt market economics as a consequence of pressure, but because [he was] convinced it was the correct thing to do for the country.' According to the President, the NRM acted in a realistic, pragmatic manner to avert an economic catastrophe: the shift was not ideological or made under duress. Others insist the NRM government had no choice, given the state of the economy, which was about to collapse (Hansen and Twaddle, 1998a). According to Brett (1998: 323), 'the influence exercised by the donors resulted from the new regime's economic vulnerability, which forced it to ask for support in 1986, and accept radical changes in its policy stance in 1987 before the donors would agree to support it through a structural adjustment policy.' During the 1986–7 policy debates, 'the inner core of the NRM leadership favoured policies which retained extensive state controls. However, these were rejected by the donors, who insisted that the Ugandan government accept a market-based reform programme involving devaluation of the currency, a reduction in budget deficits, liberalization of the marketing system and privatization of many parastatals' (Brett, 1998: 324). In the final analysis, it seems the NRM government did not act in a realistic or pragmatic manner to avert an economic catastrophe as it claims. Rather it buckled under World Bank/IMF pressure.

The NRM government launched the Economic Recovery Program (ERP) in May 1987 after sixteen months in office. The goals of the ERP, which lasted until 1995, were 'restoring economic stability, establishing more realistic prices for primary products and rehabilitating the country's productive and social infrastructure' (Hansen and Twaddle, 1986b: 8). Positive aspects of the ERP were evident primarily at the macro-economic level. For example, the growth rate improved 'from negative growth in 1985 to 2 per cent per annum in 1986 to 10 per cent in 1995, while inflation ... dropped to 5 per cent from 240 per cent in 1986' (Museveni, 1997: 182). However, critics argue that 'the first SAP to be imposed on the country paid far too little attention to either the poverty dimension or to social expenditure, because of its predominantly macro-economic character' (Hansen and Twaddle, 1998b: 14). As a result, the ERP did not reduce poverty or improve the well-being of most Ugandans. Indeed, levels of poverty remained high and access to health and education was minimal. To attend to the needs of the poor, there was a heavy reliance on NGOs and community-based organizations (CBOs) as well as local 'Resistance Councils'. For example, the *Entandikwa* Credit Scheme or 'Seed Money', which started up in 1994, gave each constituency a loan of 30 million Ugandan shillings (equivalent to US$30,000), making the total for the whole country about US$6 million. Although the scheme was intended to serve as a *revolving loan fund*, providing more people with access to funds, it was implemented through Resistance Councils, and thus heavily politicized as recipients considered the funds a *political gift* from the NRM government and never repaid the loan. The scheme failed miserably due to a combination of failure to repay and misuse of loan funds.

Hansen and Twaddle (1998b: 9) observe that during this period, 'the song was still one of state retreat, but not of complete retreat from the economic sphere. Also, the needs of the poorest people (who at least benefited by the structural adjustment policies in the short term), were now recognized.' Social sector needs were salient because of security concerns over the 50,000 demobilized National Resistance Army (NRA) soldiers and hundreds of retrenched civil servants. The Program for Alleviation of Poverty and the Social Costs of Adjustment (PAPSCA) was launched by the World Bank and the IMF to ameliorate the *harsh effects* of structural adjustment programmes on the poor and marginalized segments of the population. The PAPSCA programme, implemented primarily through international and local NGOs, engaged in income-generating activities and employment creation enterprises, received little donor funding and is considered to have had little impact on the poor.

Donors such as the Danish International Development Agency (DANIDA) and the World Bank went to the extent of making the redirection of funds to the social sector an additional condition of assistance to Uganda. The policy of redirecting funds to the social sector was declared in 1995 at the Social Summit in Copenhagen 'where the 20:20 principle was introduced whereby donors would allocate 20 per cent of all their aid to health and education in return for the recipient government itself allocating 20 per cent of its budget to the same sectors' (Hansen and Twaddle, 1998b: 9). It was not possible to sustain this expenditure due to inadequate government revenue. More importantly, support for the social sector seems to have been driven by security concerns over demobilized soldiers and retrenched civil servants, rather than a desire on the part of donors and the NRM government to address the problems of the poor. The NRM government desperately needed large sums of money to compensate the demobilized soldiers and retrenched civil servants so as to avoid the threat of political unrest in the country. Hence, the increased social assistance from 1987 to 1995 seems to have been diverted from the poor to payments made to achieve some internal political stability.

Privatization, one aspect of the first SAP policies undertaken by the NRM government in 1992 at the behest of the World Bank and IMF, may have contributed to Uganda's high annual growth rates of 7–8 per cent per annum. However, evidence shows that privatization has not significantly increased employment opportunities, or even encouraged any growth in Ugandan entrepreneurs. Privatization has done nothing to reduce poverty (Hansen and Twaddle, 1998b: 14). Finally, due to widespread corruption, privatization has failed to add significantly to the NRM government's revenue and savings (Kibikyo, 2008: 18–19).

It appears that President Museveni was not only attracted to the private sector as the engine of economic growth from the beginning but that, over time, he has become an ardent supporter of neoliberal policies, seeing them as the only way out of Uganda's economic crisis. In his view, the role of the state or government in Uganda is 'to ensure peace and to build the infrastructure such as constructing roads because these problems are too large for the private sector to solve. Once the government has done that, then the individual must do his part' (Museveni, 1998: 184). The President came to believe that the private sector, by freeing prices for agricultural producers, can help transform Uganda's rural sector and thereby eliminate rural poverty. According to him the NRM government:

> has advised people to survey the market and if the price of a particular crop goes down, they should switch to another one. In other words, they should receive maximum returns from their plots of land. The source of poverty in this respect has been small-scale farmers producing low-value crops on a small-scale and being unable to balance their households' budgets as a result. (Museveni, 1998: 183)

The President also seems to have confused *sectarian tendencies* in Uganda with support for continued subsistence farming, which he sees as an obstacle to the modernization of agriculture in the country. He has therefore come to the erroneous conclusion that, by undermining sectarianism or tribalism, he could liberate the land from subsistence farmers. This, he thought, should happen as social or community relationships, associated with sectarianism and tribal groups, were replaced by exchange (economic) relationships focusing on economic interests. The President asserted that 'when subsistence farming is undermined and the exchange of commodities is introduced, there will be more efficiency and, in time, savings, which will in turn result in investable capital. Eventually, the society will be transformed and modernized. The moment that process takes place, one's tribe or religion ceases to be of much consequence' (Museveni, 1997: 189).

However, this is not what has actually transpired. With increased poverty and inequality in Uganda, sectarian tendencies have *intensified*, contrary to the President's predictions. The experience of the Green Revolution in Asia clearly shows that the transformation of subsistence farming depends on state help to introduce new high yield seeds, irrigation and use of fertilizers, rather than on efforts to undermine existing social or cultural values (Sachs, 2005: 70). Medium and large-scale farmers in Uganda – a tiny minority of politically well-connected individuals – can survive and thrive in the market-driven economy that the President talks about. But this does not seem to apply to the majority of subsistence farmers throughout the country, who are trapped in a vicious cycle of poverty. Such producers need and deserve government support with agricultural inputs and with finding markets for their produce, so they can receive *market prices* as opposed to the low *farm-gate prices* offered by middlemen.

At a rhetorical level and in their manifestos, almost all African countries stress the key role of the agricultural/rural sector in modernization efforts. In reality, however, 'there is not yet the basic conviction among many African policy-makers that the small-holder agricultural sector can and will have to be the engine of broad based economic development and eventual modernization' (Lele, 1984: 439). Very often, peasant agriculture is perceived as a *holding sector*, that is, a *stop-gap* measure to ensure rural welfare and employment until industrialization and commercial agriculture can absorb the surplus labour on the land. It is, therefore, not surprising that the agricultural sector is a low priority in planned development expenditure. Modernization plans for agriculture do not seem to focus on peasant and subsistence agriculture; rather they put their emphasis on industrialization and commercial farming. The analysis of Uganda's Plan for Modernization of Agriculture (PMA) considered later in this section demonstrates this all too well.

2.1.1 From SAPs to PEAP/PRSP

Structural Adjustment Programs (SAPs) dominated the earlier part of the 1980s, before the launching of the Economic Recovery Program (ERP) at the end of the decade. The ERP, considered the 'first SAP' under the NRM government, lasted until the late 1990s. A Poverty Eradication Action Plan (PEAP), originally established during the 1995–7 period, was revised, updated and approved by the World Bank as Uganda's Poverty Reduction Strategy Paper (PRSP) in 2000. The PEAP had four pillars, namely: (1) sustainable economic growth and structural transformation; (2) good governance and security; (3) increased ability of the poor to raise their incomes; and (4) enhanced quality of life for the poor (Kamanyi, 2003: 2). However, the primary focus of the Plan was to reduce poverty from 44 per cent in 1997 to 10 per cent by 2017 (Nyamugasira and Rowden, 2002: 1). The PEAP served as an overarching framework for government policy and budgetary decisions and allowed limited stakeholder participation and monitoring of its operations.

A variety of initiatives between 1997 and 2000, such as the Poverty Action Fund (PAF) and the Participatory Poverty Assessment Project (UPPAP), helped to institutionalize and operationalize the PEAP. The PAF was specifically created, using debt-relief funds under the Highly Indebted Poor Countries scheme (HIPCS), to supplement the government's education and health budgets. Although the debt relief plan saves Uganda US$90 million annually, it can safely be said that these savings are not adequate to meet the funding needs of education, health, and the infrastructure needed for them (Makoba, 2010: 91). And even if some of these funds were used to create Universal Primary Education (UPE), primary education throughout the country is characterized by overcrowded classrooms, poor teacher-student ratios, poor quality of learning and poor results. This is shown in the 2008 Primary Leaving Examination results:

'only 17,021 pupils out of 463,631 passed in division one, an almost 50 per cent drop compared to 2007 results which returned 31,985 first grades out of 404,985' (Gyezaho, 2009: 4).

Outwardly, the Ugandan economy experienced consistently high growth rates when the PEAP and PRSP were being implemented between 1997 and 2008, due to large infusions of aid. Despite the high rates, though, the NRM government acknowledges that the 'living standard of the majority of rural Ugandans has not improved; there has not been any significant productivity growth in agriculture and no structural transformation of the peasant-based agricultural sector' (Uganda National Development Plan, March 2010: 1–2). This shows that Uganda's decades of high rates of growth are analogous to the notion of *growth without development* (a situation in which growth has failed to translate into concrete improvements in the well-being of the majority of the population). The NRM government claims that its efforts are directed towards transforming Uganda from a predominantly peasant-based economy toward a modern, prosperous middle-income country (Uganda National Development Plan, March 2010). However, the reality is that the agricultural sector is not the top priority sector for investment or for development budget allocation. According to Sachs (2005: 270), the existing poverty reduction strategies 'are not yet designed with enough rigor or ambition to enable countries [such as Uganda] to achieve the Millennium Development Goals (MDGs). The programmes are often ingenious but are chronically underfunded compared with what is needed to achieve the MDGs'. And, he adds, even for notable plans such as Uganda's PEAP, 'the Millennium Development Goals are expressed only in vague aspirations rather than operational targets' (Sachs, 2005: 271).[1] In other words, there have been no serious efforts made to link the achievement of PEAP goals with MDGs or to fund its programmes

---

1   The Seven Millennium Development Goals (MDGs) to be achieved by 2015 are: (1) reduce the proportion of people living in extreme poverty by one-half; (2) enrol all children in primary school; (3) eliminate gender disparities in primary and secondary education; (4) reduce infant and child mortality rates by two-thirds; (5) reduce maternal mortality ratios by three-quarters; (6) provide access for all who need reproductive health services; and (7) reverse the loss of environmental resources (Dunford, 2006: 3).

adequately. Furthermore, there has been no major collaboration between the government and the non-governmental sector. And yet as a practitioner of a major international Private Voluntary Organization (PVO) observes, 'microfinance ... offers opportunities to contribute to the achievement of all seven (MDGs) goals, primarily through its direct impact on poverty, which can support improvements in schooling, gender equity, health and even resource conservation' (Dunford, 2006: 3). The same practitioner adds: 'There is already enough evidence to say with cautious confidence that microfinance can and does contribute to achievement of the Millennium Development Goals, and in a major way has already done so in Bangladesh, if not in other developing countries' (Dunford, 2006: 13). In addition, gender has not been adequately mainstreamed into PEAP/PRSP priorities, whether at the grassroots or district levels. Hence, it is difficult to assess the impact of enterprise development on women hoping to make a living from small businesses and microenterprises within PEAP/PRSP (Kamanyi, 2003: 7).

Some critics assert 'that the World Bank and IMF have simply re-packaged past structural adjustment policies and given them a new name'. They raise serious doubts whether the new loans 'can support Uganda's poverty reduction goals under PEAP/PRSP or even the achievement of MDGs' (Nyamugasira and Rowden, 2002: v, 50; Craig and Porter, 2003: 57). In particular, PRSPs are seen as 'being implemented in order to *mitigate* the negative effects of SAPs, rather than to bring about sustainable economic development' (Kline, 2000: 1). Also, 'the new loans [under PEAP/PRSP] lack an assessment or corrective strategy to avoid the previous adverse social impact of abandoning trade barriers and subsidy cuts' (Nyamugasira and Rowden, 2002:v, 50). For example, the loan plans did not take into account how price increases for privatized water (a directive of the Poverty Reduction Support Credit or PRSC) would undermine the health-related goals of the PEAP/PRSP.

The critics further believe that, unless the NRM government addresses the serious issue of *growth with equity*, poverty reduction goals within its PRSP or MDGs may never be achieved. While improved macroeconomic indicators may give an appearance of growth, such superficial advances cannot address issues of inequality or show, in concrete terms, how this may lead in the villages to 'increased safe water sources ... wipe out the studying under trees by children ... or provide more drugs in health units' (Nyamugasira and Rowden, 2002: 11). In other words, there is a need to show concretely how growth in the economy translates into improved well-being and poverty reduction.

2.1.2 *The Current National Development Plan, 2010–2015*

A National Development Plan (NDP) replaced PEAP/PRSP in 2008 and now serves as the NRM government's policy and budgetary framework. The Uganda National Development Plan, which covers the period 2010–15, still gives prominence to the market or private sector as the engine of growth and poverty reduction. In the foreword to the National Development Plan, President Museveni observes that:

> The development approach of the NDP intertwines economic growth and poverty eradication. This will be pursued in a quasi-market environment where the private sector will remain the engine of growth and development. The Government, in addition to undertaking the facilitating role through provision of conducive policy, institutional and regulatory framework, will also actively promote and encourage public-private partnerships in a rational manner. (Uganda National Development Plan, March 2010: i)

The claim is that the NDP has incorporated the PEAP/PRSP lessons with the following differences in approach:

- While the PEAP/PRSP stressed poverty eradication and prioritized social services, the NDP maintains the poverty eradication vision with an additional emphasis on economic transformation and wealth creation thereby intertwining sustainable economic growth with poverty eradication.
- The NDP has been designed as the key plan shaping all processes, incorporating all political thinking as well as the existing and emerging government initiatives and programmes for poverty reduction, growth, prosperity for all, and reconstruction in post-conflict areas in northern Uganda.

- Over the next five years, the NDP will guide decision-making and implementation of government programmes, including the annual budget process and the prioritization and direction of NRM government actions.

Perhaps the most important difference between PEAP/PRSP and the NDP is the proposed creation of public-private partnerships in a few selected 'flagship' industries within manufacturing and export-oriented industries. It is expected that the government share of funding in such industries 'will be 55 per cent while that of the private sector will be 45 per cent' (Uganda National Development Plan; March 2010: 60). Unfortunately, this mixed model of economic development (similar to one promised in the Ten-Point Programme) will not be extended to cover the agricultural sector (or even agri-based industries).

The exemplar of the developmental state in Southeast Asia in the 1980s and 1990s – and more recently, emerging states like China and Brazil – indicates that such states tend to take the lead role in public-private partnerships and provide investment capital. They are also proactive in finding markets abroad for local products. Weak, inept and corrupt, the Ugandan state may not be able, or willing, to undertake such a substantial role in the economy. Already, the NRM government has reiterated its belief in the role of the private sector as the engine of economic growth and poverty reduction. 'It is government policy that the private sector will remain the engine of growth, employment creation and prosperity for socio-economic transformation in the country during the NDP period' (Uganda National Development Plan, March 2010: 72).

It is evident that high rates of growth do not readily translate into poverty reduction or improve people's well-being unless accompanied by employment creation and economic transformation. Unfortunately, despite the high growth rates, the rate of unemployment in Uganda has been very high, even among university graduates. Above all, NDP goals do not seem to be connected in a meaningful way with previous poverty-reduction initiatives and programmes under PEAP/PRSP, such as the Plan for Modernization of Agriculture (PMA), Prosperity for All (PFA), or the proposed use of Savings and Credit Cooperatives (SACCOS) to achieve growth and poverty reduction in rural areas. The analysis of these poverty reduction programmes that follows reveals a fundamental disconnection between government rhetoric or intent and the reality of life in the country. It also shows how the initiatives started under PEAP/PRSP have failed to reduce the level of poverty to any substantial degree or to improve the majority of people's livelihoods. The failure of the PRSPs can in part be attributed to the fact that they were really SAPS in disguise and did not fundamentally address problems of rural poverty.

2.1.3 Impact of Poverty Reduction Programmes under PEAP/PRSP

The Plan for Modernization of Agriculture (PMA) launched in 2001 is part of the Government of Uganda's broader strategy for poverty eradication contained in the PEAP/PRSP. The PMA was expected: (1) to increase incomes and improve the quality of life of poor subsistence farmers; (2) to improve household food security; and (3) to promote gainful employment coupled with sustainable use and management of natural resources (Plan for Modernization of Agriculture, 2000: v). To achieve these objectives, the PMA had to convert the subsistence farmer, and the agricultural sector in general, to commercial agriculture. The authorities concede that 'smallholder agriculture can offer a route out of poverty for many [rural households] – but only if it is productive, commercially oriented and well linked to modern markets' (IFAD Rural Poverty Report 2011, 2010: 9). Unfortunately, the PMA did not come up with a clear and concise development strategy to transform the agricultural and rural sectors. Uganda's agricultural development strategy is not clear cut, but straddles between export-oriented commercial farming for a few individuals and subsistence farming for the majority of the population. In the final analysis, neither sub-sector of the rural economy is receiving adequate resources and support from the NRM government or from donors.

Under the PMA, the government identified three categories of farmers: subsistence farmers; semi-commercial (or 'medium') farmers; and commercial ones. For better targeting of planning and support, the quasi-public National Agricultural Advisory Services (NAADS) has further categorized farmers into 'demonstration', 'lead', 'model' and 'nucleus' farmers. NAADS provides advisory agricultural services (AAS) to all of these. Different farmers are expected to graduate to a higher category (starting with 'demonstration' farmers and moving all the way up to 'nucleus' paragons). They are meant to graduate at different times, showing the level of successful adoption and implementation of agricultural practices. Aside from the 'demonstration' farmer (who may belong to a subsistence farmers' group), 'lead', 'model' and 'nucleus' farmers appear to be medium and commercial farmers who are likely to be politically savvy and well-connected to the NRM regime. It is semi-commercial and commercial farmers who seem to have been the main beneficiaries of government funding. It is reported that the NRM government 'has pledged Shs 60 billion to support agricultural mechanization and agro-processing' (Okello, 2009: 15).

In addition, under the PMA, the government was expected to establish an agricultural credit facility with an initial fund of Shs 30 billion, 'to be accessed by commercial farmers and agro-processors at interest rates not exceeding 10 per cent per year for a maximum period of 8 years' (Okello, 2009: 16). Loans and credit facilities were arranged to be accessed through commercial banks, which are profit-oriented, rather than through development banks or microfinance institutions. This has made the funds on offer too expensive for agriculture and inaccessible to subsistence or 'demonstration' farmers in rural areas. Under PMA, the majority subsistence farmers who produce for household consumption (an estimated four out of five households) were to be targeted for government expenditure and support, in order to increase their production and income. Unfortunately, this category of farmers has not benefited from either NAADS or PMA programmes.

Several factors account for the lack of funding and support to subsistence farmers in particular, and to the agricultural sector in general. First, resource allocations to the agricultural sector have often been inadequate as 'a result partly of donor preferences for the social sectors and partly because of the Treasury's general suspicion of the capacity of the Ministry of Agriculture, Animal Industry and Fisheries (MAAIF) to implement programs' (Joughin and Kjoer, 2009: 7). As Joughlin and Kjoer observe 'A recent evaluation of the poverty reduction strategy (Uganda's PEAP) emphasizes that, generally, health and education, in line with international development priorities, have been funded while investment in infrastructure and agriculture has been considered secondary' (Joughin and Kjoer, 2009: 8). Unfortunately, neo-liberal policies treat rural poverty 'as a residual phenomenon, destined to be eliminated eventually by vigorous and continued industrial growth' (Uphoff et al., 1998: 2).

Although the agricultural sector contributes over 70 per cent to employment, public expenditure on agriculture 'declined from about 10 per cent in 1980 to 5.7 per cent in 2005/6, to 3.8 per cent in 2006/7, to 4.1 per cent in 2007/8, and further to 3.7 per cent in 2008/9' (Okello, 2009: 13). And over the plan period 2010–15, agriculture will receive on average 5.4 per cent of government spending, ranking about sixth when it comes to proposed spending on priority sectors. In its rhetoric and promises, the NRM government has prioritized agriculture, yet in reality it has continued to make minimal budgetary allocations – lower than those recommended under the Maputo Declaration, which proposed that 10 per cent of the budget should go to the agricultural sector. (This is in spite of the fact that the Ugandan Government has signed both the Maputo Declaration and the CAADP Principles.) It is reported that 'to-date only eight [African] countries have reached the target of allocating at least 10 per cent of their national budgets to agriculture, while the majority of governments [including Uganda] are averaging no more than 4 per cent' (Africa Progress Report, 2010: 38).

A second reason for lack of funding is that small farmers have had problems of access to the services NAADS provides – not least, problems of saving the money to afford them. These extracts give an indication of their plight:

> The National Farmers Association has projected that 95 per cent of Uganda's small farmers will be unable to afford the full costs of the agricultural extension services in the new NAADS program. Many civil society organizations are concerned that small farmers will either go without the increased costs for extension services or go deep into debt and ultimately lose their plots in efforts to finance such services. (Nyamugasira and Rowden, 2002: 38)

Furthermore, [evidence] shows that liberalisation has not improved real incomes of farmers, particularly the small ones. The obvious reason being that prices of agricultural inputs rose in the wake of higher producer prices; thus increasing production costs and undermining profit. Therefore, liberalisation in as far as it means higher income can only benefit those who have resources to grow those crops that are attracting higher prices on the market at that moment. In other words, these could be rich farmers and capitalists as opposed to poor farmers that do not own adequate land and do not have access to infrastructure, and are affected by high transport costs due to the high taxes on petroleum products. (Bazaara, 2001: 43)

Thirdly, low allocations to the agricultural sector may be attributed to the ideological battle between the technocrats in the competing ministries of Finance and Agriculture. The technocrats in the powerful Ministry of Finance, Planning and Economic Development (MOFPED) believe 'that agricultural sector growth happens best when left to the market and therefore should not be sponsored by public moneys' (Joughin and Kjoer, 2009: 9). Treasury technocrats, who believe in the market model, have the ear of the President who converted (early in the 1990s) and the strong backing of the proponents of liberalization among World Bank and IMF officials both in Kampala and Washington DC. In contrast, technocrats in the Ministry of Agriculture (MAAIF) have never accepted the rhetoric about the market and the private sector as the engine of growth and agricultural transformation. It is reported that 'many MAAIF officers are essentially interventionist by nature, which reflects their training as scientists and their perceived status as key people' (Joughin and Kjoer, 2009: 10).

Finally, most of the poverty reduction programmes under PEAP/ PRSP, including PMA and NAADS, have been heavily politicized. In the case of NAADS services and PMA loans, these have ended up benefiting the politically well-connected, semi-commercial and commercial farmers in the same way as proceeds from the privatization of state-owned enterprises ended up in the pockets of the NRM political elite (Kibikyo, 2008: 18–19). Because of political pressure at the highest levels of the NRM government, NAADS has moved away from promoting demand-driven measures for farmers where 'demonstration' farmers in the groups 'themselves are meant to decide what to invest in and which farms to use'. Instead, 'there is new political leverage in deciding the model farmers. These farmers are likely

to be local elite who will be able to mobilize votes for Museveni' (www.
independent.co.ug/2009). The NRM government proposes to select six
'model' farmers per parish to receive benefits and run demonstration farms
for the rest of the village or community. This parallels the way members of
SACCOS are to be selected to receive credit.

In most cases, these anti-poverty programmes were launched or re-
launched during general election cycles (1996, 2001, 2006, and more
recently in 2011), so they have been viewed by opponents of the NRM
government as meeting political rather than economic objectives for economic development. For example, although Parliament has a supervisory
role over anti-poverty programmes in the country, it was marginalized
during the drafting of the poverty reduction strategy in 1997 – the strategy that became known as the Poverty Eradication Action Plan or PEAP
(Tumukwasibwe, 2010). President Museveni admitted: 'the question of
lingering household poverty [is] partly due to the weakness of our own
NRM leaders, many of whom are no different from other opportunistic
politicians; they simply want to be in power and use it for no other purpose
than serving their own interests' (Museveni, 1997: 208). To cover up for
such individuals within NRM, President Museveni claimed that:

> There are things the government can do to end poverty in the rural areas, but there
> are others which must be done by the individual ... However, what I had to cover
> up in order to protect our inefficient NRM politicians was the fact that one func-
> tion of leadership in a backward country is precisely to teach the people the means
> of tapping wealth [flowing like God's rain onto the roof of the house and for the
> occupant to trap it and put it into a container, otherwise, the house will remain
> without water], because they do not know how to do it on their own. (President
> Museveni, 1997: 208)

The President goes on to claim that: 'this imagery helped me tremendously
to explain these issues to the people. In fact, I had started using it before the
start of the [1996] election campaign, bearing in mind what the opportunistic politicians were saying in the newspapers. By the time of the campaign,
I had immunized the public against the position of the opposition' (Museveni, 1997: 208). It seems that, during the general election cycles, the NRM
government has attempted on several occasions to switch back and forth

between demand-driven and supply-driven approaches to delivering agricultural services. This was particularly evident in 2006, 'when, as elections drew closer, political concerns of gaining popularity in rural areas became more urgent, and the President got more impatient with the fact the PMA was not showing results on the ground fast enough' (Joughin and Kjoer, 2009: 14). As a result, the 2006 NRM election manifesto called for state intervention in the area of rural development. According to the manifesto, 'a trained cadre shall be appointed to drive and motivate development at each parish –it shall act as a proactive catalyst for the much desired social economic transformation of Uganda'. The manifesto also emphasized the need for improved state action, such as providing seeds and state support for microcredit associations (Joughin and Kjoer, 2009: 14). In spite of efforts by President Museveni and his comrades to appear partly in favour of state-driven policies in rural development, the dominant development model pursued by technocrats in the Treasury still remained the market.

Given such a political context, it is not surprising that the government-sponsored rural credit scheme (*Entandikwa*) and a large livestock service project failed. It was because these programmes were heavily politicized. In the same way, the Prosperity for All (PFA) and SACCOS schemes for receiving government loans are being politicized and they are expected to meet the same fate as *Entandikwa* – catastrophic failure.

The Rural Credit Scheme (*Entandikwa* or Seed Money) was part of the Poverty Alleviation Scheme. The scheme, launched in 1994 (before the expected general elections held in 1996), aimed at improving the well-being of poor people who had no access to credit from traditional commercial banks. As noted earlier, each constituency received Shs30 million, equivalent to US$30,000. There was a total of US$6 million for the whole country. *Entandikwa* money was intended to serve as a revolving loan fund to benefit thousands of poorer people in the rural areas. However, the funds were handed to political operatives and government supporters at no interest or interest free. The credit scheme failed due to low repayment rates and a colossal misuse of funds by the NRM political elite. The low repayment rates of 50 per cent or less may be attributed to the fact that recipients perceived the loans as 'reparations for damages or as inducements or rewards for political support' (Joughin and Kjoer, 2009: 11). Prior to *Entandikwa*, the Rural Farmers Scheme (RFS), launched by the government and implemented through the defunct Uganda Commercial Bank (UCB), had failed largely because of political reasons too. Under the RFS, money was loaned to individuals with potentially viable projects and deep political connections, but with no collateral to secure the loans according to commercial lending practices. Hence, individuals who received loans did so on the basis of political ties and personal integrity. They were so-called 'character loans'.

The Livestock Services Project, initiated in the late 1980s and expected to end in 1998, was a major government intervention in the livestock industry. The project was to serve the dual purpose of reversing the decline in the numbers of livestock through disease control and improving services supporting livestock. It included provision of water through the construction of a hundred small valley tanks. The project, headed by the former Vice President, Dr Specioza Kazibwe, failed due to widespread corruption and incompetence, not lack of funds. The failure of government-led credit schemes forced the government to use microfinance institutions to reach rural populations. However, MFIs proved both too independent and too hard to control for the NRM political elite. As a result, the government withdrew its support and funding for MFIs in 2007 in favour of Savings and Credit Cooperatives or SACCOS. SACCOS, though member-organized and owned, tend to be vulnerable to political influence and control, as we discuss below.

2.1.4 *The Prosperity for All Programme and SACCOS*

Under the politically-driven Prosperity for All (PFA) programme (*Bona Bagaggawale*) and the Rural Development Scheme, the NRM government sought to integrate the old PMA with more active government involvement: providing credit through SACCOS and offering a range of other inputs to increase agricultural production. The PFA programme seems to be an ambitious government initiative claiming it will move people from poverty to prosperity, but really achieving neither growth nor poverty reduction. It is like putting the cart before the horse. It is reported that, following the 2006 elections, a new programme structure was established under the control of the President's Office, running in parallel with the Secretariats of NAADS and PMA (under the Ministry of Agriculture, Animal Industry and Fisheries) (Joughin and Kjoer, 2009: 15). In reality, this move appears to have been used to give the President more powers to intervene and direct the affairs of NAADS. This included suspending the activities and operations of NAADS altogether in 2007 – ostensibly because of the slow rate of progress it was making in national transformation. Then, as a result, the restructured NAADS was brought under direct government control. In his 2009 'State of the Nation' speech, the President said:

> The restructured National Agricultural Advisory Service (NAADS) has completed the roll-out exercise to cover all districts with a renewed emphasis on ensuring that 30,000 demonstration farmers, organized into farmer groups or cooperatives, will every year, be provided with the necessary planting or breeding inputs, skills and knowledge to transform their production systems into commercially viable agricultural ventures. This intervention will ensure that farmers are able to produce economically viable volumes of produce and can more easily be linked to agro-processing industries and consequently access the market with higher value goods. (President Museveni, State of the Nation Speech, June 2009: 4–5)

The President's direct control of NAADS meant it shifted away 'from the demand-based idea ... where farmers themselves ... decide what to invest in and which farms to use as demonstration farms in their groups. Instead, there is new political leverage in deciding the model farmers. These farmers are likely to be local elites who will be able to mobilize votes for Museveni' (Joughin and Kjoer, 2009: 16). In addition, as a result of such control, the PFA unit is involved in organizing presidential tours around the country. Known as 'poverty tours', these are occasions when President Museveni 'visits model farmers and gives them tangible benefits such as pick-up trucks or cash' (Joughin and Kjoer, 2009: 16). The major challenges facing the PFA programme include lack of clear policy guidelines, no well-defined structure for implementation and too much politicization of its activities and operations. Indeed, as the 2011 general elections approach, the intensity of political intervention is expected to intensify in the PFA programme and other rural development schemes. Critics of the PFA believe that sooner or later, it will fail in the same way as the *Entandikwa* scheme, due to political interference and mismanagement (UCSD Secretariat, May–June 2007: 3).

The majority of the Savings and Credit Cooperatives (SACCOS) in Uganda are recent – first seen in early 2004 and during the 2006 general election, then launched 'politically' in February 2007 as part of the PFA programme. But there are a lot of them: already by December 2008 there were an estimated 1,500 SACCOS with about 650,000 members. Created in every sub-county throughout Uganda, these 'political' SACCOS are expected to provide micro-level finance to thousands, and eventually millions, of people throughout the country. SACCOS are seen as a vehicle for fulfilling President Museveni's vision of having each family earn at least Shs 20 million per annum. Embedded in such a vision is the transformation of Uganda into a middle-income country (Uganda National Development Plan, March 2010; see foreword by President Museveni). Most of the political SACCOS are neither regulated nor independent of political interference. According to Deshpande et al. (2006: 18), 'SACCOS operate in what amounts to a supervisory vacuum. Ugandan SACCOS benefit from no legal status, regulation, or supervision system which recognizes their distinct nature from non-financial types of cooperatives'. Furthermore, participants at the Third African Microfinance Conference in Kampala in August 2007 were surprised to learn that, in response to the Uganda government's push to spread the initiative, 'institutions originally set up as microfinance simply added the word "SACCO" to their names but remained MFIs. Applying SACCOS standards to them [has], at best, turned out to be inappropriate and confusing to the clients, the public and the regulators' (Wavamunno, 2007: 5). And, crucially, they are the only financial institutions allowed to take savings or deposits without being licensed by the Bank of Uganda. 'As a result, deposits in SACCOS have little external protection' (Deshpande et al., 2006: 18).

In fact, this situation has led the Delegation of the European Commission to Uganda to urge the Ugandan Government to pass a Savings and Credit Cooperative Organizations (SACCOS) Act and to appoint an independent regulatory body to guarantee the cooperatives' independence (Duscha, 2008: 4). In contrast to political SACCOS, traditional SACCOS are member-owned and managed, and are legally organized under the Cooperative Act and with supervision from the 'umbrella' or apex cooperative organization, the Uganda Cooperative Savings and Credit

Cooperative Union (UCSCU). However, even if the supervision of all
SACCOS were delegated to UCSCU, this body does not currently have
'the ability to enforce even basic transparency standards ... such as regular reporting requirements, disclosure of institutional performance, and
code of conduct for SACCOS managers' (Deshpande et al., 2006: 18).
UCSCU has 241 member institutions but only eight staff members to
oversee their operations – an average of one staff member to thirty institutions! In addition, UCSCU has been plagued by poor management
and failure to adapt its policies and procedures to a changing market and
political environment.

SACCOS fall broadly under the Rural Financial Services Strategy
(RFSS) and they were in part 'conceived following the failure of earlier
interventions – *Entandikwa*, the Youth Entrepreneurship Scheme (YES),
the Plan for Program of Alleviation of Poverty and Social Costs Adjustment (PAPSCA)' (Kairu, 2009: 1). It is becoming increasingly clear that
the NRM government created SACCOS as a deliberate alternative to
microfinance institutions which were providing financial services to the
rural poor. According to the former Vice President and recently dismissed
Chairperson of the Microfinance Support Centre (MSC), Dr Specioza
Kazibwe, MFIs are being bypassed by the Government of Uganda in favour
of SACCOS because 'money has not been reaching the poor, it has been
stopping in the hands of technocrats in [microfinance] institutions' (Lee,
2010: 4). In a speech to the NRM parliamentary caucus meeting in August
2006, the President attacked microfinance institutions for charging high
interest rates and ordered Ministers from the Finance Ministry to investigate the rates they charged customers (http://microcapitalmonitor.com/
August 24, 2006). Uganda is among several developing countries that 'have
threatened to cap [MFI] interest rates and tighten usury laws' (Meyer, 2007:
7). In addition, local 'newspapers have published articles about exploitative
microfinance providers and parliamentarians have repeatedly accused MFIs
of usury. While these incidents may be partly due to ignorance regarding
microfinance best practices, individual Members of Parliament ... also seem
to engage deliberately in MFI-bashing campaigns, expecting to gain some
popularity out of it' (Carlton et al., 2001: 28).

Normally, MFIs charge modest or market interest rates with the aim of using interest revenue to cover necessary expenses (operating and financial costs). Indeed, this is one of the ways MFIs strive to achieve sustainability over time. The other way is to cut costs and improve efficiency. It appears that the Association of Microfinance Institutions in Uganda (AMFIU) – the premier association of MFIs in Uganda – has been unsuccessful in explaining the issue of higher interest rates charged to clients. Although NRM government officials often claimed that MFIs charged high interest rates and did not support the poor adequately, the government still supported them through its Microfinance Support Centre (MSC) until the launching of SACCOS in 2007. One observer has suggested that the government withdrew its support of deposit-taking microfinance institutions (MDIs) 'because MDIs did not fulfil government's expectation of massively branching out shortly after transformation. Government changed its focus of microfinance assistance to SACCOS. Thus, indirectly the shift to support SACCOS was partly a result of unfulfilled expectations regarding the MDIs' (FSDU, 2007: 38). I myself believe the NRM government withdrew its support for unregulated MFIs because, as largely independent organizations (with their established methodologies and adherence to universally accepted best practices), MFIs do not do the government's political bidding, even if they are funded by MSC. By contrast, government supported SACCOS are easy to control and influence.

In an official speech launching PFA, President Museveni explained how SACCOS were to be formed in each sub-county and how much interest was to be charged:

> We start with 30 homesteads per sub-county in order to demonstrate to the others what we are talking about is possible. We select the 30 homesteads according to the speed at which they can learn and adopt the new strategy. We give them the necessary requirements ... [including] ... Shs 8 billion, for this year, for microfinance. ... These SACCOS will pass on government money to borrowers and savers at the interest rates not exceeding 13% per annum for crops, livestock, fish farming and artisanship; and 17% for trading and commerce. (Presidential Speech at the official launch of the Prosperity for All Programme, 8 October, 2007: 2)

In addition to determining criteria for SACCO formation and interest rates, the NRM political elite are heavily involved in the mobilization and start-up of SACCOS. Given such pervasive political involvement in the operations and funding of the cooperatives, it is not surprising that the Parliamentary Committee on Finance, evaluating developments, recently concluded:

> During [the] tour, we have noted with keen interest that there is an issue of poor governance. There is political interference that is having a negative [impact] on the operations of SACCOS all through districts ... [The] politicians think that because they played roles in the start-up of the SACCO, then when they take loans from these SACCOS, they are not obliged to pay back ... If the leaders can't set an example, then that is why this might as well end up like *Entandikwa* because the rest of the members will also refuse to pay back money loaned to the SACCOS by government. (Kairu, 2009: 1)

Unlike traditional SACCOS that raise their loan funds from members' savings and share capital, political SACCOS rely heavily on government funding. The Microfinance Support Centre (MSC) lends the money obtained from the government wholesale to SACCOS. In a recent interview, Dr Kazibwe, the former chairperson of MSC, pointed out that:

> [In the Government] budget lasting up to 2014 ... we shall have gotten Shs 500 billion in the countryside to finance agriculture directly. It will be implemented through loans, because people are rarely challenged to put to good use money that was given to them freely. We are not going to have any interest-free loans. We shall sustain the sector to have the money to revolve so that it doesn't run out. We have an agriculture fund and we know to whom we have lent money for agriculture. And we shall work with the Uganda Bureau of Statistics so that if we give you agriculture enterprise money for a tractor, we want to know the impact it has had. If we have loaned money for storage, we need to know what impact it has had on household income. We shall look to other indicators of success. (Namazzi, 2010)

The interview reveals that MSC does not have criteria for deciding which SACCOS qualify to receive the loan funds; and the monitoring and evaluation of the performance and impact of SACCOS would be left to the Uganda Bureau of Statistics rather than to technocrats in the Ministries of Finance and Agriculture, who possess the relevant expertise about agriculture and rural development credit schemes.

Post Bank Uganda is another government finance institution designated to provide loan funds to SACCOS. However, in June 2007, the Managing Director of Post Bank Uganda, Mr. Stephen Mukweli, acknowledged that the government had provided the bank with only Shs 500 million, out of the total Shs 20 to 35 billion expected to come from the PFA programme (UCSD Secretariat, May–June 2007: 2). At the same time, voices in Parliament cited the Post Bank's low capital base and limited outreach to many parts of Uganda as major obstacles to the success of implementing the PFA programme. According to the concerned MPs:

> This is a bank with small capital and all of a sudden [it] wants to take on a huge project. We realize they only have two billion shillings as working capital which is far below what one can use to open up branches ... With just 21 branches country wide, Post Bank will be hard pressed to roll out the project in all 964 sub-counties in the current 80 districts within one year as is expected by the government. (UCSD Secretariat, May–June 2007: 2)

It should be noted that the Post Bank's current outreach and capacity problems are a result of actions taken by the Bank of Uganda on the direction of the NRM government. For example, 'in 2002, the Central Bank ordered the restructuring of Post Bank including a reduction from 91 to 20 service locations' (Deshpande et al., 2006: 4). A combination of several problems seems to confront the performance of SACCOS and the PFA programme. In addition to poor governance, political interference, lack of coordination and fraud, SACCO members perceive government loans to be a 'government handout' as was the case with the *Entandikwa*. Among the major factors considered harmful to the success of the PFA are 'fear over government's involvement and political influence' (UCSD Secretariat, May–June, 2007: 2).

An important study on the impact of wholesale or external lending to SACCOS in Uganda has concluded that such lending does more harm than good, especially in the cases of SACCOS with weak performance or poor portfolios. Extending external credit to weak SACCOS has not only changed the orientation of individual SACCOS from savings-led functioning to a preoccupation with disbursement of member savings and external loans, but has introduced dangerous attitudes to debts. As Fiorillo

(2006: 6) recounts: 'many SACCO members were negatively influenced by politicians who presented external funding as a government grant. In such cases, delinquency rates increased after the loan'. Indeed, loss of confidence in SACCOS and the PFA programme (just as with *Entandikwa*) would spell disaster.

In contrast to SACCOS, Village Savings and Loan Associations (VSLAs) are independent, self-selected and self-managed (http://www.microfinancegateway.org/2008). VSLAs allow groups of people to pool their savings in order to have a source of loan funds. The associations do not receive any external funding. CARE's Community Based Trainers (CBTs) in Uganda 'promote the formation of groups that meet regularly to accumulate savings and disburse part or the totality of the amount saved to one or more members of the group' (Singer, 2008: 1). VSLAs may scale up their services or build institutional linkages to MFIs, credit unions or commercial banks. However, in general, they tend to operate for nine to twelve months, conduct an *action audit* and then disband or reconstitute themselves with new and different members. VSLA members have more control over their financial services than SACCOS ones. Hence, VSLAs seem to *complement* MFIs, while political SACCOS are increasingly used by the NRM government as *alternatives to* MFIs. Finally, traditional rotating savings and credit associations (ROSCAs) provide members with an opportunity to save, but do not permit savers to earn interest on their savings as a formal account would, or provide a means of borrowing.

2.2 High Growth Rates, Inequality and Poverty

Although Uganda has experienced high rates of growth since the mid 1990s, structural transformation of the economy has not occurred. In addition, the high growth rates have not improved the well-being of the majority of the population or substantially reduced poverty levels. Poverty levels are persisting – especially in the north and east and in rural areas throughout the country (Okello, 2009). An important World Bank study found that 'economic growth alone won't alleviate global poverty, in part because political and economic systems favour the rich over the poor and the powerful over the powerless. Facilitating the empowerment of the poor people – by making state and social institutions more responsive to them – is also the key to reducing poverty' (Phillips, 2000: A2). The same World Bank report concluded: 'In a world where political power is unequally distributed and often mimics the distribution of economic power, the way state institutions operate may be particularly unfavourable to the poor ... [The] poor are often excluded from benefits of government health or education programs meant to help them, and are unable to fight back against public corruption' (Phillips, 2000: A2).

In the case of Uganda, various programmes intended to promote growth and reduce poverty in rural areas have not only excluded the poor (especially subsistence farmers) but have been mismanaged due to widespread corruption and political interventions at all levels. According to critics, 'Museveni's politics of patronage and neo-patrimonialism may have had negative consequences for the economy. Rather than use national resources for priority development programmes, they are instead wasted on rewarding loyalty, buying off opposition, bribing voters and investing in forces of coercion' (Muhumuza, 2008: 41). State resources are wasted through corruption and a bloated administrative apparatus which provides employment to cronies and the NRM political elite. According to Transparency International's (TI) Corruption Perception Index, '[while] Uganda's ranking in the corruption league table dropped from 105th position to 111th position, its average CPI score edged up from 2.7 in 2006 to 2.8 in 2007' (AFDB/OECD, 2008: 612). In their recent communiqué issued at the Episcopal Conference in Kampala, Catholic bishops in Uganda expressed concern over Parliament's selective handling of corruption cases. In particular, they said that 'in spite of a highly incriminating probe by the Parliamentary Public Accounts Committee, the accused ministers were exonerated by the 8th Parliament after the members of the majority ruling NRM were whipped, causing widespread condemnation from donors, activists and the public' (http://www.monitor.co.ug/news). Such inadequate measures by government have led to a culture of impunity among violators and potential corrupt public officials in the country.

Although the recent 'walk-to-work' protests against high fuel and food prices were initiated and directed by major opposition leaders in the country, the protests seem to have tapped into a reservoir of discontent associated with high levels of unemployment and under-employment, poverty, inequality and corruption at various levels of government. These conditions are a result of the economic policies pursued by the NRM government since the late 1980s, continuing on into the present. Denying this, the NRM government has maintained that rising fuel and food prices are due to external factors beyond its control – factors such as drought and the unrest in the Middle East, which are affecting global oil prices. However, the important thing is that, in people's minds, the nascent 'walk-to-work' movement has successfully managed to link spiralling fuel and commodity prices in Kampala and elsewhere in the country with government corruption and spending or budget decisions (Kron, 2011: A10). Particular resentments towards government spending decisions relate to a US$250 million supplementary budget for conducting general elections in February, 2011, the spending of US$720 million for the purchase of fighter aircraft from Russia, and the earmarking of funds for an extravagant and costly inauguration of the President during his sixth five-year term, on 12 May 2011 (Kron, 2011: A7).

The economic crisis and political repression of the late 1980s and early 1990s contributed greatly to the wave for democratization that hit many countries in Sub-Saharan Africa during this period – akin to what is now happening to countries in North Africa and the Gulf States. What seems to connect political changes in the 1990s to current protests in Burkina Faso and Uganda, is a 'combination of economic malaise and political repression' in both countries (Makoba, 1999: 61). The potential for the fledgling 'walk-to-work' movement to bring about political changes in Uganda, including regime change, will depend on several factors – such as the extent, organization and depth of protests, and the potential or actual split within the NRM political and military elite. As critical factors for the success or failure of moves for regime change, the intra-elite split theory suggests we keep an eye on potential or actual split and conflict within the governing elite plus the resources available to both the regime and opposition forces (Przeworski, 1986: 53–6). Though protests in Uganda first started for economic reasons, they are beginning to turn political and demands for regime change are growing. These political demands may inadvertently have been accelerated by the government's evasive responses, threats and use of violence against unarmed, peaceful protesters. Government over-reaction, avoidance of dialogue and use, instead, of overwhelming force may have the unintended consequence of strengthening and popularizing the fledgling 'walk-to-work' movement throughout the country. In contrast to the NRM government's violent reaction to peaceful protesters in Uganda, the Burkina Faso government has reacted in a peaceful and calm manner to contrastingly violent protests in the capital city of Ouagadougou. There President Compaoré, who has ruled for twenty-four years, decided to negotiate and compromise. He has avoided the use of excessive force and has remained above the crisis (Nossiter, 2011: A5). In addition, the Compaoré regime seems to have faced a weak and fragmented opposition and a public bent on blaming individual army or police commanders and particular political leaders for the corruption and the economic crisis in that country. This may explain why the protests are dwindling and things appear to be returning to normal in Burkina Faso. However, this may be both deceptive and temporary since the underlying economic conditions of high food and fuel prices and poverty have not been addressed by the Compaoré regime.

So far, efforts by President Museveni to convene a meeting with opposition leaders under the auspices of the Inter-Party Forum for Dialogue (IPOD) have failed, in part due to the pre-conditions set by the opposition, which include an apology from the government for its 'brutal' treatment of the protesters and the leader of the main opposition, Dr Kizza Besigye (*New Vision*, Editorial, 2011). At the time this study was going to press, it appeared that the opposition was not interested in negotiations, while the NRM government believed that continued crackdown on the opposition and protesters would severely undermine the 'walk-to-work' movement's momentum and thus prevent it from succeeding. In addition, the President has announced that once the 9th Parliament has convened on 19 May 2011, he will introduce 'plans to amend the Constitution to deny bail for murder, rape, treason, defilement and riot suspects as well as economic saboteurs [and media houses engaging in 'irresponsible reporting'] until they [have served] a mandatory 180 days on remand' (http://www.monitor.co.ug/news/national/).

The international community is concerned about the escalating violence the government is directing at the protesters and has urged the NRM
government to respect the right of its citizens to demonstrate in a peaceful
manner. Some donors have threatened sanctions, while the prosecutor for
the International Criminal Court (ICC) has said government actions are
under its watchful eyes. Human Rights Watch too has called 'on the Uganda
Government to conduct a prompt, independent and thorough investiga-
tion into the recent use of lethal force by security forces' (DeCapua, 2011:
1). It is not clear what will become of the fledgling 'walk-to-work' movement. Following a recent government crackdown on opposition leaders and
protesters, movement organizers have now decided to call on the public to
honk car horns five times at five o'clock in the afternoon in a bid to 'drum
the message of escalating food and fuel prices' into the government's ears
(http://www.monitor.co.ug/news/national). The 'drive-to-hoot' tactic
seems to be supplementary to the 'walk-to-work' method of protesting.
However, it may foreshadow political upheaval in Uganda, similar to political uprisings in North Africa and the Gulf States.

2.2.1 Growth Rates and Development Aid

Uganda's improved macroeconomic performance since the mid-1990s has
been primarily the result of massive aid inflows. Under the direct budget
support (DBS) and sector-wide approaches (SWAPS), donors including
the World Bank 'have been increasingly offering large sums to be used for
broader, overall sector-wide reforms while moving away from particular
project lending' (Nyamugasira and Rowden, 2002: 13).

In Uganda, all donors (except USAID) have agreed to provide aid *in
one basket*, as part of the national budget to be spent on priority areas of the
National Development Plan, the successor to the PEAP/PRSP. In spite of
the shift in donor lending strategy, aid has in most cases been inadequate
or has not been delivered in a timely manner. According to Sachs (2005:
337), 'the aid flows have neither been massive nor scaled in any way to
the levels needed to spur economic growth'. For example, foreign aid 'per
person in Sub-Saharan Africa ... expressed in constant 2002 dollars, fell
from $32 per African in 1980 to just $22 per African in 2001, during a period

in which Africa's pandemic diseases ran rampant, and needs for increased public spending were stark' (Sachs, 2005: 82). The 2001 report commissioned for the World Health Organization (WHO) by its Commission on Macroeconomics and Health (CMH), showed that improved health is a critical requirement for economic development in poor countries. As a result, the CMH 'calls for health spending at about [US]$34 per head in order to plan for adequate investments in health, allowing the world's poorest people to live longer, have more days of good health, and be able to earn more' (Nyamugasira and Rowden, 2002: 24). Unfortunately, because of inadequate overall aid, the World Bank insists on spending between US$13 and US$15 per head, a much lower figure than CMH's US$34 per head or the Uganda Ministry of Health's US$28 per head (Nyamugasira and Rowden, 2002). Overall, aid to Sub-Saharan Africa was to increase by US$25 billion per annum over the following three to five years (2008 to 2010). This, it was believed, would help to increase the growth rate in Africa and improve progress toward the achievement of Millennium Development Goals by 2015 (rather than 2017 in Uganda's case). According to current projections, Africa is not only behind target on reaching all MDGs by 2015, but unfortunately, 'the halving of poverty will come ... by 2150 – that is 135 years late' (Commission for Africa, 2005: 64). Hence, there is an urgent need to increase aid. According to the Commission for Africa Report:

> Doubling aid to Africa may sound ambitious. In reality, it amounts to giving every man, woman and child on the continent just an extra US 10 cents a day. If efforts now are too small and uncoordinated to be effective, the world will be faced with the prospect of a permanent aid program to Africa. (Commission for Africa Report, 2005: 60)

2.2.2 *Export Trade and Development*

Like that of other Sub-Saharan African countries, Uganda's share of global trade is small to modest. However, in the past twenty years, it has tried to increase and diversify its exports. The European Union (EU) is the country's largest trading partner, with more than one third of exports consumed in the EU market (http://www.deluga.ec.europa.eu/). Under the EU's Everything But Arms (EBA) programme, Uganda increased and diversified its exports between 1988 and 2001 as follows:

> During these 13 years, fish and tobacco have taken a substantial part of the products exported from Uganda to the EU, increasing respectively from US$24,000 to US$61 million for fish and fishery products and from US$89,000 to US$31 million for tobacco. Coffee and tea still represent the major share of the trade flows between Uganda and the EU. This share stands now at 36 per cent instead of 90 per cent, which means that much diversification has taken place. (http://www.deluga.eu.europa.eu/)

As a result of the EBA initiative, Uganda's exports to the EU increased. They were duty-free and had adjustable quota restrictions. However, in spite of this open access, Uganda has never reached or exceeded its existing quota limits in the past twenty-five years. Within the African region, export of Ugandan goods continues to grow. It was estimated at US$ 2.8 billion for the financial year 2008/9, but, as Museveni states 'most of the increase was on account of regional informal cross-border trade which is estimated at US$1.242 billion in [the same financial year]' (Museveni, June 2009: State of the Nation Address/www.statehouse.go.ug/). In spite of improved exports, Uganda's terms of trade are deteriorating, because it imports more than it exports. In 2008, for example, the country's total value of exports was estimated at US$1.72 billion, while its imports were estimated at US$4.5 billion (US State Department, February 2010; http://www.state.gov/).

Like other Sub-Saharan African countries, Uganda lacks the capacity to produce and export quality products that can benefit from either AGOA or EBA. At the conclusion of the Doha Round, the value of such preference schemes is expected to erode or disappear altogether, making exports from African countries less competitive. However, as we noted in Chapter One, Africa could benefit if the developed countries back Doha Round trade reforms which may help build Africa's capacity to trade and adjust to the new trade regime.

It is clear that trade alone is not adequate to bring about economic growth, sustainable development or poverty reduction. Hence, trade reform and economic reform must be linked at the national level. In the current National Development Plan there is no serious effort to link the transformation of the agricultural sector to exports or to high value commodities that would also increase incomes and employment (or self-employment) in the rural sector.

2.2.3 Recent Discovery of Oil and Potential for Development

In a recent speech, President Museveni made statements about the discovery of both oil and gas in Uganda. He reiterated the fact that the oil or petroleum resource would be 'used for infrastructure development and not for consumption' (20 March, 2010: 1, http://www.statehouse.go.ug/). At the same event, the Minister of Finance and Economic Planning echoed the President's message and 'assured Ugandans that the oil resources will be managed prudently in order to avoid the so-called oil curse' (http://www.statehouse.go.ug/news: March 2010). However, other observers believe that:

> Significant discoveries of oil ... in western Uganda in 2008 pose both a major challenge and a major opportunity for Uganda's economy and development. As of late 2009, the private sector had invested considerably in the oil sector, but production had not yet begun pending further feasibility studies on the funding and construction of the necessary infrastructure to support industry. (U.S. State Dept., February 2010; http://www.state.gov/)

In a speech made during the launching of the Uganda Country Economic Memorandum (CEM), Paul Collier, a long time student of Uganda's economy and adviser to the government, cautioned the government against 'throwing a party over the recent discovery [of oil], saying that Uganda must first carefully auction petroleum rights and then invest oil revenues wisely through an honest and efficient public investment process' (Collier, 2007: 2). Experts believe there is a negative correlation between natural resource endowments and economic growth. The 'resource curse hypothesis' predicts that resource-rich countries are likely to fail, for various reasons including 'higher prevalence of indolence, rent seeking, conflict between stakeholders, corruption, and predation' (Hillbom, 2008: 201). Whether considered an 'oil curse' or the 'Dutch disease', evidence from the past thirty to forty years about resource-rich countries shows 'corrupt leaders selling off natural assets and pocketing profits, individuals and international companies becoming wealthy while governments stayed poor' (Hillbom, 2008: 201).

Although the NRM government formulated a National Oil and Gas Policy in 2008, there is plenty of scepticism both at home and abroad about how oil revenues will be spent (speech by Minister of State for Mineral Development, August 2010). The policy articulates the goal and objectives of using the oil and gas revenue to achieve poverty eradication and to create value for all stakeholders; but it does not address concerns about how the revenue will be spent or how to prevent corruption from 'eating up' the revenue.

Donors, civil society groups and the opposition are all concerned about the rampant corruption in government spilling over into the newly discovered oil and gas sector. In a recent interview, a leading member of the opposition alleged that 'based on the current record, all [the] money [estimated at US$2 billion a year] would be swindled'. He went on to say, 'all this is being handled personally and exclusively at the kitchen table of the President. We know nothing about it' (Nichols, 2010). Recently, the Ugandan Parliament passed a bill taxing 'pre-production activities, handling advancements in oil exploration and production of oil in Uganda' (*New Vision*, 2010: 1). Members of the opposition and other critics of the bill argued that the government should have had the Petroleum Bill tabled and passed by Parliament before considering a bill to tax oil revenues or related pre-production activities. The critics observe that the action of the government is 'putting the cart before the horse'.

The discovery of oil is mentioned in the current National Development Plan as one of the priority areas, but nothing is said about the creation of a Petroleum Law to govern the allocation of the expected revenues or how such revenues would be utilized over the plan period (2010–15). It is imperative that such a law be enacted as soon as possible. The NRM government should do more than it is currently doing to pass legislation to ensure full contract disclosures between the government and oil companies and increase transparency and accountability about the amount of oil revenue received and how it is spent on the country's development projects and infrastructure. Furthermore, Uganda should become a member of the Extractive Industries Transparency Initiative (EITI). It is:

> A coalition of governments, companies, civil society groups, investors, and international organizations that participate in a voluntary global compact for improving transparency in countries dependent on extractive industries. It aims to strengthen governance by improving transparency and accountability in the extractive sector in resource-rich countries through the verification and full publication of company payments and government revenues from oil, gas, and mining. (http://www.eitransparency.org/)

Finally, the government should plan prudent management of the oil revenue and seek to avoid the 'oil curse' and the 'Dutch disease' endemic in resource-rich countries. This could be achieved through medium to long-term planning enabling the government to determine how to utilize the oil revenue to benefit all Ugandans. A recent commentary from a prominent Ugandan jurist proposed the creation of a National Oil Council that would be 'the supreme governing body of the oil industry and only subject to government policy and parliamentary control' (Kanyeihamba, 2011). The proposed council would be representative of different segments of the Ugandan population and would be insulated from politics or political interference in a similar way to the proposed autonomous development fund model discussed in Chapter Six.

2.2.4 Investment and Growth

Public and private investment in Uganda, though modest, has contributed to recent economic growth. In particular, 'private investment in the services sector, especially in construction and telecommunications, [has] attracted sizeable foreign direct investment (FDI). Uganda's foreign direct investment (FDI) as a percentage of GDP has been modest; 17 per cent of GDP in 2006/07 compared to 15.7 per cent in 2002/03. Hence, Uganda's percentage investment to GDP is a good deal below the Sub-Saharan average of 20 per cent of GDP' (Carlton et al., 2001: 12). However, private sector investment, primarily financed by remittances or private transfers from abroad, was 20 per cent of GDP in 2006/07 (U.S. State Dept., 2010). Remittances from Ugandans in the diaspora have continued to be a significant portion of private sector investment. For example, while remittance flows to Sub-Saharan Africa made up an average of 2.6 percent of the GDP in 2009, the share of GDP in Uganda was 4.3 percent in the same year (World Bank, 2011: 92; Table 2A: 1). According to the 2011 joint World Bank and African Development Bank Report, Ugandans working abroad sent US$694 million in remittances in 2010 and are expected to send home about US$773 million in 2011, an increase of about 12 percent in one year. This implies that in 2011 diaspora remittances to Uganda will constitute 25 percent of its national budget and nearly equal the donor contribution, which is less than 30 percent (http://www.weinformers.net/).

In contrast to the practice in countries like Mexico, where remittances are channelled through hometown associations and cooperatives for community development projects (Brown, 2011), in Uganda remittances are sent to individuals and families and are largely used for consumption, education and health (UNDP Human Development Report, 2009: 92). Like some other countries on the African continent, Uganda has sought to encourage diaspora participation through dual citizenship and the adoption, in 2004, of a flexible labour policy which encourages and supports skilled Ugandans who leave home to work in North America and the United Kingdom. Despite concerns that such a policy deprives the country of its skilled labour force, especially in the health sector, remittances from the diaspora seem so far to show that the benefits outweigh the negatives. Hence, there is a need for the government to develop a more comprehensive policy framework that links skilled migration and remittances to economic growth and poverty reduction.

The increasing level of remittances has tended to mask the total foreign direct investment in Uganda and other African countries in recent years. 'In 2002, Africa received US$12 billion in remittances, 15 per cent of the global total' (Bakewell, 2007: 16). Increasingly, emigration and development are perceived as co-existing and creating a 'win-win' situation for the country of origin, the migrant, and the country of destination. Oil exploration, already discussed, has continued to attract increased foreign investment (AFDB/OECD, 2008: 603). However, since this is relatively new, its impact on the Ugandan economy is still unknown.

Under the facilitation (not leadership) of the Uganda Investment Authority (UIA), the NRM government is developing several industrial parks to provide investors with land and other critical infrastructure in central locations in Kampala and other sites around the country. The industrial parks are based on the Public-Private Partnership (PPP) business model, which aims to include: 'third party developers who are allocated land to invest in pre-built factories and warehouses for renting to investors; private developers who are allocated plots of land for their investment projects; and the Business Park Manager company to whom is outsourced the day-to-day running of the park' (Business Parks Implementation Manual, 2007; Section 2.3). Rather than provide overall leadership for the development and implementation of the industrial parks policy, the UIA stresses that it 'will be the landlord for all government-sponsored business parks' (Business Parks Implementation Manual, 2007; Section 3.1). The UIA's facilitation role contrasts very sharply with that of Japan's Ministry of International Trade and Industry (MITI) as the leader or architect of its country's industrial policy. MITI, created in 1946 and reorganized in 2001 as the Ministry of Economy, Trade and Industry (METI), 'served as an architect of industrial policy, an arbiter on industrial problems and disputes, and a regulator. A major objective of the Ministry was to strengthen the country's industrial base' (http://www.fas.org/).

The UIA is charged with setting up twenty-two new industrial parks throughout the country, with no fewer than four new parks every financial year. However, in 2007, only three business parks were reported to be under development: the Kampala Industrial and Business Park, Luzira Industrial Business Park, and the Bweyogerere Industrial Estate (AFDB/OECD, 2008). Additional locations for new industrial parks around the country are proposed in several districts including Mbarara, Mbale, Soroti, Gulu, Kasese, Kabale, Masaka, and Arua. It is reported that:

> In 2007, the Uganda Investment Authority licensed a total of 330 projects with planned investment of USD 1.75 billion and estimated employment of 42,950. This represents a 100 per cent increase over the previous year in terms of investment value and a 26 per cent increase in terms of employment. Foreign capital accounted for 57 per cent of new investments in 2007. (AFDB/OECD, 2008)

Despite this positive record,

> In 2007, Uganda's global ranking in the World Bank *Doing Business* indicators fell
> from 107th to 116th (out of 175 countries). Uganda performed relatively well regard-
> ing the ease of employing workers, protection for investors and ease of making tax
> payments, but performed poorly on the cost of starting a business, dealing with
> licences, registration of property, securing credit and trading across borders. (AFDB/
> OECD, 2008)

In virtually all the areas where Uganda performed poorly, corruption is
rampant. Although the goal of the industrial park policy is to transform
the Ugandan economy into a middle-income country by 2020, there is no
link with investment in agro-processing industries in the agricultural sector
or priority flagship industries in the manufacturing sector, as stipulated in
the current National Development Plan. Critics contend that the government has no coherent industrial policy operating across the various sectors
of the economy and society. They claim that:

> Most industries established have minimum forward and backward linkages and
> remain largely import dependent. Financing of the industry sector has not escaped
> patronage politics and networks. Rather than enhancing local industry through
> financial support, the NRM Government has on a number of occasions sunk massive
> resources in ailing companies where the political leadership seems to have personal
> stakes. Most beneficiaries have been Asians and entrenched entrepreneurs. (Okello,
> 2009: 23)

The lack of an overarching development strategy seems to undermine efforts
to build 'an independent, integrated and self-sustaining national economy'
envisaged in the now abandoned Ten-Point Programme (Museveni, 1997:
217). Africa is resource-rich, but its resources are generally not processed
into value-added products on the continent. The export of unprocessed
minerals and commodities, prevents the emergence of competitive manufacturing sectors and 'reduces the potential positive domestic carry-on
effects of resource extraction to a mere trickle' (Africa Progress Report,
2010: 46).

2.3 Summary

In summary, critics of the NRM government charge that it lacks a coherent vision and development strategy for the country, and that the government simply lurches from one programme or initiative to another, seeking the one that is the most politically expedient. As a consequence, the government favours programmes or initiatives that make political sense in the short term, but often at the expense of schemes that could bring about the desired economic growth and poverty reduction in the medium- and long-terms. Programmes in the rural agricultural sector seem to fit this pattern. Overall, 'while Uganda has excelled and been exemplary in technical policy formulation and innovation, the major problems have often been implementation of such policies and plans' (Civil Society Perspective Paper, 2009: 30). Uganda, like other Sub-Saharan African countries, lacks both the political will and the human and institutional capacity to ensure that its policies of economic growth and poverty reduction are effectively implemented (ACIR, 2011: 27 and 37). Reducing poverty in Uganda should be conceived as a development problem that requires a broad or multi-pronged development strategy (Jamal, 1998b: 85–6). Indeed some development experts believe that focusing on poverty reduction alone is not sufficient to get Uganda's population out of abject poverty. For example, Collier argues that:

> As a land-locked country ... Uganda must attain a higher and faster growth if it is to converge with middle income countries ... [A] renewed focus on infrastructure, regional markets, agriculture, and fast job-creating e-services, such as call centres could help attain that desired growth. (Collier, 2007: 2)

In the final analysis, Uganda's growth, poverty eradication, and sustainable development will require more aid, increased remittances, trade and investment (both foreign and domestic) and a strong triple partnership between the public, private and NGO sectors. None of these sectors on its own will enable Uganda to achieve Millennium Development Goals or become a middle-income country. Furthermore, the Ugandan situation shows the need for the state to balance policies promoting economic growth with those aimed at achieving poverty reduction and enhancing people's well-being. Hence, the role of the developmental state should be to promote economic growth with equity (Makoba, 1998: 20–1).

The next chapter examines the importance of NGOs and MFIs in their efforts to achieve the twin goals of empowering customers and promoting overall economic development. Again there is a special focus on Uganda.

CHAPTER THREE

NGOs, Microfinance Institutions and Grassroots Development: Focus on Uganda

3.0 Introduction

Non-governmental organizations (NGOs) and microfinance institutions (MFIs) are perceived as a powerful alternative strategy for promoting social and economic development in developing countries, including Sub-Saharan Africa. Although NGOs and MFIs tend to have two goals – improving the daily lives of poor people and achieving long-term economic development in less developed countries (Yilirim, 2010) – most impact studies focus on the first goal and overlook the second. However, we consider below the impact of NGOs and MFIs on national economic development. For decades in Sub-Saharan Africa both states and markets have failed to promote economic development or deliver basic services such as education and healthcare, and NGOs and MFIs have been used to fill in the 'development gaps or spaces' left or created as a result of such failure. By serving as important gap-fillers and trouble shooters, NGOs and MFIs seek to promote stability and reduce potential political unrest. And in conflict and post-conflict areas, they perform an important role, providing relief and rehabilitation services.

Critics, especially neo-Marxists, blame MFIs for focusing on the market and provision of financial services to women and the poor rather than considering the underlying class structure and patriarchy that exploit the women and the poor (Hulme and Moore, 2006). In addition, neo-Marxists contend that such programmes contribute to inequality and poverty because they restrict the potential of the poor to become politically aware and to mobilize against the power elite (Petras and Veltmeyer, 2001). My general response to such criticism is that you do not let the poor starve in order to foment a revolution; rather it makes sense to organize and mobilize them through self-help groups that increase their political awareness and economic empowerment, thereby enhancing chances for social transformation. Most governments in Sub-Saharan Africa (regardless of their political or ideological orientation) find NGOs acceptable and useful. Even authoritarian regimes have tolerated NGO activities, provided they operate within the framework of relief assistance and economic development rather than espouse advocacy for human rights and democratization.

It is estimated that there are over 30,000 international non-profit organizations (NPOs) worldwide, with about 20,000 of these active in developing countries (Salamon, 1994). The relationship between international non-profit organizations (NPOs) and national or local NGOs, tends to be hierarchical: international NPOs provide technical assistance and raise private and public funds for development aid, while national and local NGOs (including community-based organizations or CBOs) receive and allocate such funds to various projects and use technical assistance at the grassroots level for implementation (Smith, 2007). As discussed in Chapter One, four major reasons have been advanced to account for the rapid growth and expansion of NGOs and MFIs at the global and national levels. These can be summarized as follows: (1) a changing attitude of the international donor community about results-oriented development aid; (2) declining levels of development assistance from the leading industrialized countries, especially the G8; (3) a new emphasis on targeting aid to benefit the poor and other marginalized segments of the population – especially after the end of the Cold War; and (4) the desire to fill in development vacuums left by retreating states and inadequate markets, especially after the failure of SAPs in Sub-Saharan Africa.

3.1 The Impact of NGOs and MFIs on Grassroots Development in Developing Countries

Most studies on the impact of NGOs and MFIs tend to focus at the individual, household, and enterprise or community levels. However, there are a few studies that seek to analyse the impact of development-oriented NGOs and MFIs on a country's economic growth and poverty reduction. Studies on the *wider impact* in the area of development are still in their infancy. Baum and Lake (2003) observe that development-oriented NGOs have both a direct and indirect effect on economic growth in developing countries. For example, development-oriented NGOs and MFIs promote economic growth by supplying capital or credit for business development or large-scale development projects, leading to the creation of employment and self-employment. According to Eid (2006: 21), MFIs in North Africa and the Middle East have shown 'a job creation rate of five times the average rate of labour market growth in the region ... Job-creating entrepreneurial initiatives can exist at all levels of the economy, from water collection and jam production by village micro-enterprises, to mechanic shops and wedding dress rental boutiques in both rural and urban areas.'

Increasingly, NGOs and MFIs receive significant amounts of development aid and their projects are designed to help achieve UN Millennium Development Goals (MDGs) or goals set by a specific developing country for economic growth and poverty reduction. From the year 2000, the microfinance industry has aimed to satisfy unmet demand on a much larger scale, as well as play its role in reducing poverty (Campion, 2001: 57). According to Getu (2007: 173), 'there is a huge gap between demand and supply, as only 130 million of the 600 million estimated potential global micro-entrepreneurs are currently being served.' Dunford (2006: 3) explains how MFIs will not, meanwhile, lose sight of societal objectives: 'microfinance (and its attendant services, such as group formation, training and social capital-building) offers opportunities to contribute to the achievement of [the MDGs] goals [by 2015], primarily through its direct impact on poverty reduction, which can support improvements in schooling, gender-equity, health and even resource conservation.'

In addition to financial services, NGOs and integrated MFIs provide training and educational services. Recent studies on 'human capital' consider investments in this area more broadly, extending them to increased knowledge and production capabilities as well as improved health and life expectancy. And such investments tend to have important implications for economic growth. Studies looking at the impact of human capital indicate that an increase in female secondary school enrolment tends to have an immediate impact on economic growth, while improved female life expectancy has only a gradual impact (Acemoglu and Johnson, 2006; Baum and Lake, 2003; Meyer, 2001).

Increasingly, country poverty reduction strategy programmes include microfinance as an important element of national development. This is because:

> Financial services are recognized now as playing multiple roles in development so that improved access can have a far greater and more comprehensive impact on poor households than previously assumed. In addition to the virtuous production and investment cycle, financial services can smooth consumption and improve food security. Moreover, supplying financial services to women may be an especially important way to empower them to play more active economic and social roles in society. (Meyer, 2001: 2–3)

In a review by Cartwright et al. examining previous studies on how MFIs empower women, the authors concluded:

> Results are consistent with the view that women's participation in micro credit programs helps to increase women's empowerment. Credit programs lead to women taking a greater role in household decision making, having greater access to financial and economic resources, having greater social networks, having greater bargaining power vis-à-vis their husbands, and having greater freedom of mobility. They also tend to increase spousal communication in general about family planning and parenting concerns. (Cartwright et al., 2006: 817)

Furthermore,

> Evidence from the millions of microfinance clients around the world demonstrates that access to financial services enables poor people to increase their household incomes, build assets, and reduce their vulnerability to the crises that are so much a part of their daily lives. Access to financial services also translates into better nutrition

and improved health outcomes, such as higher immunization rates. It allows poor people to plan for their future and send more of their children to school for longer. It has made women clients more confident and assertive and thus better able to confront gender inequities. (Littlefield et al., 2003: 1)

In other words, the 'evidence shows that microfinance interventions have indeed the capacity to reduce poverty, contribute to food security, and change social relations for the better' (Carton et al., 2001: 9). The United Nations Capital Development Fund (UNCDF) believes that 'where financial services are made available to the poor, poverty is greatly reduced' (Kapper, 2007: 1).

Though all accept that 'microfinance produces benefits in some places at some times for some people' (Moon, 2007: 49), there are some critics who claim that the impact of microfinance on poverty reduction is overstated (Labie, 2005). It is true that the social and economic improvements brought about by development-oriented NGOs and MFIs are often insufficient to lift households or nations out of poverty (Hulme and Moore, 2006). This is in part because not all the economically active poor participate; and for active microfinance participants, assistance is rarely continuous or permanent. Even if on balance MFIs appear to be contributing to poverty alleviation and food security in developing countries, the more sceptical voices say 'the universal effectiveness of microfinance institutions in alleviating poverty is still in question' (Westover, 2008: 1).

3.2 Growth and Expansion of NGOs and MFIs in Sub-Saharan Africa

The growth and expansion of NGOs and MFIs in Sub-Saharan African countries, including Uganda, has primarily been due to inadequate markets and lack of government resources reaching the vast majority of the population – a result of the diminished role of the state. In addition, MFIs may serve as 'an important financial development strategy in the face of weak, incompetent or corrupt governance, and in post-conflict reconstruction efforts' (Barr, 2005: 284). During the 1970s and 1980s (the period of the SAPs), church-related service organizations were greatly expanded to fill the gap created by government cutbacks in educational and health services to the poor. Furthermore, new national NGOs were created with the support of international non-profit organizations (NPOs) to develop and implement small-scale development projects catering for the needs of the poor and other marginalized segments of the population. Also, government cutbacks forced retrenched civil servants and middle class professionals in various African countries to search for alternative strategies to assist the poor. These included forming NGOs and community-based organizations (CBOs) for self-help projects at the village or community level. As we discuss later, the expansion of the NGO sector in Sub-Saharan Africa is clearly evident at the country level. The growth and expansion of NGOs and MFIs in Uganda is explored in detail further on in this chapter.

Within the NGO sector, the most important and promising entities are microfinance institutions that provide financial services to the economically active poor.[1] In many instances, NGOs tend to operate microcredit programmes to achieve sustainability and outreach (Buss, 2008). In particular, 'NGO-MFIs have both social missions and commercial motives. Social mission assumes that more and more poor people should be covered and the continuity of the service should be maintained through plough back of the recovered fund' (Rahman, 2001). NGO-MFIs are 'motivated by the social returns and poverty alleviation that micro-financing activities offer' (Kapper, 2007: 8). MFIs that focus on women seek to improve the opportunities and status of the women and their families by providing access to credit and other financial services. Considered the *missing piece* in grassroots development, access to credit by low-income women is said to contribute to 'broader empowerment and community development of the poor' (McKee, 1989: 1001). There are added benefits: this process can

---

[1]   In this chapter, 'microfinance institutions' (or MFIs) refers broadly to 'financial institutions dedicated to assisting small enterprises, the poor, and households who have no access to the more institutionalized financial system, in mobilizing savings, and obtaining access to financial services' (Basu et al., 2004: 3).

also 'be an effective strategy for improving child welfare on a large scale' (Dunford, 1996: 11–12). This is because the 'cash controlled by women, especially poorer women, is more likely to be used for the direct benefit of children (food, healthcare, clothing, etc.) than cash controlled by men' (Dunford, 1996: 12). According to a major study reported by Lapenu and Zeller:

> The database of MFIs from 85 developing countries shows 1,500 institutions (790 institutions worldwide plus 688 in Indonesia) supported by international organizations. They reach 54 million members, 44 million savers (voluntary and compulsory savings), and 23 million borrowers. The total volume of outstanding credit is $18 billion. The total savings volume is $12 billion or 72 per cent of the volume of the outstanding loans. MFIs have developed at least 46,000 branches and employ 175,000 staff. (Lapenu and Zeller, 2001: ii)

The same study shows that in developing countries an average of 1.5 per cent of the total population are MFI members. 'The volume of credit disbursed is around $5 per inhabitant and $3 per inhabitant are mobilized savings' (Lapenu and Zeller, 2001: ii).

Although the number of micro-borrowers had increased to 94 million worldwide by 2006, seven of every eight borrowers (47 per cent) live in the densely populated countries of Asia. In Latin America coverage is 15 per cent – most borrowers being among the 'entrepreneurial poor' living in cities. And Africa, with the Middle East, lags behind with only 9 per cent coverage (Ashe, 2007: 1). Nevertheless, microfinance flourishes in some parts. Lapenu and Zeller (2001: 11) report that MFIs 'in eastern and southern Africa (Kenya, Uganda, Zimbabwe and Zambia) are particularly dynamic as well as in some countries in the CFA-franc zone (Mali, Benin, Burkina Faso, Ivory Coast, and Togo)'. The Inter-Africa Financial Institution or IAFI, a regional network of fifty-two MFIs in twenty-four African countries has reported that 'as of February 2006, these institutions were collectively servicing approximately 3.8 million poor clients, 66 per cent of them women. The combined membership had a loan and savings portfolio of over US$571 million and US$313 million, respectively' (Mwaniki, 2006: 5).

According to the main technology or methodology used to provide financial services, MFIs in Africa are classified into five major types. These are: (1) cooperatives; (2) solidarity groups; (3) village banks; (4) individual contracts; and (5) linkage models. Mixed MFIs tend to combine different methodologies, such as individual and solidarity group models. Based on this classification, 'the largest MFIs are cooperative and individual models, with a small number among the solidarity groups. The linkage system and the village banks remain small, most of [them having] fewer than 50,000 members each' (Lapenu and Zeller, 2001: 17). Overall, the rural depth of MFIs is very low in Africa, compared to Asia; yet the majority of the population in Sub-Saharan Africa is predominately rural. Hence, Africa remains under-served by MFIs and 'agricultural finance for small holders remains underexploited' (Lapenu and Zeller, 2001: 31). In particular, rural Africa has the lowest MFI outreach because the cost of delivering financial services is much higher than in other developing countries.

It is reported that, 'unlike trends in most regions around the globe, more than 70 per cent of the reporting African MFIs offer savings as a core financial service for clients and use it as an important source of funds for lending' (Lafourcade et al., 2005: 1). The dominance and inclusion of savings and credit cooperatives under African MFIs may explain the focus of activities. In a study of 163 African MFIs published in 2005, it was found that the overall performance of the MFIs lagged behind other regions; but a growing number of regulated MFIs and cooperatives (not SACCOS) tended to be profitable (Lafourcade et al., 2005). The same study indicated that rural unregulated MFIs were more likely to target poorer clients, but often at high costs due to the small volume of operations. The study recommended that such smaller MFIs try to scale up, transform or merge with other institutions to achieve levels of efficiency that can safeguard their continued operations. MFIs involved in the mobilization of savings from the public and customers should be regulated, while small MFIs should be left unregulated. The implementation of a regulatory framework in a country 'does not necessarily mean that unregulated MFIs should disappear. It may be important to accept that two kinds of MFIs can coexist' (Lapenu and Zeller, 2001: 23). In Uganda, both unregulated and regulated micro-finance institutions coexist. The regulated MFIs (also known as deposit-taking institutions or MDIs) seek to mobilize savings from customers and the public to facilitate their rapid expansion into commercial financing. However, as we discuss later, regulatory requirements from the Bank of Uganda have made it cumbersome for the MDIs to capture deposits and expand outreach, especially to rural areas where there is insufficient credit for low-income people.

3.3 NGOs and MFIs in Uganda

As we noted in earlier chapters, the severe economic crisis that hit Uganda during the 1980s and the SAPs imposed by the World Bank and IMF gave rise there to the emergence and expansion of development-oriented NGOs and MFIs in the early to mid 1990s. These bodies emerged in Uganda to fill in the *vacuum* left by the state, forced to retreat by the implementation of the neo-liberal policies. Thus, due to 'various forms of failure by the market or state' (Tvedt, 1998: 42), NGOs emerged to provide unmet needs in neglected basic services such as education and health care. Many official donors supported the NGOs rather than local states (Dicklich, 1998b: 6). NGOs have not only provided basic social services as the state abandoned this field, but have also been involved in providing solutions to poverty alleviation through MFI programme creation. Uganda has been selected for special focus in this chapter because the country 'is generally seen as the [one] with the most vibrant and successful microfinance industry in Africa' (Carlton et al., 2001: 10). In addition, Uganda has incorporated development-oriented NGOs and MFIs as part of its larger development strategy to improve economic growth and reduce poverty.

An estimated 1,000 registered foreign and indigenous NGOs have emerged over the years to provide self-help solutions to the poor. They have been involved in basic social services and in providing solutions to poverty reduction. They own and operate many MFIs, with most of the funding coming from multilateral development agencies and, to a smaller extent,

private charities and host governments' (Ingves, 2005: 3).[2] It is reported
that annually NGOs in Uganda receive and disburse 'an estimated 25 per
cent of all official aid' (Dicklich, 1998a). In general, many MFIs are owned
and operated by non-governmental organizations (NGOs).

The emergence of microfinance institutions in Uganda is therefore
linked to the evolution of development-oriented NGOs:

> In their bid to alleviate poverty through a social agenda, a number of NGOs and other
> aid organizations started developing some form of microcredit as departments or
> functional areas in the 1980s and early 1990s. About the same time, a few specialized
> MFIs also started operations, mainly delivering microcredit backed by compulsory
> savings used as collateral substitutes. Owing to the real need for financial services
> by low income people, these microfinance programmes grew fairly fast in number
> and size. (FSDU, 2007: 10)

Between the late 1990s and early 2000s, the paradigm of microcredit shifted
to microfinance and a focus on the *best practices* in the industry. This was
due to 'a combination of donor programmes, government support and keen
interest to learn on the part of the MFIs' (FSDU, 2007: 10). In addition,
the failure of past government rural credit schemes seems to have prompted
recourse to microfinance as a new approach for delivering financial services to small-holder farmers. Government schemes had failed them for
four decades (since independence in 1962): attempts to reach the rural
poor with credit lines had no sustainable impact; the Savings and Credit
Bank Scheme, the Cooperative Credit Scheme, the Group Farm Scheme,
the Rural Farmers Scheme, *Entandikwa*, and the Youth Entrepreneurial
Scheme had all failed because they 'were often politically motivated, had
a large grant element, were not linked to savings mobilization and broadly
lacked linkages with the wider network of the financial sector' (IFAD,
2002: 2–3). In these years 'politically well-connected individuals' had often
received funding instead of those really in need, and a buy-votes-with-

---

2   In addition to NGO-owned MFIs (or NGO-MFIs), there are MFIs owned by their
     members (as in the case of SACCOS or cooperatives in Uganda), by the govern-
     ment, by social investors or by commercial investors. In some developing countries,
     commercial banks have units with an MFI niche as well.

subsidies mentality had been encouraged by loans often lent at unreasonably low rates. Because of the low rates, 'sustainable informal and formal lenders alike were unable to compete, and this led to a subsidy trap' (Babri and Vom Dorp, 2009: 23). In fact, because of this history of failure, especially with *Entandikwa* in the 1990s (Kasirye, 2007: 1), both donors and the NRM Government adopted a rural credit policy in which the public sector divested itself of direct delivery of credit; and instead, focused on creating and maintaining an enabling environment for MFIs to operate unimpeded. This hands-off attitude of the government lasted until the declaration of the NRM political manifesto in 2006.

Microfinance in Uganda grew very rapidly between 1998 and 2003, due to several additional factors: 'significant donor funding (approximately US$40 million); a shared stakeholder vision for the sector, including active government support ...; skilled human resources; and intensive collaboration among the major stakeholders [such as] practitioner organizations, donor agencies, and government bodies' (Goodwin-Groen, 2004: iv). As a result of this strong collaboration and commitment among MFI stakeholders, there were 'approximately 1,500 MFIs ... serving more than 935,000 small savers and close to 400,000 borrowers' by the end of 2003 (Goodwin-Groen, 2004: iv).

The need for regulation and supervision of MFIs increased as the number of institutions and clients grew. Initial attempts at this seem to have begun in the late 1990s with one or two larger MFIs (out of an estimated 102). It is clear that donors and the Bank of Uganda influenced transformation of the first four NGO-MFIs into deposit-taking institutions (Tumusiime-Mutebile, 2010: 3–4). The stakeholders had different expectations for supporting the regulation of MFIs, but all seem to have accepted the following reasons: (1) safety of public deposits; (2) increased savings mobilization; (3) safeguarding the public against unfair lending by MFIs; (4) overall stability of the financial sector; (5) increased outreach to rural areas; and (6) giving the regulated institutions increased sustainability (FSDU, 2007: 13). In 2003, the Uganda Government passed the Microfinance Deposit Taking Institutions (MDI) Act, 'which regulates MFIs in their operations of raising rural savings' (Kasirye, 2007: 2). Under the MDI Act, four tiers of financial institutions were established. Tier 1 applied to commercial banks and Tier 2 covered credit institutions. But Tier 3 applied to the four micro-deposit taking institutions just mentioned, which were authorized by the Bank of Uganda to take voluntary deposits from the public; and Tier 4 constituted Savings and Credit Cooperatives (SACCOS) and unregulated MFIs (Deshpande et al., 2006).

Despite the changes in the financial sector brought about by the MDI Act of 2003, financial dualism in Uganda still persists (Nannyonjo and Nsubuga, 2004). It combines both formal and informal institutions, with the latter controlling a larger proportion of the market in the rural areas of the country (Mpuga, 2004). According to a 1999 District Resource Endowment Profile Survey (DREPS), an estimated '79 per cent of all borrowers in rural areas of Uganda obtain their loans from non-traditional sources [such as] ... individual money lenders, friends and relatives and the local revolving credit systems under the self-help arrangements' (Mpuga, 2004: 7). However, emerging micro-finance and 'Tier 4' rural financial institutions such as SACCOS and unregulated MFIs now constitute a *new* sector, the semi-formal sector, which is rapidly evolving. Increasingly, people in the rural areas are served by these informal and semi-formal financial institutions – SACCOS and unregulated MFIs.

According to a 2007 FinScope Uganda Survey, '38 per cent of Ugandans use financial institutions of any type, leaving a majority of 62 per cent *unserved*' (FinScope Uganda Survey, 2007: vii). Of those receiving some form of financial services, about 3 per cent (or 400,000) are at least, semi-formally served by SACCOS and unregulated MFIs. Both MDIs and MFIs serve an estimated 3 per cent of those with access to some form of credit or financial services. The Centenary Rural Development Bank (CERUDEB), licensed in 1993 as a micro-lending bank to low-income Ugandans, has the largest portfolio loan size. It is reported that CERUDEB 'has almost 50,000 micro-borrowers and a loan book of US$44 million' (CGAP Focus Note, 2006: 5). Overall, it is estimated that '5 per cent of all households in the country receive services of the microfinance institutions' (Mpuga, 2007: 9).

Although the process of passing the MDI Act was considered participatory and involved the major stakeholders, it was largely donor-driven and had the aim of achieving the twin goals of commercialization and sustainability (discussed in Chapter Five). Donor influence was felt strongly in provision of funds and technical assistance (or capacity building) and in developing the vision for the MFI industry. From 1997 onwards, a strong collaboration emerged among key stakeholders in the microfinance sector in Uganda – the donors, the government and the central bank (Carlton et al., 2001). However, donor coordination through a formal and informal mechanism called the Private Sector Donor Sub-Group (PSDSG) has had the greatest impact on the Ugandan microfinance industry. Through the PSDSG mechanism, donors were instrumental in developing the microfinance vision in 2000:

> The single most important recent donor meeting was the donor workshop facilitated by AFCAP in April 2000. After a period of less intense cooperation in mid-1999, the workshop brought people together again and donors mutually agreed on a joint vision for the sector. Donors sketched very ambitious plans regarding client growth rates (50 per cent per annum) and rural outreach expansion (from ... 80 per cent urban and 20 per cent rural, to 60 per cent to 40 per cent respectively) for the next five years. In order to meet these targets, donors agreed that a coherent strategy for demand-driven capacity building and an active promotion of product development for rural areas would be needed. (Carlton et al, 2001: 32)

Furthermore, donors led an initiative to develop uniform performance indicators and reporting standards including a local rating system. The donors did *not* support two initiatives, however – the District Resource Endowment Profile Survey (DREPS), supported by the United Nations Development Programme (UNDP) and the Government of Uganda and the Microfinance Study conducted by Consultancy Within Engineering (COWI) and funded by the government (Carlton et al., 2001: 33).

Despite setting a goal of reaching 60 per cent urban and 40 per cent rural clientele by 2005, neither the donors nor government had a coherent strategy for rural outreach. Donors resisted the implementation of the Microfinance Outreach Plan (MOP) because they felt the government had 'sidelined [them] during the development of the MOP and felt that the precedent of close collaboration and good practice microfinance ... had been abandoned' (Goodwin-Groen, 2004: 26). Because many donors resisted the MOP, it was not possible for the government and donors to reach a meaningful solution on the rural outreach plan. In addition, funding gaps and a lack of funding priorities, especially for the rural areas, undercut the Microfinance Outreach Plan. Between 1999 and 2003, the donor community provided an estimated US$40 million for microfinance activities in Uganda. While total funding to MFIs, as well as direct loans and guarantees for loans, increased during this period, direct grants and investments in MFIs declined over the same period. Although this may have been beneficial to the four transforming MFIs, it was particularly difficult for promising MFIs that had yet to achieve sustainability. Because of funding gaps and a lack of prioritization, 'some donors put money into MFIs that [would] never be sustainable and [would] not [contribute] to either outreach or innovation. Other donors gave grants to MFIs, instead of helping them get access to commercial financing' (Goodwin-Groen, 2004: 5). Still other donors pulled the rug from under promising MFIs like FOCCAS Uganda, which was contributing substantially to both rural outreach and innovation in eastern Uganda. The fate of FOCCAS Uganda has been discussed elsewhere.[3]

From 2003 onwards, donor funding to MFIs in Uganda shifted from grants or soft loans to commercial loans and leveraging access to credit in commercial banks. However, experiences learned elsewhere suggest that 'the transformation from grant or soft loan funded operations to commercially funded institutions has proven difficult in other parts of the world and will require substantial capacity building and a revision of MFI ownership and management structure' (Carlton et al., 2001: 35). The donors compelling MFIs to work with commercial banks had failed to take note of this, and there were difficulties. In particular, the *premature* reduction and then withdrawal of grants and soft loans from financially weak MFIs, such as FOCCAS Uganda with a significant rural outreach of 85 per cent (in 2006), undermined the rural outreach efforts envisaged under the microfinance outreach plan. And starting from 2006 onwards, the Government of Uganda used the Microfinance Support Center (MSC) and

---

3   See Daniel Rozas (2009), his article 'Throwing in the Towel: Lessons from MFI Liquidations'.

the Post Bank to channel government funds directly to SACCOS rather than microfinance institutions. Hence, by 2007, neither the donor group nor the government was supporting non-regulated MFIs with grants or soft loans. This was the case despite an earlier industry recommendation that 'donors could do more to ensure that their individual actions did not pull in different directions' or undermine promising MFIs (Howes, 1997: 35). Unfortunately, neither government nor donors have heeded such advice or recommendation.

While a few international non-profit organizations (such as Freedom from Hunger which assisted FOCCAS Uganda) have played an important role in improving MFI capacity and professionalization, donor capacity builders within Uganda have had little outreach and have proved inadequate in their capacity building initiatives. This is because donor-led capacity building programmes undertaken in the past ten years or so 'have worked in isolation with little or no coordination and synergies' (Nannyonjo and Nsubuga, 2001: 21). Also in some cases, the training was not very relevant as it failed to address specific entrepreneurial or operational problems. In particular, the so-called *vaccination approach* to training favoured by donor capacity builders 'exposes as many institutions as possible to training [and] tends to spread resources evenly, but thinly'. This is the view of Deshpande et al. (2006: 15). As the same authors point out, 'parcelling out capacity building in small packets also begs the question of whether donors and government programmes have the resources needed to build up many small institutions, or would be better advised to concentrate on developing fewer, stronger ones.'

As noted previously, the emergence of microfinance and rural financial institutions was a result of government and donor support as well as the actions of those trying to arrange self-help solutions to meet the credit and savings needs of low-income groups throughout the country. Government rural credit schemes (including *Entandikwa*) having failed, both donors and the government saw microfinance as a new approach for delivering credit to the rural poor. The Poverty Eradication and Action Plan (PEAP), the Plan for Modernization of Agriculture (PMA), and the Medium-Term Competitiveness Strategy (MTCS) all saw microfinance as part of their larger development strategy to promote economic growth and reduce poverty (Carlton et al., 2001). The current National Development Plan (2010–15), the successor to the PEAP/PRSP, recognizes the importance of microfinance in rural development and transformation. At a policy level, 'the NRM government prioritizes the promotion of savings and the restoration of public confidence in the financial sector, with emphasis on small deposits' (Goodwin-Groen, 2004: 3). The government strongly supported the role of MFIs in providing rural finance until 2007, when it launched the Prosperity for All (PFA) programme which was to be implemented through SACCOS.

The government's initial support was very strong. Through PAP and *Entandikwa* Programs it was directly involved in the delivery of rural credit. Following the failure of *Entandikwa* in the late 1990s, PAP was transformed into the Rural Microfinance Support Project (RMSP). The RMSP, established as an independent legal entity, was charged with 'providing capacity building as well as lines of credit to existing MFIs' (Carlton et al., 2001: 28). The current Microfinance Support Center (MSC), a company limited by guarantee and owned by the Government of Uganda is funded under the Rural Microfinance Support Project (RMSP). MSC's original goal was to bring financial services to the rural poor through the extension of wholesale loans to microfinance institutions and other partner organizations for the purpose of on-lending to rural clients. Hence, from the 1990s the government's involvement in the delivery of rural credit was indirect. It focused on creating regulations and an enabling environment for the financial sector. From 2006 onwards, however, the government was not happy with the pace of outreach MDIs and MFIs were achieving or with the efforts made under PEAP/PMA to reduce rural poverty. It was reported at the time that within government 'there [was] a broad consensus that regulations governing MDI operations have ... slowed the pace of branch openings and rural outreach' (Deshpande et al., 2006: 17).

In order to speed up outreach to rural areas, the government started channelling credit directly through SACCOS under the PFA programme. Compared to MDIs or MFIs, political SACCOS are easy to organize and control by the political elite. At the same time, SACCOS can easily be capitalized by government and used as populist vehicles to reach people at every sub-county throughout the country. Indeed, the government saw

SACCOS 'as a bridge gap measure ... to facilitate ... access [to] wholesale funds for lending to their clients at interest rates below the market rates' (Saleh, 2009). As we noted in the previous chapter, government efforts to expand the SACCOS under the PFA are expected to intensify with the upcoming general elections in 2011. Currently, SACCOS, which are unregulated and unsupervised, are receiving external funds from government through the Microfinance Support Center and Post Bank Uganda for on-lending to their members at below-market interest rates. Unfortunately, political interference and external financing of SACCOS threatens to undermine their viability. Empirical evidence shows that 'excessive lending [to SACCOS] can serve as a disincentive to pursue additional deposits or, worse, threaten the very incentive structure holding SACCOS together' (Deshpande et al., 2006: 13). Furthermore, evidence of MFI financial sustainability indicates that 'excessive political interference in the microfinance industry appears to be one of the main threats to financial sustainability' (Ingves, 2005: 8). For MFIs to succeed, they need to avoid direct government involvement in their operations (Babri and Von Dorp, 2009). Furthermore, growing evidence shows that 'the performance of MFIs depends critically upon [their] having autonomy in management decision-making, including the setting of deposit and lending rates with an appropriate profit-making spread; being vigilant to avoid non-performing loans; and building institutional capacity, addressing skill shortages' (Basu et al, 2004: 21).

3.4 The Impact of MFIs in Uganda

Although combined MDIs and MFIs provide financial services to an estimated 3 per cent of Ugandans (FinScope Uganda Survey, 2007), 'the entire credit portfolio of all MFIs corresponds to more than 6 per cent of national domestic credit and the savings portfolio makes up 15 per cent of the national savings, showing the importance of the microfinance sector'

(Carlton et al., 2001: 41). In terms of employment or self-employment, micro and small enterprises (MSEs) combined employ the greatest number of people. Carlton estimates that the microfinance sector provides a full 90 per cent of non-farm employment in some regions (Carlton et al., 2001: 12). Surveys of microfinance institutions indicate they are involved in supporting agriculture-related activities, but also manufacturing, commerce, service industry and other smaller sectors' (PSD/CB, 2001: 11): '38 per cent of total loans made by rural MFIs in 2006 went to agricultural activities and 62 per cent to [these] other investments' (Meyer, 2007: 4). Agriculture remains the key driver of non-farm economic development, though, 'with each dollar of additional value added in agriculture generating another 30 to 80 cents in second-round income gains elsewhere in the economy' (IFAD Rural Poverty Report 2011, 2010: 21). In general, financial services impact clients in three important areas: (1) asset building; (2) reducing vulnerability to shocks and other financial crises; and (3) empowering women in decision-making in households or communities (C-GAP, 2008).

Various impact assessment studies carried out in Uganda over the past several years confirm the positive effects of microfinance services on poverty reduction (see Carlton et al., 2001: 9). An important comparative impact assessment study was carried out between 1997 and 1999 by FINCA Uganda, FOCCAS Uganda and PRIDE Uganda on their clients and non-clients. It indicated that the three programmes:

> help client households reduce their financial vulnerability through diversification of income sources and accumulation of assets. Program participation was found to be strongly associated with client households establishing new enterprises and clients increasing the number of crops they cultivate. Diversification is a strategy for spreading risk across a number of income sources. Also, the microfinance programs had an impact on the amount of money clients spent on durable assets and client households becoming owners of their residence. Durable assets and houses represent a store of wealth that can be diverted, liquidated, or rented out to meet a financial crisis. The assessment findings suggest that the strategies of the three MFI programs result in clients acquiring valued skills and knowledge. Also, the assessment found that program participation was linked with increases in the number of ways micro-enterprises save and their level of savings. In addition, on the average, clients spent more on agricultural inputs than did non-clients. In these ways, participation in the three MFI program branches studied has empowered clients who were primarily women. (Barnes et al, 2001:xiv)

Women's access to credit, though critical, is a necessary but not sufficient condition for their empowerment and improved well-being (Cheston and Kuhn, 2002). An important empirical study of women in the Arua and Mukono districts of Uganda found that participation in microfinance empowers women's decision-making in the two areas of agricultural production and use of household income (Wakoko, 2010). The same study indicated that 'individual-level factors such as occupation (farming, trading), and household-level factors, notably household headship, have a profound influence on women's empowerment in both traditional and non-traditional spheres of decision-making' (Wakoko, 2010: iii). In other words, the studies confirm that participation in microfinance programmes reduces women's vulnerability to economic risks, so that they are able to cope with shocks or economic stress. Participation also leads to the acquisition of valued skills, especially entrepreneurial ones, and it increases the empowerment of clients in terms of household decision-making and community participation through local councils.

These findings mirror a study of the Uganda Women Finance Trust (UWFT), which concluded that 'the impact of the program has been manifested in education, health, nutrition, accommodation [i.e. shelter] and in savings mobilization' (Matovu, 2006: 36). It was found that the 'borrowers of the Uganda Women's Finance Trust ... place an extremely high value on having access to ... credit and savings facilities since it is helping them in becoming less vulnerable to shocks and crises such as theft, fires, and chronic illness' (Van Santen, 2010: 5). Furthermore, 'Ugandan rural farmers who have the opportunity to obtain loans or make deposits in savings accounts have a higher likelihood of affording a nutritious meal, meeting medical care expenses and improving their farm production than those who do not have access to credit and savings at all' (Wakoko, 2010: 61). Finally, a study of the impact of rural microfinance in Uganda found that 'the primary impact of microfinance in the short term is an improved social standing for the client which can lead to increased self-confidence, better access to other financial services, and larger acceptance within the local business community' (Maggiano, 2006: iii).

In a survey of gender access to microfinance services in Uganda, it was found that about 70 per cent of the active borrowers in surveyed institutions were women, and women made up 65 per cent of the active savers (Nan-nyonjo and Nsubuga, 2004: 15). The most important reason why MFIs worldwide focus on women is, lending to women benefits the whole family and strengthens society, as women more readily spend their incomes to meet household needs such as better food, education and healthcare or fees for children. As Kabeer (2001: 83) pointedly observes, 'the entire family is much more likely to benefit economically, and women are much more likely to benefit personally and socially', when loans are directed at them rather than at men.

Studies done in Uganda in the late 1990s found that women's participation in the MFIs helped them 'to protect themselves and their households against risks by rendering their enterprises more competitive, diversifying their income sources, broadening their asset base, restocking their business and smoothing consumption' (Carlton et al, 2001: 24). An impact study by CERUDEB, the only microfinance bank that lends to both women and men, found that 'women clients have greater positive overall and specific impacts relative to female non-clients than do male clients over comparable male non-clients' (Gail et al, 1999: 4). According to Kabeer (2001: 83), 'loans to men do little to challenge the internal gender inequalities of households, and indeed appear to reinforce them by giving men an affordable base from which to prevent their wives from engaging in their own income-earning activities.' Furthermore, a study referred to previously, involving men and women participating in rural agricultural credit in Arua and Mukono Districts of Uganda, found that rural men's empowerment is associated with their patriarchical position rather than with household level conditions as was the case with women participants (Wakoko, 2010).

However, even if more Ugandan women are served by MFIs (in part because they are the target group), they have yet to escape poverty or achieve gender equality. There are two explanations why women's status has changed so little over the years. First, the average loan size is quite small and savings are still limited. Secondly, most of the largest MFIs in Uganda are located in urban or peri-urban areas, while the majority of women living in rural areas are under-served or unserved. This implies that, rather than perceiving microfinance as a 'magic bullet' or 'panacea' against poverty, it should be seen as a well-defined tool that will be most efficient in combination with other tools' (Kilibo and Schmidt, 2006: 5). A pro-poor financial strategy requires financial services to interface with specific production spheres such as subsistence farming and increased investment in rural infrastructure. In this way, microfinance could be a more promising approach than any tried in previous schemes in Uganda (Barr, 2005: 296).

3.5 The Relationship between NGOs/MFIs and the Government of Uganda

The relationship between NGOs/MFIs and the NRM government has evolved from the government's enthusiastic support in the 1990s to a situation of near hostility in the late 2000s. Initially, microfinance was seen as part of Uganda's overall development strategy. In particular, the government had identified lack of access to credit in rural areas as a major obstacle to achieving the goals of economic growth and poverty reduction. MFIs were perceived as part of the solution of reaching the poor and providing them access to credit.

All the three major policy frameworks – PEAP, PMA and the Medium Term Competitiveness Strategy (MTCS) – emphasized how credit and savings institutions such as MFIs would provide smallholder producers access to credit (Goodwin-Groen, 2004; Nannyonjo and Nsubuga, 2004; Carlton et al., 2001). This assumption permeated even the highest levels of government. For example, it is reported that: 'President Museveni believes that financial services are key to his nation's future and keenly follows MFIs, from the outreach they achieve to the interest rates they charge. His interest, fostered by the sector's success, means that microfinance receives much more government attention in Uganda than in most other countries' (Goodwin-Groen, 2004: 3).

As we argued previously, the past failure of government-led rural credit services combined with donor pressure on the government to withdraw from delivering credit directly, intensified government resolve and support for MFIs. It is also believed that when the government put through the 2003 MDI Act, it did so 'in order to increase poor people's access to financial services' (Microfinance Institutions Data Base Survey Report, 2002: 2). In other words, the government's support for MFIs and MDIs was based on the assumption that they would increase both rural outreach and access to credit. The support the government provided to MFIs through the Rural Microfinance Support Project (RMSP) included capacity building and lines of credit. However, the government's expectations for increased outreach and access to rural credit were not achieved (FSDU, 2007). This was because 'regulations governing MDI operations ... slowed the pace of branch openings and rural outreach' (Deshpande et al., 2006: 17).

The government's frustration with the slow pace of MDI and MFI outreach to rural areas was palpable. I believe it led to its promotion and support of SACCOS as an alternative vehicle for delivering rural credit. The frustration also seems to have influenced the government's hostile attitude towards MFIs expressed in 2006 during the declaration of the NRM Manifesto when it emphasized reliance on SACCOS to achieve the PFA programme in all sub-counties throughout the country. By the end of 2007, the Microfinance Outreach Plan had been completely abandoned in favour of supporting political SACCOS at the sub-county level. Top government officials, including the President, blamed MFIs for ostensibly charging high interest rates to their customers (http://microcapitalmonitor.com/Uganda). It also appears that the Association of Microfinance Institutions in Uganda (AMFIU), the apex organization for Ugandan MFIs, failed to explain to the government and the public why its member institutions charged high interest rates. MFIs charge market interest rates even on grants and soft loans with the aim of improving cost recovery for service delivery and to move toward financial self-sufficiency. However, I believe the real reason for government hostility towards MFIs and the subsequent withdrawal of funding support had to do with the MFIs' failure to achieve rural outreach and provide credit to the rural poor. Indeed, the desire significantly to increase breadth and depth of outreach was the fundamental motive for transformation (Fernando, 2004: 3). Evidence on the performance of the four MDIs that transformed in 2003 seems to suggest they have failed to achieve both breadth and depth of outreach (at least in the short and medium terms). As we noted previously, the government's frustration intensified as the 2006 general elections approached – hence, the NRM Government Manifesto of the time was aimed at speeding up rural outreach through SACCOS.

In Uganda, as elsewhere in Africa, the scope for collaboration or confrontation between the government and NGOs/MFIs is determined 'not only by the attitudes and ideas of individuals [managing] these institutions, but also by broader political, social and economic factors' (Wellard and Copestake, 1993: 5). In the case of Uganda, economic and political factors were decisive. Initial NGO/MFI-State collaboration was based largely on compatible development goals of promoting economic growth and poverty reduction. However, when these institutions failed to meet the NRM government's expectations of increasing rural outreach and access to credit, it led to government frustration, hostility and ultimately, a withdrawal of funds. As previously noted, prior to government hostility, a sense of shared goals among all stakeholders prevailed:

> A spirit of cooperation among microfinance stakeholders in Uganda led to the creation of several highly active, formal mechanisms for collaboration, including the PSDG (for donors), the Microfinance Forum (for all stakeholders, including high level government representatives, where they meet regularly to discuss sectoral issues), its subcommittees (for technical consultations on key issues, such as capacity building, financing MFIs, consumer affairs, regulation, and lobbying), and the industry association AMFIU. (Goodwin-Groen, 2004: iv)

It should be emphasized that government hostility towards NGOs/MFIs did not arise from ideological or fundamental policy differences. Rather, it was a result of failure to meet expectations or achieve the government's goals of rural credit access and outreach. However, one area where the NGO-State relationship in Uganda has been truly confrontational is in cases where NGOs have advocated human rights, democratization and the rule of law. As a quasi-democratic regime (Ekman, 2009), the NRM government has been 'highly suspicious of NGO activities, especially those that may be construed as political in any way' (Dicklich, 1998b: 24). And, 'because government's first concern is almost always to retain power, independent-minded grassroots movements generally seem more of a threat than an ally' (Durning, 1988: 1). In general, NGOs are 'viewed with suspicion by governments because, as competitors, they pose a direct threat to their legitimacy' (Hyden, 1995: 44). The Uganda government's desire to monitor or control NGO activities, may explain why the NGO Registration Board is under the Ministry of Internal Affairs (dealing with internal security), rather than the Ministry of Finance, Planning and Economic Development. At the same time, the NRM Government has tried to co-opt development-oriented NGOs into its national development strategy. NGOs in Uganda, as in other African countries, tend to work with the government when their social mission and government goals are compatible (Paul and Israel, 1991). However, the NGOs will resist or fight back if government seeks to constrain their activities (especially in the realms of human rights and democratization). While the NRM Government has *tolerated* human rights advocacy groups (or pre-empted them by creating the Uganda Human Rights Commission), it has effectively deflected international pressure and opposition allegations of repression and anti-democratic tendencies, by pointing to decentralization and the existence of local councils (formerly Resistance Councils) that allow citizens to participate in the political process at the grassroots level.

3.6 The Future of MFIs in Uganda

It is assumed that Uganda's microfinance industry has reached a critical point in its development. Either it will evolve into a dynamic market, fully integrated into the national financial system and providing a wide range of financial services to most of the population, or it will decline into 'a successful, but marginal, development niche' (Goodwin-Groen, 2004: iv). Donor and government support of MFIs has declined considerably in the past few years. Currently, the government's funding is directed towards political SACCOS operating at the sub-county level throughout the country. Although the government has no strategic vision for re-orienting the financial system to serve the rural poor, populist and ad hoc initiatives such as Prosperity for All and the creation of SACCOS have enormous political appeal to both the electorate and the political elite. Donors have cut back on MFI grants and soft loans. They have also cut back on development aid to the government because of widespread corruption. Increasingly, major donors provide 'funding to MFIs on more commercial terms and facilitated MFI borrowing from commercial banks through the use of partial guarantees' (Goodwin-Groen, 2004: 5). The guarantees include a mix of market interest rate loans and credit lines from the commercial banks. This process, known as commercialization, is explored further in Chapter Five.

Under the 2003 MDI Act, only four MFIs transformed into deposit-taking institutions or MDIs. Nearly seven years later, there is only one MFI contemplating transformation, while one of the four transformed MDIs is having second thoughts about its current status and may upgrade to Tier 1 as a commercial bank. So far, the experience of the MFIs that transformed shows that 'compliance with prudential rules is also costly to the supervised entities and may be especially burdensome to MFIs, adding to their already high operational expenses' (Ingves, 2005: 13). Furthermore, empirical evidence shows that external governance mechanisms such as imposed regulations have little positive impact on outreach and performance (Babri and Von Dorp, 2009: 30). Empirical evidence of regulated MFIs shows they too do not 'perform better in terms of either sustainability or outreach as compared to non-regulated MFIs' (Hermes et al., 2008: 7). In particular, over-regulation and stringent and costly Bank of Uganda capitalization requirements of between US$1 million to US$3 million for each MFI have prevented the expansion of current MDIs and halted any prospects for the transformation of the new ones. The costs of transformation, regulation and internal development may vary from country to country, but essentially they include: adding and training staff; modifying or replacing management information systems; feasibility study; registration and legal costs; and supervision fees (Kapper, 2007; Christen and Drake, 2002).

In addition, MDIs have been required to meet higher capital standards than either commercial banks or credit unions. It is reported, for example, that: 'MDIs are now finding themselves *over-regulated* because of some requirements which are more stringent for them than is the case is with commercial banks or credit unions'. According to the Governor of the Bank of Uganda (Tumusiime-Mutebile, 2010: 5–6), 'minimum core capital and total capital to risk weighted assets ratios for MDIs were set at 15% and 20% respectively (while for banks and credit institutions, they stand at 8% and 12% respectively).' The MDIs may consider converting

into commercial banks if the law continues to disfavour them compared
to banks. 'At least one MDI plans to graduate into a commercial bank
in the years to come. If MDIs turn into banks and mature Tier 4 institutions continue to seek transformation into Tier 1 or 2, Uganda might
soon have a redundant law called the MDI Act 2003' (FSDU, 2007: 40).
MFIs transforming into deposit-taking institutions 'require a lot of work
to meet licence requirements, and major operational changes must be
made' (Kapper, 2007: 19).

Because of such unprecedented burdens experienced by MDIs, it is
reported that by the end of December 2009, one of the four MDIs had
converted into a bank under Tier I (Tumusiime-Mutebile, 2010). And after
the passage of more than seven years since the transformation of the first
MFIs, there are only three out of 102 large MFIs that are regulated financial
institutions (RFIs). In Bolivia and other countries in Latin America, the
demonstration effect of BancoSol on commercialization of the microfinance
sector was powerful. In contrast, it seems that the transformation of MFIs
into MDIs in Uganda has radiated a rather negative effect. A MicroRate
Report (2004: 10) of the Uganda Finance Trust (formerly the Uganda
Women's Finance Trust) concluded that MFI 'transformation into a supervised financial intermediary is a traumatic process which further stresses the
institution'. Furthermore, it seems that neither donors nor government took
the total costs of transformation or the implications of MFI transformation
for outreach and access to credit properly into account. DeSousa-Shields
and King (2005: 28) explain how 'deposit funding is typically slower to
materialize and more costly than MFIs originally [planned] and it can
take many years to reach ideal deposit to debt ratios and cost structures'.
High costs of transformation and internal development, plus slow deposit
mobilization, tend to limit the growth and outreach of newly transformed
MFIs. In particular, 'regulation may direct attention away from outreach, if
regulatory requirements focus too much on financial goals such as capital
adequacy (or) financial sustainability' (Hermes et al., 2008: 7). Hence,
it could be argued that it was lack of government support for MDIs and
MFIs that was in large part responsible for their failure to achieve the rural
outreach expected of them.

According to the governor of the Bank of Uganda, outreach of MFIs will be greatly improved through more MFI transformation, banks scaling down to offer microfinance products and better service delivery by other sectors of the economy (Tumusiime-Mutebile, 2010). Unfortunately, this is unlikely to happen in the short and medium terms as the cost of MFI transformation is prohibitively high (estimated at over US$1 million per MDI) and downscaling by banks to offer new microfinance products has not happened since 1993 when CERUDEB, the only microfinance bank in the country, decided to provide individual microloans to low-income people. Also, the rise in number of MDI branches has been considerably less than the government expected – an increase of only twelve (to seventy-six) in the four years up to the end of 2009 (Tumusiime-Mutebile, 2010: 8). Moreover, as was the case with some Latin American NGO-MFIs, Tier 4 institutions in Uganda will remain untransformed for years to come, 'either because their boards of directors prefer to maintain the non-profit status – often to target the most poor – or because the regulatory system is not suitable for MFI regulation' (Berger et al., 2006: 74).

One of the most promising avenues for increasing both the breadth and depth of outreach of rural finance is through linkages or linkage banking. The creation of linkages helps to 'reduce risks and costs of delivering financial services to the customers' (Meyer, 2007: 6), and it allows MFI 'clients to become direct clients at banks, where they can open individual savings accounts and ... apply for larger or individual loans' (Babri and Von Dorp, 2009: 54). Already, Post Bank Uganda has pioneered several such linkage initiatives, but these have so far had mixed results. Some of them are notably good: it is reported, for example, that one partnership between Post Bank and an MFI 'yielded a UGS 300 million increase in deposits in several branches in northern Uganda, with Post Bank making several loans to the MFI for on-lending' (Deshpande et al., 2006: 12). The complementarity between MFIs and SACCOS or VSLAs makes experimentation with linkages or partnerships in both rural and urban settings critical and possible. Currently, Rural SPEED is 'engaged in a partnership with Simba Telecom to develop a payments system using SMS text messaging over mobile phones' (Deshpande et al., 2006: 16). The major constraint to linkage banking right now is the Bank of Uganda's regulation that prohibits 'co-branding of products between regulated and unregulated entities and banning unregulated institutions from collecting deposits on behalf of an MDI or bank' (Deshpande et al., 2006: 19). The Bank of Uganda is said to allow mobile vans, but they are restricted to credit operations and do not engage in savings activities.

Uganda's financial sector is still 'largely underdeveloped and concentrated in urban areas, leaving the majority of the agricultural producers in rural populations with no access' (Mpuga, 2004: 1). It is high time that the government, with the support of donors and collaboration of the non-governmental sector, develops a comprehensive pro-poor rural financial services strategy (rather than rely on ad hoc initiatives being undertaken by politically motivated SACCOS). Such a policy would facilitate the emergence and expansion of the *new* semi-formal financial sector linking several rural financial institutions under Tier 4. This would be a welcome development for millions of rural poor without access to credit. It would also go a long way to improve peoples' well-being and reduce poverty.

The next chapter reviews the literature on microfinance performance and impact and considers major reasons for the conflicting evidence about both issues in the industry. It also suggests that, in spite of disagreements, all stakeholders agree on the ultimate goal of microfinance intervention: it is to reduce poverty and empower clients.

CHAPTER FOUR

Microfinance Reconsidered: Performance and Impact Assessment Methods

4.0 Introduction

Microfinance is a popular and increasingly powerful strategy for sustainable development and poverty reduction worldwide (Westover, 2008). In various developing countries, microfinance institutions provide credit, financial services and savings, and other products such as insurance to millions of poor people excluded from the formal financial sector. At the 1997 First Micro-Credit Summit in Washington DC, major developed countries and international financial institutions such as the World Bank and supporters of microfinance pledged to expand credit to 100 million poor people by 2005. The United Nations even designated the year 2005 as the International Year of Microcredit. However, at the Latin America/Caribbean Microcredit Summit in April 2005, these objectives were changed. Now, the summit aims to reach 175 million of the world's poorest families, especially women and children, by the end of 2015 (Microcredit Summit, 2005; Getu, 2007).

The microfinance sector has undoubtedly experienced impressive growth since the late 1990s. Between December 1997 and December 2005, the number of MFIs increased from 618 to 3,122, and they were able to serve nearly 113 million poor people (Hermes et al., 2007). MFIs continue to grow both in size and clientele at an annual average rate of 21.6 per cent (Guierrez-Nieto and Serraro-Cinca, 2007). In 2005, it was reported that an estimated 7,000 MFIs served approximately 233 million poor families in developing countries (Westover, 2008; Kapper, 2007).[1] In 2006, there were an estimated 10,000 MFIs, an increase of 43 per cent within a year. It is reported that the majority of MFIs are small; over 90 per cent of them have fewer than 10,000 customers' each (Kapper, 2007: 12).

Despite the importance of microfinance as a tool for poverty reduction and sustainable development, experts do not consider it to be a panacea or 'magic bullet' for ending poverty. Furthermore, there is conflicting evidence about the impact of MFIs on improving poor people's livelihoods. Buss notes that 'even though microcredit programs have proliferated across the globe and many international donor organizations have funded evaluations of them, they remain enigmatic. There appears to be confusion or disagreement among researchers, practitioners and funders about what to evaluate and how to evaluate it' (Buss, 2008). This situation is further complicated by the fact that MFIs focus on the 'double bottom line', which seeks to achieve a balance between business objectives and a social mission (Dunford, 1999: 1). While 'financial performance can be tracked with relative ease, mainly because there is a good consensus about what should be measured and how ... social impact measurement is far more difficult' (Dunford, 2001: 4).

Beyond the challenges of what and how to measure impact is the issue of who should undertake such an evaluation or assessment. Copestake (2007: 1722) has proposed three options for carrying out an assessment of MFIs: 'One view is that impact assessment is a task better left to independent researchers and oriented towards informing public policy. At the other extreme is the view that the potential of microfinance as a development tool can only be realized if financial institutions themselves systematically and routinely investigate their own development impact. An intermediate position favours a mix of more rigorous *proving* impact assessment research for public policy and less rigorous *improving* research for internal use by financial institutions.'

---

1   It should be noted that 'no systematic and comprehensive data on MFIs are collected and there are no authoritative figures on key characteristics of the microfinance industry, such as the number and size of MFIs, their financial situation, or the population served' (Westover, 2008: 2–3). Furthermore, direct and indirect MFI clients/customers may or may not be included, leading to wide variations.

Current research and scholarship on the impact of development-oriented NGOs, as well as MFIs, falls into two categories: that stressing the success and positive impacts, and that attesting to failure or lack of meaningful impact. This chapter explores reasons for the conflicting evidence regarding the impact and performance of MFIs on the poor in developing countries. It also considers emerging pro-practitioner tools such as *ImpAct* and *Progress Tracking* that seek to bridge the gap between performance and impact assessment. Such tools seek to prove and improve impact or track progress toward desired outcomes.

4.1 Performance and Conflicting Evidence about MFI Impact

There are three major explanations for the conflicting evidence about MFI impact. First, there is a problem of what to measure and how to measure it. Even if their ultimate goal is poverty reduction, most MFIs tend to pursue a 'double bottom line' of financial and social goals. And striking a balance regarding this dual mission is difficult to achieve. The second problem has to do with a tendency to confuse performance indicators (or 'best practices' in the industry) with impact assessment – the socio-economic impact on clients or customers. Performance indicators such as outreach or client satisfaction are not identical to measures of impact such as income generation, poverty reduction or client empowerment (Goetz and Gupta, 1996). Third, impact studies derived from emerging integrated or embedded approaches such as *ImpAct* or *Progress Tracking* seek both to prove and improve the effectiveness of microfinance. Such studies try as well to provide the link or continuity between MFI performance and impact on outcomes.

MFI performance is concerned with improving the delivery of services, while impact assessment deals with proving the effectiveness of the services provided to customers (Sharma et al., 2000). In addition, the focus of performance tends to be on the institution, whereas impact is concerned

with the customers or their livelihoods. Some commonly used performance indicators include: governance; management and leadership; mission
and plans; products; portfolio quality; and financial analysis (Verhagen,
2001). The World Bank's Consultative Group to Assist the Poor (CGAP)
has developed an appraisal format which contains practical guidelines and
indicators used for measuring MFI performance. For example, their Poverty
Assessment Tool (PAT) considers 'current economic status and fulfilment
of basic needs, the means to achieve a level of welfare in the present and
future, such as assets, human and social capital'. PAT also 'elucidates on the
other aspects of ... [poverty alleviation] such as health status and access
to healthcare, access to food, shelter, clothing and degree of vulnerability
to future shocks' (Babri and Vom Dorp, 2009: 36). CGAP's performance
tools have encouraged transparency and the development of standards for
financial analysis and financial sustainability. CGAP Standards for MFI
Performance, for instance, have given rise to the 'best practices' approach
used by donors, practitioners and rating agencies. Such 'best practices' are
approved and sanctioned by both the World Bank and the United States
Agency for International Development (USAID).

Since MFIs are 'double bottom line' institutions, simultaneously pursuing financial and social goals, there is a need to consider both financial and
social performance. Social performance is defined as 'the effective transla-
tion of an institution's social mission into practice in line with accepted
social values' (ACCION, 2007: 1). Social performance entails serving more
clients (often poorer ones), broadening the range of the services they receive
and offering such services on a sustainable basis (Copestake, 2006). Despite
the fact that social goals often drive the strategies and processes of many
MFIs, most MFIs are assessed primarily in terms of financial performance
(ACCION, 2007). 'While financial return benchmarks are standardized
and universally accepted; social performance metrics are qualitative, not
standardized and more difficult to track' (IAMFI Position Paper, 2008:
3). As a result, there has often been little effort to *balance* financial and
social performance or impact properly (yet both missions are crucial for
the success of microfinance as a tool for poverty reduction). However, currently, there are promising initiatives underway to develop industry-wide
guidelines to evaluate social performance *together with* financial performance (ACCION, 2007).

In contrast to performance indicators, indicators used to assess the impact of MFIs include: growth of material assets or increase in individual or household income; reducing vulnerability to shocks or risks; and empowering women clients (Duscha, 2008; Snodgrass, 2002; Verhagen, 2001). Such impact indicators are used as tools for determining the effectiveness of microfinance as a strategy for poverty reduction and sustainable development. Evidence of microfinance impact shows that credit or financial services help to increase 'the standard of living of the people, an awareness, decision-making and reduction of poverty among the rural [clients]' (Adnan, 2004: 2). Impact assessment, like performance, tends to focus on financial analysis while ignoring or marginalizing social analysis, and stakeholders, such as donors, policy-makers, practitioners and researchers, tend to concentrate on different priorities and different standards, with diverging uses and approaches in mind (Cohen and Sebstad, 1999: 3).

Some of these stakeholders advocate linking performance and impact assessment using Hulmes' (1997) continuum of objectives to prove and improve the effectiveness of microfinance (Goldberg, 2005; Cohen and Sebstad, 1999). Other stakeholders view MFI impact assessment as serving a dual role, due to the shift in MFI objectives from *proving impact* to *improving impact* (Verhagen, 2001). The dual role entails determining whether MFI services are having a positive impact on the poor customers they serve, and assessment is seen as a management tool to improve operational efficiency, product design and social effectiveness. Donor agencies such as USAID focus on MFI outreach and reducing vulnerability to shocks rather than increasing household income and reducing poverty per se (Cohen and Sebstad, 1999). However, once customers have income, it is assumed they can use it to smooth consumption and reduce vulnerability to the risks associated with hunger and poverty.

In general, *donors and policy-makers* often want proof of MFI effectiveness in terms of achieving mission or development objectives. Beyond concern for programme sustainability, outreach and deepening financial markets, they want to know whether MFI services are reaching the poor and helping to reduce poverty and empower customers. On the other hand, *practitioners* are driven primarily by a mix of proving and improving MFI goals. They want to ensure that MFI financial services and products really do reach the poor and that they are responsive to customer needs and wants. It is generally believed that 'most practitioners recognize a strong link between program performance and client level impact' (Cohen and Sebstad, 1999: 3).

In the past, therefore, donors and practitioners tended to go their separate ways with impact assessments. This was because donor-driven impact assessments focusing on financial sustainability were intended to justify funding rather than assist MFI management learn and improve their operations. However, the emerging *practitioner-oriented* approach to impact assessment considers such assessments as serving 'a variety of objectives, including internal learning for MFI staff, improving operational efficiency, enhancing management and information systems, [and] proving the positive impact of financial services to external donors' (http://micro-financegateway.or/section/resourcecenters/impact/assessment/what/). Such an embedded impact assessment tool is intended to benefit donors, practitioners and customers alike. Examples of such tools outlined here are *ImpAct* and *Progress Tracking*. These tools seek to improve service delivery and assess impact or track progress towards desired outcomes.

Despite the desire by practitioners of MFIs to link performance to impact assessment, there is a tendency to confuse the two or to focus on performance as a proxy for impact assessment. Some MFIs assume that financial performance indicators are sufficient proxies for impact on customers. Such MFIs contend that if customers are willing to pay for financial services and other products, it can be assumed they are satisfied with what they are getting. From this point of view, satisfied customers, good repayment rates and customer retention are considered positive indicators of impact (Epstein, 2005). However, such performance cannot be equated with improvement in poor people's livelihoods or well-being. For example, customers who have fallen into debt may repay their loans even when their businesses fail and they themselves are facing considerable personal hardships. Such customers may be assisted by their solidarity groups or they may simply borrow from a competitor MFI to pay off what they owe in order to get the next loan. The practice of clients borrowing from multiple MFIs in order to settle outstanding loans is a serious problem in Latin America where the microfinance industry has reached saturation point (Sebstad et al., 1995). This problem, though less acute in Africa, is becoming increasingly evident. It is possible, then, for effective MFI performance to lead to positive results or outcomes, but the two concepts should not be equated or confused, as is so often the case.

With the current push toward financial sustainability and outreach, client level impact assessment has tended to be marginalized or replaced by the assessment of institutional performance. MFIs that stress financial sustainability tend to equate institutional sustainability with the socioeconomic impact of customers. They automatically suggest that their operations are making a positive difference to the lives of the customers when this may or may not be the case. As a result of such one-sided analyses, the overall quality and rigour of microfinance impact evaluations can vary greatly and may be diluted: it depends on the programme objectives (Goldberg, 2005). Thus, the greatest challenge facing MFIs is to demonstrate the effectiveness of microfinance and its impact on customers. To this end, USAID – under the AIMS Project (developed by the Small Enterprise Education and Promotion Network (SEEP) – has been critical in redefining the impact assessment agenda. It has developed a range of reliable, lower-cost tools which yield data people can trust to prove and improve the effectiveness of microfinance. In a similar way, some emerging middle-range approaches consider both MFI performance and impact. The aim to serve the poor more effectively and reduce poverty among clients has thus been integrated into impact assessment.

4.2 Emerging Performance and Impact Assessment Tools

The emerging middle range approaches to impact assessment such as *ImpAct* (funded by the Ford Foundation) or *Progress Tracking* (developed by Freedom from Hunger) 'seek to integrate impact assessments into organizational learning and development, so that the understanding of clients and their wider situation becomes central to the work of microfinance organizations' (Simanowitz, 2001: 26). These approaches focus on the need by MFIs to improve the delivery of services and to assess impact, or at least progress toward poverty reduction (Dunford, 2005). Both *ImpAct* and *Progress Tracking* have two interrelated goals. The first is to link impact assessment to existing staff and work patterns, building on existing knowledge and experience, and producing results that can be applied easily by management. The second goal is to design and improve methodologies for assessing wider poverty reduction impacts of microfinance. Thus, *ImpAct* or *Progress Tracking* can be used to identify indicators for performance and also impact objectives the microfinance institution might take up (Simanowitz, 2001; Copestake, 2006). At the moment, various MFIs and practitioners are in process of implementing and assessing the effectiveness of such tools. SEEP and Freedom from Hunger (based in Davis, California) have each developed tools designed to assess impact or progress toward impact.

SEEP is a membership organization of microfinance institutions and practitioners. Underwritten by USAID, under the AIMS project, it has developed a package of five tools intended to service a combination of programme improvement and impact objectives (Cohen and Sebstad, 1999: 7). The tools developed by SEEP include a mix of quantitative and qualitative instruments such as household surveys, exit surveys, loan and savings tools, and focus group discussions on client satisfaction and client empowerment. Taking a different line, Freedom from Hunger (an MFI and member of SEEP) recommends the design of simpler tools to assess impact and progress toward impact (Dunford, 2005). Instead of requiring rigorous cause-effect research (which is not easily attainable), Freedom from Hunger aims to work through *Progress Tracking* embedded in routine operations and aimed at improving the impact of services. Freedom from Hunger has worked with various partners around the world (such as FOCCAS Uganda, CRECER in Bolivia, and CARD in the Philippines) to develop and implement three progress-tracking tools which fill the gaps in the earlier impact assessment systems. The tools include: (1) observational checklists to ensure linkage of required inputs to outputs; (2) pre- and post-mini surveys linking outputs to desired outcomes or impacts; and (3) participatory learning action (PLA) to assess client response to the outputs in an open-ended way. These tools are designed to be used by field staff during regularly scheduled field visits or meetings with clients, so there is no need for specialist staff or consultants to conduct special studies. Senior staff have to make some specific initial decisions on improving service delivery or product performance. The MFIs are then free to develop their capacity to use collected information to promote a culture of learning, service quality, and responsiveness to client demand. Ultimately, the effective implementation of *Progress Tracking* depends on senior management with a strong client service orientation.

4.3 Major Approaches to Evaluating the Impact of MFIs

There are four major approaches used to evaluate the impact of microfinance institutions. These are: (1) the Household approach (or 'narrow' approach); (2) the *'wider impacts'* perspective; (3) the Benefits Process approach; and (4) the Livelihoods Framework.[2] A growing number of impact assessments provide a range of benefits that accrue to MFI customers. Such benefits include increase in household income, self-employment and employment generation, asset accumulation, reducing vulnerability to shocks or stress, empowerment, and improving food security and nutrition (Park and Ren, 2001).

The Household approach differs from the conventional approaches as it considers impact at household, individual and community levels (Sebstad, et al., 1995). In so doing, it 'not only improves our understanding of dynamics

---

2   Though the focus here is on major approaches, there are several different ways of measuring impact including Social Performance Assessments (SPAs), Assessing the Impact of Microenterprise Services (AIMS), and Internal Learning Systems such as *Progress Tracking* or *ImpAct*; also use of a sustainable Livelihoods Framework. Most assessments use quantitative research tools such as surveys, financial ratios and participatory tools; and qualitative tools such as focus group discussions and participant observation. For more on *ImpAct* as a global action research program to explore ways of improving the measurement and management of poverty-reduction MFIs, see Copestake (2007: 1721–38).

and impacts at the enterprise level, but also allows us to widen the impact lens to consider impacts beyond the enterprise' (Sebstad, et al., 1995: i).

At the household level, microenterprises promote growth by contributing to household income, asset accumulation, the smoothing of consumption during tough or lean times, and a range of subsidiary things. Hence, measuring change at the household level involves consideration of three impact paths or domains: income; expenditures on household consumption (including debt); and assets. At the individual level, individuals should experience well-being and be empowered; household welfare should improve and the household economy be more diversified. Three particular domains of impact at the level of the individual are: independent control of resources; empowerment in terms of decision-making within the household; and community participation. Finally, at the community level, microenterprises contribute to growth by attracting new income from outside the community, preventing income flight, and creating self-employment and new employment opportunities for household or community members. At this level, change is measured in terms of four paths of impact: net changes in employment and income; forward and backward linkages; social networks; and civic participation. These changes, when considered together, 'indicate the movement of households toward (or away from) greater economic security; the movement of enterprises between stages of enterprise development; and changes in individual well-being, in civic participation, and the economic development of communities' (Sebstad, et al., 1995: iii). In this way, microenterprise intervention is said by proponents of the Household approach to contribute both to poverty reduction and to economic development.

The Household approach claims to combine both specific (narrow) and broader (wider) impacts, but there is increasing concern among development experts, MFI practitioners and researchers over the narrowness of its focus on individuals, enterprises and households in most of the studies (Zohir and Matin, 2004). Critics of the Household approach insist that *wider impacts* are not included within the narrow focus regardless of its claims, making the two types of impact mutually exclusive. In short, the Household approach is viewed by its critics as providing a too 'narrow perspective of wider impacts'.

The critics' concerns about the Household approach centre round three major issues. First, even if individual/household variables may be aggregated to arrive at impact at the community or national level, there is a mismatch of achievements at the micro- and meso-levels. Second, there is an increasing understanding that achievements of microfinance institutions, especially in countries like Bangladesh, which has a large and mature industry, have been underestimated. Third, studies with a narrow focus consider impacts of individual programmes or comparisons across them, but rarely examine impacts on both participants and non-participants when there are several MFIs operating in the same marketplace.

In contrast to the Household approach, the *wider impacts* perspective considers 'all other impacts, which are not included within the narrow focus' (Zohir and Matin, 2004: 305). It thus facilitates a shift in focus away from individuals or households to meso- or macro-levels and broadens the scope of impacts to include both participants and non-participants. The *wider impacts* perspective is based on the assumption that the total impact of microfinance intervention has been underestimated in conventional studies, because these studies do not take into account 'the possible positive externalities on spheres beyond households and the subsequent feedback effects on both participants and non-participants' (Zohir and Matin, 2004: 301).

Impacts within the wider community relate to poverty within it as well as to social inequalities and lack of participation by the poor (especially women) in public-decision processes (*Insights*, 2004). Furthermore, proper consideration of wider impacts plays a critical role in achieving the broader goals of poverty reduction and development. Imp-Act has made a study of the Foundation for International Community Assistance (FINCA) project in Uganda, which provides savings and insurance services. The study 'demonstrated that micro-insurance increases income stability of both MFI clients *and* non-clients within the community as the local economy benefits from a more stable circulation of money and increased trade' (www.id21.org). Another study by Imp-Act, this time on a bank involved in microfinance in Uganda – CERUDEB – showed that loans given to small farmers have contributed to substantial increases in part-time and permanent wage labour for non-clients (Wrenn, 2005).

Finally, the use of group-based approaches by MFIs in various countries such as Indonesia, India and Bangladesh has been found to play a critical role in achieving wider impacts including: the generation of labour market opportunities for the poor; trust among members; and improved relationships within the wider community. For example, a study by Zohir and Matin (2004: 301–5) found that 'many MFI loans are used for agricultural production, trading and transport, resulting in an increase in the use of agricultural inputs and increased outputs of agricultural production'. Clearly this benefits both participants and non-participants. It should be noted, however, that sometimes group-based strategies contribute to conflict among members and may result in the exclusion of the poorest and increased inequality within the community.

The *wider impacts* perspective does not just broaden the scope of assessment at meso/macro levels; more importantly, it lays out impact paths or domains. These cover four broad sectors: economic, social, political, and cultural. However, because financial services are the core activity of microfinance, bias towards the economic domain and institutional analysis tends to be unavoidable (Zohir and Matin, 2004). In the economic domain, wider impacts occur in two ways. First, through credit or financial services, individuals and households are linked to various markets. Second, microfinance institutions in the course of their operations, engage with markets or other MFIs as well as partnering up with a range of other formal and informal institutions (including the state or government). The institutional context within which MFIs operate may impose new roles, requiring them to provide a larger package than basic financial services to participants and non-participants. This is particularly the case if MFIs partner with public financial institutions.

While impacts of the use of loans by borrowers are often studied, less attention is usually paid to the impacts of MFIs as new actors in the financial market and the ways in which they interact with other formal and informal institutions. For example, with their innovative products, MFIs have enlarged the financial market, increased household incomes and savings, and induced competition in the rural financial markets. Thus, it is important to study certain areas of wider impacts that may not be captured by the Household approach. In addition to their (potential) contribution towards promoting economic growth and providing employment, MFIs have induced competition in several markets. There is competition with government in delivery of social services, with the private sector in the production and marketing of private goods, and with the formal banking sector in the financial market. The gains for the national economy are much higher than those captured by the 'narrow' Household approach.

Though studies on *wider impacts* in the area of economic development are still in their infancy, serious efforts have been made by both development experts and practitioners to examine the impacts on development of MFIs coupled with development-oriented NGOs. These centres of activity (both local and international) are said to have both a direct and indirect effect on economic development. Directly, they help foster development by providing capital and credit, supporting business and entrepreneurship, facilitating economic stability, and governmental accountability. Indirectly, they increase the human capital necessary for the promotion of sustained economic growth (Baum and Lake, 2003), leading to enhanced employment opportunities for the wider community. Recent observers of such microfinance believe it will play a pivotal role in achieving the Millennium Development Goals (Dunford, 2006; Wrenn, 2005). Such observers believe that microfinance has the capacity to deliver social benefits on a sustainable basis and is suited to eradicating poverty, promoting education, improving health and empowering women. However, not all experts and observers are enthusiastic about the role of microfinance in promoting development or reducing poverty.

Studies on the use of microfinance to eradicate poverty show that well-designed programmes by MFIs that understand and cater to the needs of the poor can indeed improve the incomes of the destitute and struggling and help move them out of poverty (Wrenn, 2005). Both qualitative and quantitative studies 'support the view that access to finance provides the poor with opportunities to invest in income-generating activities, smooth consumption and thus reduce their vulnerability to income fluctuations during emergencies' (Economic and Social Survey of Asia and the Pacific, 2005: 262). However, some microfinance specialists contend that increasing the income of the poor does not necessarily reduce poverty. Such specialists argue that improvements in economic security (rather than increase in income per se) should be the first step in poverty reduction, as this reduces the overall vulnerability in society of people who have nothing beyond the very basics.

The Sustainable Livelihoods Framework (SLF), which is part of the *wider impacts* perspective, transcends the economic impact of microfinance. A livelihood security approach 'aims for a holistic analysis and understanding of the root causes of poverty and how people cope with poverty' (Wrenn, 2005: 6). People's capacities to withstand or cope with shocks or risks, such as natural disasters and drought, political instability and economic crises, as well as resources they have such as education and local infrastructure, have to be taken into consideration when assessing the impact of microfinance on well-being. This means that in addition to the economic impact, the social impact of microfinance on the poor must be considered. The social impact of microfinance, as it relates to aspects of human capital such as nutrition, health, education and interpersonal networks, must be carefully analysed. Such social analysis should go beyond the individual or household to include the local community, economy and society. A comprehensive study of sixteen different microfinance institutions world-wide showed 'that having access to microfinance services has led to an enhancement in the quality of life of clients, an increase in their self-confidence, and has helped them to diversify their livelihood security strategies and thereby [increase] their income' (Wrenn, 2005: 7).

The Benefits Process approach like the Sustainable Livelihoods Framework takes into account root causes of poverty and food insecurity as well as the direct and indirect impacts of microfinance on participants. Furthermore, it analyses the benefits accruing to participants in microfinance in terms of 'ultimate goals of improved household food security and better health and nutrition status by acting through the necessary intermediate benefits of poverty alleviation, empowerment, and behaviour change' (MkNelly, 1992: 18).

Though seemingly simple and clear, the Benefits Process approach tends to be complicated by the practical and methodological challenges of measuring, and even defining, benefits. (How, for example, do you define and measure 'empowerment'?). It is difficult to agree on acceptable levels and time frames for change, and to assess possible trade-offs between differing program objectives – for example, scale and impact' (MkNelly, 1992: 19). The Benefits Process approach raises the critical issue of potentially confusing financial performance with programme impact. While important for measuring the potential of microfinance to reduce poverty, positive financial indicators (such as high repayment rates) cannot substitute for data reflecting the social impact on participants. This is because serious trade-offs exist between institutional (financial) performance and economic or social impact at the individual or household level. For example, 'an evaluation of a credit program for women in India found that while women were maintaining good repayment rates, the small profits they were able to make were used to pay the interest on loans' (MkNelly, 1992: 21).

As previously indicated, three major problems confront efforts aimed at determining the impact of microfinance on the well-being of participants. The first problem is what to measure and how to measure it. The second problem has to do with confusing performance with impact. And the third problem concerns the use of embedded approaches (such as *ImpAct* or *Progress Tracking*) that seek both to prove and improve the effectiveness of microfinance. What follows is an analysis of the impact of microfinance, so far as it can be determined, together with an account of the challenges often encountered while attempting to make assessments. It is important to note that, so far as the overall impact of microfinance on poverty alleviation is concerned, results are mixed (Westover, 2008). In the analysis below, however, we consider some of the positive impacts.

4.4 Impacts of Microfinance Institutions

Although the assumed or stated goal of microfinance institutions is poverty reduction, in reality the goals of MFIs vary quite a bit. Some focus on poverty reduction, while others seek to provide financial services and other products to the poor (Epstein, 2005). Some MFIs claim that measuring financial performance is adequate for determining MFI success, while others contend that measuring real impacts on the lives of the poor is the way to establish success. (Criteria include: increase in income; empowerment; change in assets; and improvements in education and health.) Practitioners and experts may be divided over MFI goals or potential impact, but most scholars do concur that the ultimate goal of MFIs is poverty reduction, whether or not it is stated as a primary goal (Epstein and Crance, 2005; Khandker, 2005).

The dearth of available data, combined with the absence of operational transparency, makes it difficult and expensive to assess the impact of microfinance on participants in any comprehensive way (Copestake, 2007; Aghion and Murdoch, 2005). As a result of these difficulties, some studies have tried to connect the poverty-reducing success of MFIs to proxy variables such as changes in household income and consumption. Other empirical studies of MFIs have used financial performance indicators such as high repayment rates, outreach or profitability as proof of poverty reduction (Datar et al., 2008). However, the use of financial performance indicators as proof of poverty reduction by MFIs is not a reliable measure (Datar et al., 2008). In the same way, reliance on consumer satisfaction or high repayment rates as ways to measure positive impacts on clients are of limited value. Despite the challenges presented by impact assessments of microfinance, however, a handful of empirical studies focusing on increases in household incomes and consumption smoothing have demonstrated significant rates of poverty reduction among MFI participants (Mel et al., 2007: Epstein, 2005). According to these studies, increases in household income and consumption show economic improvement among participants, suggesting that the borrowers of microfinance loans are emerging above poverty.

In a recent study of microfinance borrowers, it was found that 'small loans to existing businesses have significant returns to capital. In fact, the loans given to business owners increased real income by profits of 68 per cent. This real annual return is significantly higher than nominal market rates of 16–24 per cent for a two-year term' (Mel et al., 2007: 21). The study showed significant gains for borrowers from small loans, suggesting that providing the poor with access to credit and other financial services they need promotes consumption smoothing, reduces risks and vulnerability to financial shocks and serves as an important tool against poverty (Epstein, 2005). Critics of this and similar studies argue that the studies tend to target existing businesses that are closely supervised to ensure loans are used for productive purposes (Arun et al., 2006). They insist further that most MFIs neither track the specific use of loans nor lend only to existing businesses.

The largest and most important study to date is that undertaken by Khandker in 2005 on the participants of The Grameen Bank (Khandker, 2005; Goldberg, 2005). This study used panel data of income and consumption to measure the impact of microfinance loans on the clients. Khandker (2005) contends that, since the overarching objective of microfinance is poverty reduction, any impact assessment of microfinance and poverty reduction should 'assess whether program participation increases household consumption over its level before program participation' (Kandker, 2005: 14). The study, which was carried out between 1991/92 and 1998/99, found evidence of increased income and consumption for both participants and non-participants. According to its findings, 'the household annual per capita expenditure grew by 30.5 per cent for all households, compared with 34.5 per cent for borrowers' (Khandker, 2005: 19). The increase in overall household consumption levels is attributed to the 'multiplier effects' of borrowers' improved economic conditions and to benefits accruing to non-participants due to growth in the local economy. The same study demonstrated that, as a result of increased consumption in the sample villages, 'overall poverty declined by 17 per cent between 1991/92 and 1998/99 and extreme poverty by 13 per cent' (Khandker, 2005: 20). The findings of the study show that 'not only does the increase in consumption resulting from borrowing raise the probability that program participants will escape poverty, but the microfinance intervention also benefits non-participants through growth in the local economy' (Khandker, 2005: 23). These findings suggest that 'a raise in borrowers' income is sufficient to show poverty alleviation' (Goldberg, 2005: 46). Another important income and consumption study – made on participants of the Khushbali Bank (KB) in Pakistan – not only found a positive correlation between MFI lending and increase in client income and consumption levels, but also found that spending on children's education increased significantly (Montgogomery, 2005). The findings of both studies appear to support the assumptions of the *wider impacts* perspective discussed earlier.

Critics of income-consumption-poverty studies claim that such studies fail to account for the underlying causes of poverty or powerlessness among MFI participants. They contend further that, even if access to credit permits consumption smoothing and the reduction of risk or vulnerability to financial shocks, real economic development and poverty alleviation may not necessarily occur as envisaged (Epstein, 2005). For example, such critics argue that 'despite the large amount of outreach to the poor reported in Bangladesh, the poverty situation has not improved dramatically' (Economic and Social Survey of Asia and the Pacific, 2005: 262). But in an apparent acknowledgement of the criticisms, proponents of income and consumption studies call for the need to look deeper than the observable changes before asserting any improvements in the financial condition of the borrowers (Vanroose, 2007). Hence, alternative approaches to income and consumption tend to consider changes in the behaviour or assets of participants before and after programme participation (Hatch and Frederick, 1998).

4.5   Assessing Impact in Poverty-Centred MFIs

While financially-oriented MFIs use household income and consumption levels to assess impact on participants, poverty-centred ones track changes in education, health or assets of participants. Poverty-centred MFIs, also known as '*microfinance plus*', often monitor very closely how borrowers use their loans, and they tend to provide business and health education to their clients. The close monitoring of loans is often expensive, but some recent studies indicate that social and economic impacts are greater in cases of close monitoring than in unsupervised ones (Arun et al., 2006). Furthermore, participants who are closely monitored and provided with business education training tend to have businesses that are more likely to be sustainable (Arun et al., 2006). Overall, these studies seem to suggest that 'when MFIs closely monitor the use of loans, group performance increases, lowering default rates as well as increasing the chances of success' (Hermes and Lensink, 2007: 6). In addition to loans guided through tracking and monitoring, the provision of education services is said to increase the human capital of the clients and their children (Vanroose, 2007; Maldonado, 2002). According to Vanroose (2007: 7), '*microfinance plus* programs have the ability to increase the level of human capital which in the long run, allows for sustainable poverty reduction and development.'

Proponents of *microfinance plus* believe that MFIs should play a much more dominant role than traditional banks or credit institutions 'by offering financial services ... education, training and close monitoring of the use of loans and profits generated from loans to maximize social and economic impacts' (Datar et al., 2008: 40). Furthermore, the proponents believe that education and training offered to clients should be extended to loan officers and field staff as well, to ensure a robust monitoring regime and maximize the desired impacts (Datar et al., 2008). Currently, a handful of microfinance institutions, such as Freedom from Hunger and Opportunity International, offer both financial and comprehensive educational services. Below, briefly, we consider the impact of such services on the participants.

In 1991, Freedom from Hunger carried out an impact survey of randomly selected participants from its *Credit with Education* programmes in Honduras and Mali. In the Mali survey, controls were selected from other communities not participating in the programme but having similar socioeconomic characteristics; in the Honduras survey, the controls were non-participants in the programme communities themselves. According to the results, in both programme sites, 'a greater percentage of the program participants reported having more income than non-participants' (MkNelly and Lassen, 1991: 1). It is also reported that participants in both programmes spent increased incomes on food, clothing, health and school costs – in that order (MkNelly and Lassen, 1991). In terms of women's empowerment (taken as increase in self-confidence and influence), 'the results from Mali and Honduras support the findings of other more detailed studies that show that when a woman's economic contributions to the family increase, her bargaining power and influence also increase' (MkNelly and Lassen, 1991: 2–3). In both programmes, women participants reported being more confident and thought they were receiving more respect and consideration by others in the household and the communities.

Finally, the findings of the survey showed 'that in each of the two countries a greater percentage of program participants than non-participants had learned about specific types of foods that were good for young children' (MkNelly and Lassen, 1991: 3). What is interesting is that almost all respondents who reported learning about good foods also indicated they had tried the foods at least once. For example, it is reported that '65 per cent of the program participants, compared to only 20 per cent of non-participants, knew that weaning foods should be introduced when infants were from four to six months of age' (MkNelly and Lassen, 1991: 3). Overall, the 'studies showed that microcredit clients in Mali and Honduras were more likely than non-clients to have larger businesses, to see an increase in personal income and food consumption, to have personal savings (a mandatory element of the program), and to feel a greater sense of self-esteem' (*The New York Times, Op. Ed.*, 2007: A3).

In addition to the surveys in Mali and Honduras, Freedom from Hunger has carried out studies – similarly designed – on the impact of its *Credit with Education* programmes in Ghana and Bolivia (Dunford, 2001). The respective programmes are the Lower Pra Rural Bank one (in Ghana) and the Bolivian *Credito con Educacion Rural* (CRECER). In the programmes, comparisons were made between women clients with one to three years of participation in *Credit with Education* and women non-participants in either baseline or control groups. The women's young children (up to three years old) were also included in the assessments. The impact of the financial services offered by the *Credit with Education* programmes was measured and, in both countries, the study demonstrated 'increased levels of livelihood security among clients – more regular earnings throughout the year, asset accumulation and consumption-smoothing' (Dunford, 2001: 9). In Ghana, according to the survey, *Credit with Education* clients 'enjoyed a significantly greater increase in monthly non-farm earnings – almost double – as compared to non-participants in the same communities or residents living in control communities' (Dunford, 2001: 9). The findings also show positive changes in clients' health knowledge, self-reported practices and some health outcomes. In Bolivia, 'between the baseline and follow-up, a significant and positive difference was found in the percentage of clients reporting [that] they gave children with diarrhoea "more liquid than usual" (liquids of any kind, including breast milk) as compared to non-participants' (Dunford, 2001: 10). In terms of women's empowerment, the studies indicated that 'in both Ghana and Bolivia, there was evidence that access to financial and education services had positively impacted [on] women's self-confidence and status in the community' (Dunford, 2001: 11).

Another microfinance plus organization in the field is Opportunity International. Opportunity International and its affiliates provide business, educational and health training for all their clients, in addition to financial services and other social outreach programmes necessary in particular places. According to the organization, providing health education in addition to financial training tends to increase household health expenditure, thereby mitigating a major cause of poverty. Other studies back this kind of finding up. A study of the benefits of education training programmes in Bolivia by Karlan and Valdivia (2007) suggests that such programmes positively impact on the targeted borrowers' human capital; and an earlier one by Maldonado et al. (2003), which used data from the Bolivian MFIs, CRECER and SARTAWI, found a positive and significant correlation between training and changes in the households' education and health. This last study showed too that, on average, the longer clients participated in the training programmes, the more likely their children were to stay on in school. Because of such positive outcomes an increasing number of MFI programmes now incorporate education and health training with their basic financial services (Vanroose, 2007).

In addition to focusing on behaviour changes in education and health, poverty-oriented MFIs often track clients' assets as an alternative to income and consumption levels. The asset assessment approach considers the amount of land owned, quality of household shelter, presence of physical implements such as pots or pans, availability of livestock, and quality of clothing available to households (Hatch and Frederick, 1998).

The use of assets serves two interrelated functions. First, it is a good indicator of the household's poverty level. The absence of assets and basic necessities in a household often means vulnerability to risks of financial shock or hunger. Second, it permits microfinance institutions to distinguish between the economically active poor and the extreme poor, thereby allowing better targeting of clients. This enables MFIs to maximize coverage while minimizing leakage to non-targeted groups. This is important, as failure to target programme participants effectively may lead to bias in the expected impact (Coleman, 2002). Tracking clients' assets is both expensive and difficult, but a change in assets is a reliable indicator of improvements in economic conditions and real reduction in vulnerability. Currently, very few microfinance institutions have incorporated asset measurement in evaluating clients' poverty levels. The Grameen Net Worth Test for borrowers (based on 30–60 minute interviews) includes a visual inspection of borrowers' homes and is used to measure the clients' net worth based on their assets (Hatch and Frederick, 1998). The method is considered amply comprehensive and produces rich data on clients – but it is very expensive to administer. Because of the costs and technical difficulties associated with this approach, the Grameen Bank tends to restrict use of the tool to selected branches located in very small villages or communities. Some other microfinance programmes, such as the KMBI in the Philippines, rely on clients' self-assessment of their assets, and this reduces the cost to the microfinance institution, but the accuracy of the data suffers (Hatch and Frederick, 1998).

4.6 Future Prospects and Challenges for Microfinance

Many of the studies cited above show that microfinance programmes are 'able to reduce poverty through increasing individual and household income levels, as well as improving health care, nutrition, education, and helping to empower women' (Westover, 2008: 4). In other words, 'access to a small loan which enables the poor to take advantage of economic opportunities, to plan and expand their business opportunities, to pay fees or to bridge a cash-flow gap can be a first step in breaking the cycle of poverty and moving out of the poverty trap' (Economic and Social Survey of Asia and the Pacific, 2005: 250). In a similar way, 'the ability to access a safe and convenient savings account enables [the poor] to save in order to meet unexpected expenses and plan for future investments, in such areas as inventories for their small businesses, children's education and housing improvements' (Economic and Social Survey of Asia and the Pacific, 2005, 250–1).

However, critics of the microfinance approach claim that its impacts are not substantive and that it does not really alleviate poverty or promote economic development. The problems the critics cite include: encouraging self-employment over wage earning employment; promoting debt over saving; promoting reliance on credit over earning credit through entrepreneurship; encouraging low-income households to assume debt; and encouraging dependency on subsidies and grants over financial sustainability or independence (Crabb, 2007). Some critics even claim that increasing self-employment through MFIs does not contribute to poverty alleviation: they insist that it is jobs created in large industries and not through microenterprises that lift the poor above poverty (Datar et al., 2008). The scale of MFI operations has also been criticized: the impact, some say, is too small to bring about a genuine overall reduction in poverty levels (Khandker, 2005). Finally, a study by Goetz and Sen (1996) has claimed that most women borrowers do not control the loans they received or the income generated from their microenterprises.

Despite the balance towards positive news on the impact of microfinance, then, there is not yet the evidence to draw very firm overall conclusions. Much of the evidence is anecdotal or self-reported, or comes from rather narrow case studies that fail to achieve the rigorous standard needed for wider generalization or dissemination (Westover, 2008). This absence of rigorous MFI impact studies can be attributed to methodological problems and lack of data. Many studies evaluating the impact of microfinance and pointing to improvements for participants cannot conclusively demonstrate whether such improvements were a result of programme impact or of other factors (Vanroose, 2007). Both scholars and practitioners acknowledge how difficult it is to determine cause and effect patterns in practice (Simanowitz, 2008; Dunford, 2005; Dunford, 2006). The problems of impact attribution seem to be worsened by lack of key data and the absence of methodologies that convincingly isolate effects of programme participation. This means that we have no adequate answers to some important questions (Cull et al., 2007). Aghion and Murdoch (2005) also complain of a lack of transparency among microfinance institutions.

As noted previously, a comprehensive study measuring the impact of microfinance conducted by Goldberg (2005) concluded that, even from carefully considered impact studies, conclusions on both specific and wider impacts can only be tentative. For example, incomes of participants may increase because they are a self-selected entrepreneurial group and women may seem empowered due to the culture or community within which they are embedded (Coleman, 2002). Hence, studies that track changes in income, consumption or asset accumulation face too many plausible explanations outside programme impact. In a similar way, studies that compare participants and non-participants face the twin problems of client self-selection and programme placement bias (Dunford, 2006; Ingves, 2005; Snodgrass and Sebstad, 2002; Karlan, 2001).

Clients who participate in microfinance programmes tend to be more entrepreneurial and resourceful, reinforcing the self-selection bias. Non-participants tend to lack such characteristics. Programme placement bias implies that microfinance providers reasonably or wisely select better-off communities in which programme success is almost guaranteed (Dunford, 2006; Karlan, 2001). The programme placement bias may therefore invalidate sites chosen as controls or comparison sites, because they differ in key characteristics from those associated with programme success. The two types of site may not be comparable at all.

Some studies seek to get round this difficulty by using mature or veteran clients of the same schemes as the controls (rather than non-clients or people from a different area). The authors of such studies maintain that all differences between new clients and mature ones are due to the impact of participation. Against this claim, critics say that the studies are still afflicted by various biases. For example, survivor bias tends to favour clients repaying loans with interest; 'wait-and-see' bias favours clients joining after the microfinance institution has a track record; and bias due to changes in programme characteristics or requirements favours clients who have different qualifications or are located in different geographical sites. To address the methodological challenges posed above, Dunford (2006) suggests the creation of a 'randomized control trial' design. This proposed design would ensure 'that a new client or a new program site is unlikely to differ statistically from the control people or communities due to self-selection or program placement biases' (Dunford, 2006: 4). However, 'despite various efforts to assess the impact of microfinance, the reliability of the impact assessment is still open to debate' (Economic and Social Survey of Asia and the Pacific, 2005: 263).

The next chapter discusses the ongoing debate about commercialization and mission drift. It also considers divergent paths taken towards commercialization in Latin America, Asia and Africa, and speculates on the future of commercialization.

CHAPTER FIVE

Commercialization and Sustainability of Microfinance Institutions: Implications

5.0 Introduction

This chapter discusses the 'commercialization thesis' paths to commercialization and sustainability, mission drift and the future of commercialization. Commercialization in this context means using a market or business approach to manage microfinance institutions, with the aim of achieving sustainability and profitability so as ultimately to increase outreach or serve more poor people (Schmidt, 2008; Katz, 2008; Copestake, 2007; Charitonenko and Campion, 2004; Christen and Drake, 2002; Christen, 2000). In the 1990s the commercialization of MFIs was seen as critical to achieving financial sustainability in order to expand growth and reach more low-income clients (Christen, 2000; Poyo and Young, 1999). The 'Best Practices' movement of the late 1990s helped create a consensus among both MFI practitioners and leading donors (such as USAID and the World Bank's CGAP) that microfinance institutions could achieve high repayment rates, improve cost recovery, reach greater numbers of poor clients (especially women), and become sustainable within a time period of between five and seven years (Charitonenko and Campion, 2004). It was expected that once MFI sustainability was attained, donor funds could be leveraged to reach even more unserved and under-served clients. With these aspirations, the commercialization approach was seen as the ultimate strategy for increasing both sustainability and outreach or scale.

However, despite apparent consensus on what commercialization entails and what it could achieve, an intense debate and controversy continues to rage concerning its implications. The debate is between the proponents of two contrasting perspectives. One group considers commercialization to be critical for providing high quality financial services to more poor clients. The opposing group believes the profit motive will undermine the MFIs' commitment to the poor, and weaken or destroy their social mission (Christen and Drake, 2002). While proponents of the 'commercialization thesis' see it as the path to microfinance sustainability and outreach, the opposition camp is very concerned about the 'mission drift that would be associated with such a commercial approach to microfinance' which, they say, 'virtually guarantees that an MFI will move up-market, abandoning poor clients' (Christen and Drake, 2002: 4).

Since the mid-1990s, the popularity of commercialization among donors and practitioners has escalated. It is reported that between 1992 and 2003, 39 NGOs became Regulated Financial Institutions (RFIs). These transformations occurred in fifteen countries spread between Latin America, Asia and Africa (Fernando, 2004: 1). By the end of 2006, there were 43 transformed NGO MFIs in these continents (Hishigsuren, 2006) and this number excludes commercial banks that 'downscaled' services to microcredit clients during the same year. It is estimated that in 2006, the total number of commercial MFIs by region was as follows: Africa – 52, Asia – 66, Eastern Europe – 54, and Latin America – 50 (Rhyne and Busch, 2006). Although Africa had 52 MFIs, 34 of them (over half the number) were serving fewer than 15,000 clients each, compared to 16 institutions (out of 50) in Latin America which individually served over 50,000 clients (Rhyne and Busch, 2006). Hence, growth of commercial MFIs in Africa occurred, but in small institutions. The last figures given include all commercial MFIs that transformed and commercial banks engaged in 'downscaled' operations for low-income clients. Despite the growth of commercial MFIs worldwide, a recent World Bank study of 346 of the world's leading ones found that 'only 10 per cent of the MFIs consist of commercial microfinance banks' (Ballantyne, 2009: 4). And while commercial microfinance banks accounted for over 50 per cent of all the assets of the institutions in the sample, NGOs and non-profit MFIs 'make up 45 per cent of the MFIs in the World Bank sample but can only claim 21 per cent of the total assets' (Ballantyne, 2009: 4). So, in spite of the drive towards commercialization, 'not every micro-finance NGO needs to transform. There are large, efficiently run NGOs, such as ASA and BRAC in Bangladesh, that do not intend to become RFIs' (Hishigsuren, 2006: 39).

5.1 Paths to Commercialization of MFIs in Latin America, Africa, and Asia

Who is driving the commercialization process? Answers to that question are again divided between the camps. Proponents of the 'commercialization thesis' believe that MFI commercialization is a natural (some say inevitable) evolutionary process; their view is described as the 'Financial Systems approach'.[1] The critics of commercialization think the process has come about as the result of donor pressure to achieve outreach and sustainability; analysts call this line the 'Integrated approach'.[2] Those in favour of commercialization contend that the Integrated approach has 'had limited impact' on clients, has been costly, and 'could be sustained or expanded only through grant funding' (Mutua, 1994: 268). Since most NGOs are subsidy-dependent, 'they are vulnerable to pressure toward the transition to a finance-based system' (Makoba, 2001: 354). Otero and Rhyne (1994: 2) observe that due to declining donor support, NGOs are being pushed to design 'microenterprise finance models that allow for continuing program expansion'. In the late 1990s, major donors such as the World Bank (under CGAP) and USAID (under its Microenterprise Innovation Project or MIP) were unified in their desire to achieve both scale and financial sustainability, usually within five to seven years (based on the Latin American microfinance experience which is predominantly urban). It was reported that 'microcredit donors ... have been fixated on the financial bottom line and have pushed very hard for microcredit practitioners to become fully financially self-sufficient quite quickly' (Dunford, 2001: 23). In many instances, large donor agencies such as USAID or the British Department for International Development (DFID), preferred to support and work with NGOs committed to achieving institutional

---

1   The Financial Systems approach is also known as the Institutional approach or Demand-Driven approach. It stresses sustainability (i.e. profitability) and efficiency.

2   The Integrated approach is also known as the Welfarist, Credit Plus, Poverty Lending or Supply-Driven approach. It focuses on outreach and poverty alleviation. For a detailed analysis of both approaches, see the following sources: Babri and Vom Dorp (2009); Hermes et al. (2008); Makoba (2001); and Mutua (1994).

sustainability. For example, NGOs whose mission or vision statements and strategic plans contained the magic words 'achieve sustainability' or 'deliver (financial) services sustainably' were highly sought after and were funded by external donors.

Opponents of continued donor support for MFIs view the grants and soft loans as an obstacle to the commercialization process. For example, Campion (2001: 58) observes that 'while donor support for institutional capacity building is still needed, the availability of grants and soft loans for on-lending keeps microfinance institutions from pursuing more commercial sources of capital, including savings mobilization and commercial debt and equity funding.' She claims further that because the Grameen Bank continues to be donor-dependent, it has failed to implement 'credit technologies that would lower operational costs and make savings rates more attractive to clients' (Campion, 2001: 59). In spite of such a claim, leading MFIs in Bangladesh, including the Grameen Bank, BRAC and ASA, have continued to increase outreach and achieve sustainability without commercialization. Although NGOs have higher operation costs than regulated financial institutions, 'it has not been proven that subsidies [per se] reduce the efficiency of microfinance organizations' (Babri and Vom Dorp, 2009: 28). Hence the advocacy of commercialization as the 'holy grail' for sustainability in all contexts is, at the very least, misguided.

Proponents of commercialization believe that financial self-sustainability is 'a necessary pre-condition for achieving exponential growth'. Without it, they claim, 'no amount of subsidy is sufficient to preserve the long-term access of a large number of very poor clients to basic financial services' (Drake and Rhyne, 2002: 15). Some of the radical supporters of commericialization claim that it is the only approach likely to have any social and developmental impact and that any 'moral' criticism of the approach is 'wrong-headed' or 'misguided' from both an economic and ethical perspective (Schmidt, 2008). Furthermore, they claim that donor agencies are either unwilling (perhaps from 'donor fatigue') or unable (due to insufficient funds) to continue subsidizing MFIs that do not achieve sustainability. Hence, they claim that 'irrespective of whether an MFI is profit-oriented; the desire to reach a large number of low-income clients should drive it to build a sustainable model' (Drake and Rhyne, 2002: 15).

Other experts believe that the Integrated approach (in favour of institution-building) and the Financial Systems approach (for commercialization) are complementary rather than contradictory (Schmidt, 2008). Such individuals argue that 'if institutions are to be financially viable, they must be commercially oriented; and if they are to achieve the necessary commercial success to have a lasting impact on development, they must have a suitable institutional structure' (Schmidt, 2008: 8–9). While commercialization may contribute to increased competition, reduced costs and more sustainable services to the poor, a total preoccupation with the delivery of services on a purely commercial basis is unsuitable for the poorest of the poor (Doran, 2008).

The commercialization of MFIs in Latin America has come about through three processes: (1) upgrading, or the creation of RFIs by and from NGOs – the formation of BancoSol from PRODEM in Bolivia is an example; (2) downscaling, or a situation in which commercial banks and other financial institutions expand and reach down-market to micro-clients; and (3) 'green field investments', or the creation of new MFIs, often with equity investments from private or social investors from international networks (Berger et al., 2006; MicroCapital Institute, 2004; Drake and Rhyne, 2002; Christen, 2000; Poyo and Young 1999). Some experts regard the transformation of PRODEM into BancoSol, in Bolivia in 1991, as a watershed moment in the evolution of NGO MFIs into commercial MFIs in Latin America. They think the creation of BancoSol significant because of the 'demonstration effect' it has had for the rest of the financial system, not only in Bolivia but in the region as a whole (Poyo and Young, 1999: 29). However, in general, the process of commercialization in Latin America has been both gradual and multi-faceted.

As noted above, a few of the commercial MFIs in the region have arisen from partnerships between corporations and specialized MFIs (O'Neil, 2005: 1), and they are known as 'green field investments'. Formation consists of 'simply establishing a new formal bank which is oriented from the start towards offering reasonably priced loans and other financial services for small and very small businesses and other "ordinary people" on a cost-covering basis' (Schmidt, 2008: 16). This strategy can be achieved through the creation of a public-private partnership (PPP). As a result of such partnerships, networks like ACCION and microfinance groups like ProCredit participate in the equity of new MFIs or banks that specialize in lending to low-income customers or their microenterprises.

In Latin America, according to Christen and Drake (2002: 2), 'the commercialization of microfinance has been heartily embraced by industry pioneers and sought after as a prime objective. [The] most important driver of the commercialization process ... has been the desire of MFIs to grow exponentially, on the basis of borrowed funds.' It is reported there that

> pioneers realized early on that funds for their growth would necessarily come from the financial sector, as opposed to donor agencies or governments. Additionally, early loan portfolios in Latin America were based on microenterprises that grow and generate employment, rather than on poorer, marginalized women, as was the case in South Asia, particularly in Bangladesh. As a result, the boards of directors of Latin American microfinance NGOs tended to be formed by individuals from business and banking as opposed to social work or community development. [And such leaders] ... saw the road to sustainability as commercialization through financial sector funding provided to efficient institutions. (Drake and Rhyne, 2002: 5)

Furthermore, microfinance in Latin America 'has been characterized ... by a clearly profit-driven and competitive landscape that differs widely from the peer-group style lending championed by Grameen Bank of Bangladesh and other Asian and African models' (MicroCapital Institute, 2004: 1). Indeed, as the Vice President for Resource Development of ACCION put it, 'Latin America is the most commercially advanced microfinance market in the world' (MicroCapital Institute, 2004: 1). The Latin American MFI Model – with variations – is largely commercially oriented in terms of operations, financial performance, ownership structure and in targeting a broad range of customers, including the poor and the not-so-poor (Berger et al., 2006). MFIs in Latin America are known for their 'reliance on private sources of funding to fuel growth and continued operations. As compared to their counterparts in Asia and Africa ... Latin American MFIs depend more on borrowing than on deposits and equity for their funding' (Berger et al., 2006: 6). In other words, MFIs in Latin America have relied largely on funding from the private sector while those in Asia or Africa rely on both donors and governments.

In the Latin American model, with commercialization seen as a path to sustainability/profitability and outreach, the evolutionary development of a typical microfinance institution runs through four stages: (1) existence as a subsidized MFI; (2) subsequent adaptation to a for-profit system that charges market interest rates, even on grants or soft loans; (3) a move to using market-based funds (e.g. commercial loans rather than equity); and (4) final transformation into a full for-profit microfinance institution (Hogarth, 2009). This is the general evolutionary trend for South American countries, but it has not been followed in Peru and Chile, where the state has intervened to stabilize or expand MFIs. Before 1990, funds for most NGOs in Latin America came in the form of grants, soft loans or subsidies from various sources including multilateral agencies, local or national governments, and quasi-governmental organizations such as national development banks or social ministries. However, these subsidies and grants declined in the next years, and NGO MFIs were forced to accept loans or lines of credit from commercial banks, guaranteed by external lenders. Then, as the costs of such transactions escalated, most MFIs sought to transform into RFIs – Regulated Financial Institutions. It is claimed that this development arose from the desire of both MFIs and governments to have MFI activities regulated, allowing the institutions to operate at a higher level so they could mobilize more capital and offer a wider range of services to clients. Examples of such regulated microfinance institutions include BancoSol in Bolivia, MiBanco in Peru and Finansol in Colombia. In addition, from the early 1990s right into the early 2000s, both private and social investors became more involved in lending to Latin American MFIs.

Finally, increased market competition coupled with government regulation seems to have led to a dramatic rise in the number of commercial MFIs in Latin America. In most of the countries there, the regulatory framework meant that the whole financial sector 'was adapted to facilitate microcredit operations, allowing MFIs to become regulated institutions without changing their client focus, and permitting already regulated financial institutions to offer credit to a new clientele' (Berger et al., 2006: 25). However, in a few instances, such as in Peru and Chile, the state intervened either to develop microfinance programmes or to pressure banks to start lending to low-income clients (Christen, 2000). Commercially-oriented microfinance institutions now dominate the microfinance landscape in Latin America. According to the President of the Inter-American Development Bank (IADB), 'the ultimate goal is to spur private markets to triple microfinance in the region from its current portfolio level of $5 billion to $15 billion by 2011' (Berger et al., 2006: x). It is also reported that MFIs in the region rank highly in terms of both sustainability and profitability, compared to their counterparts in Asia or Africa (Berger et al., 2006). Globally, it is estimated 'that only 10 per cent of MFIs are able to survive without subsidies' (Babri and Vom Dorp, 2009: 17) or are considered to be financially self-sufficient. In Africa, 'over two thirds of the institutions are far from achieving sustainability' (Hishigsuren, 2006: 10).

In contrast to the Latin American experience, the most important characteristic of MFIs in Africa and Asia is 'an exclusive focus on the poor' (Berger et al., 2006: 2) and a desire to alleviate their poverty. In other words, MFIs in Asia and Africa tend to focus on developmental idealism, while their counterparts in Latin America seek to provide employment or self-employment and credit to the urban poor (Asian Development Bank Institute, 2004). While MFIs in Latin America have relied on private sector funding, those in Africa and Asia have relied on both government and donor support. In the case of several Asian countries, 'government ownership has played a role in some of the leading institutions, including Bank Rakyat Indonesia (BRI), a state-owned agricultural bank, and Grameen Bank in Bangaldesh, which was partly owned by the government in the 1980s' (Berger et al., 2006: 8). However, as more state-owned banks in Asia expand their operations to include the microenterprise niche, and the NGO MFIs transform into RFIs, 'there are signs of convergence between the two regions' (Berger et al., 2006: 8). For example, between 1992 and 2003, fifteen out of thirty-nine NGOs that transformed worldwide, were from six countries in Asia (excluding Bangladesh and Indonesia) – the Philippines, Cambodia, India, Nepal, Mongolia and Pakistan (Fernando, 2004). As yet, though, these regions still lag behind South America in this development (Asian Development Bank Institute, 2004).

In East and Southeast Asia, through the use of large state banks or cooperatives for rural credit, governments as well as donors have been instrumental in the creation of microfinance institutions, including RFIs.

In between government initiatives and donor support, private commercial or development banks (such as the Asian Development Bank) have either facilitated the commercialization of MFIs or expanded bank activities to serve down-market niches, albeit to a lesser extent than in Latin America. Overall, commercialization initiatives in the microfinance industry in Bangladesh, Indonesia, the Philippines and Sri Lanka are all at different phases or stages of development (Charitonenko and Rahman, 2002). In most of these countries, commercialization has been selective or targeted rather than done wholesale as was the case in Latin America.

In Bangladesh, commercialization is relatively new and is not very securely established. This is partly because the term 'commercialization' carries a negative connotation with it for many domestic microfinance stakeholders who equate commercialization with exploitation of the poor (Charitonenko and Rahman, 2002: ix; Hogarth, 2009: 5). As a result of the success of Grameen Bank and other NGOs, microfinance in Bangladesh has historically operated on a mainly non-commercial basis, 'although two of the largest such NGOs, the Association for Social Advancement (ASA) and the Bangladesh Rural Advancement Committee (BRAC), are commercially viable and currently reach about half the national market' (Charitonenko and Rahman, 2002: ix–x).

Because of continued donor and government support for microcredit programmes and minimal market competition against Grameen Bank, ASA or BRAC, the pace of commercialization in Bangladesh has been slow, and is expected to stay that way for some time to come. However, even if most of the NGO MFIs in Bangladesh are not financially self-sufficient, 'about 70 per cent of poor households are currently reached by MFIs, based on the ... government estimate of 12.2 million poor families in the country' (Charitonenko and Rahman, 2002: ix).

In Indonesia, the Bank Rakyat Indonesia (BRI), which started as a government-subsidized rural agricultural credit programme, has had its 'village units' transformed into 'full-service rural banks that provide a wide range of flexibly priced products, with profitability [being] the primary criterion of success' (Economic and Social Survey of Asia and the Pacific, 2005: 256). As a result of the transformation, at the end of 2003, BRI was estimated to be serving 29.9 million savers and 3.1 million borrowers

(Economic and Social Survey of Asia and the Pacific, 2005: 256). It is considered a successful example of a large-scale financially sustainable MFI, serving millions of the 'semi-urban and rural population with regular incomes' (Economic and Social Survey of Asia and the Pacific, 2005: 256). Transformed MFIs such as BRI offer prospects of both profitability and outreach into the rural areas (Christen and Drake, 2001; Cheritonenko and Campion, 2004).

In the Philippines, several government initiatives and strong donor support have been instrumental in the move towards MFI commercialization. The Center for Agriculture and Rural Development (CARD), in particular, has transferred part of its loan portfolio to establish the CARD Rural Bank while continuing to operate as an NGO (Economic and Social Survey of Asia and the Pacific, 2005: 257). Since 1997, the government has sought to improve the legislative environment to enable a few NGOs to transform into rural or thrift banks. As a result, 'rural banks in the Philippines are the dominant providers of microfinance' and the USAID-funded Microenterprise Access to Banking Services (MABS) programme aims to assist participating rural banks as they extend the services they provide to the micro-enterprise sector (Asian Development Bank Institute, 2004: 3). However, the government has also directed that government-owned credit programmes should be transferred to RFIs and managed according to a business model (Charitonenko, 2003). At least one expert fears that 'the requirement [by government] to include at least two independent members on the board of directors (of Regulated Financial Institutions) and to reduce NGO ownership in the new bank to no more than 40 per cent within five years of transformation' has the potential to lead to mission drift (Charitonenko, 2003: xv).

The microfinance industry in Sri Lanka 'is relatively large and diverse in terms of outreach and institutional types compared to that in other countries in the region' (Charitonenko and De Silva, 2002: ix). Apart from some cooperative rural banks (CRBs) which have become microfinance providers, there are fewer NGOs transforming into regulated financial institutions, and fewer commercial banks downscaling to the microcredit niche as well. Inadequate government oversight and negative perceptions of commercialization prevent the growth and expansion of commercially-oriented Sri Lankan microfinance. In particular, pro-commercialization experts say the government has failed 'to enforce laws against microfinance NGOs mobilizing savings deposits and offers no clear legal path for the institutions to transform themselves into formal financial institutions subject to prudent supervision' (Charitonenko and De Silva, 2002: x). As in Bangladesh, people in Sri Lanka perceive commercialization in negative terms because of concerns over potential mission drift: 'they believe that MFIs will reduce their emphasis on targeting the poorest sectors of society and will gradually increase their loan sizes' (Charitonenko and De Silva, 2002: xiv). Overall, government initiatives and donor support have been critical in the commercialization of microfinance institutions in several Asian countries considered here. While the Asian Development Bank has supported the development of viable MFIs in the region through its microfinance development strategy, private commercial initiatives have been minimal (Charitonenko and Rahman, 2002). The nature and extent of government support for commercialization has varied from country to country. The government has been very instrumental in Indonesia and the Philippines, but lukewarm in Bangladesh and largely non-supportive, even subversive, in Sri Lanka.

In contrast to the Asian experience, the commercialization of the microfinance sector in Uganda and other Sub-Saharan African countries has been largely donor-driven.[3] This is for two major reasons. First, most, if not all, NGOs and MFIs on the African continent have been donor-dependent in terms of grants, subsidies, soft loans and technical assistance; and they still are. Secondly, the costs of transformation, regulation and internal development of the NGO MFIs are prohibitively high, and in most instances, beyond the financial capacity of the institutions. These circumstances account for Sub-Saharan Africa trailing behind South America and Asia in the kind of NGO transformation the commercialization lobby advocates (Buss, 2005).

---

3   It should be noted that in a few countries in Sub-Saharan Africa such as Benin, Ghana, Guinea and Tanzania, the failure of state-owned banks to extend rural credit microfinance services has led to major restructuring of the formal financial sector. 'The success of ... restructurings [in the four countries] was possible because of the simultaneous strengthening of the regulatory environment and of the supervisory capacity to avoid moral hazards' (Basu et al., 2004: 15–17).

Between the 1980s and 1990s, the microfinance sector in Africa saw a large number of donor-supported credit-only NGOs develop and sometimes transform into 'new types of non-bank financial institutions' (Mokaddem, 2009: 3). Declining donor funds and the desire to achieve both outreach and sustainability compelled most donors to demand that NGOs use a finance-based approach for managing their activities. The case of NGO MFI transformation in Uganda clearly demonstrates the important role donors played in the process. As we discussed in Chapter One, the end of the Cold War in the early 1990s, combined with declining donor assistance and demands for accountability of donor funds by tax-payers in developed countries, all made donors 'want to fund projects and programs that [had] a greater chance of being sustainable and of standing on their own' (Ridell, 1999: 321). Major donors such as the World Bank (under CGAP) and USAID (under its Microenterprise Innovation Project) took the lead in helping NGO MFIs worldwide achieve outreach and sustainability. For example, in the late 1990s, the USAID-PRESTO Project in Uganda operated a 'Center for Microenterprise Finance' (CMF). The aim of the centre was:

> disseminating microenterprise finance Best Practices to the managers and staff of participating MFIs. These 'Best Practices' draw upon the lessons that have been learned from successful microenterprise finance programs worldwide over the past decade ... Most importantly, they include an institutional commitment to achieving financial sustainability to ensure that savings and credit services that are now being developed with donor support will be available to the poor over the long term, rather than limited to the time frame of donor interventions. (CMF, Kampala, 1997)

The influence of donors and the Bank of Uganda technocrats was critical in the transformation of the first four NGO MFIs into regulated deposit-taking institutions in 2003 (Tumusiime-Mutebile, 2010). The Government of Uganda supported and approved the 2003 MDI Act largely on the assumption that the transformation would increase access to credit and outreach.[4] But as we have already argued, the transformation of MFIs, at

---

4   See Chapter Three for a detailed discussion.

least in the short term, has *not* contributed to access to credit and has *not* increased outreach. Donors in Uganda were not only committed to the transformation of MFIs, but they also provided significant funding for the process. The total cost of transformation, regulation and development of internal systems of each of the four MFIs that became RFIs has been estimated at between US$1 million and US$3 million.

The four MFIs could not easily meet this prohibitively high cost of transformation. They were only in Phase Two of their development, compared to their counterparts in Latin America and Asia which were in Phase Three or Phase Four.[5] This means that the four MFIs identified by donors for transformation began adopting a for-profit model in which they charged market interest rates on grant funds and soft loans. However, as subsidies and grants declined, they were forced to accept loans or lines of credit from commercial banks (such as The Nile Bank), guaranteed by external lenders and donors. These transactions soon became costly to the MFIs. Hence, the donors began to prepare the four MFIs for transformation into regulated deposit-taking institutions under the 2003 MDI Act. The four MFIs that transformed were: FINCA Uganda; the Uganda Women's Finance Trust; Pride Uganda; and Uganda Microfinance Limited. With the exception of CERUDEB (the only microfinance bank), the four NGOs were non-banks which 'transformed into companies limited by shares' (Tumusiime-Mutebile, 2010: 3). The current governor of the Bank of Uganda does not

---

5   The phases of MFI development are outlined above. The progression is: (1) start as a subsidized NGO MFI; (2) the MFI adopts a for-profit model that charges market interest rates, even on grants or soft loans; (3) it uses market-based funds, especially from private investors; and (4) it transforms into a regulated financial institution (RFI) that relies solely on private funds and seeks to maximize profits. (For a detailed analysis of each phase, see Kapper (2007), especially 19–20 and 32–3.) The four phases of MFI development parallel four phases of NGO MFI market competition viz: (1) pioneer; (2) take-off; (3) consolidation; and (4) maturity (CGAP Focus Note, No. 33, February, 2006: 2–3). Schmidt (2008) indicates that NGOs go through two steps before they are commercially viable: (1) making the existing organization larger and more efficient through technical assistance and funds by donors; and (2) transformation into a regulated financial institution or bank, requiring experts/consultants in institution-building and loan funds.

seem to see the problem of mission drift as being relevant to the remaining three deposit-taking institutions (Tumusiime-Mutebile, 2010). The fifth of the original MFIs designated by donors for transformation, FOCCAS Uganda, was not able to become an MDI because of its comparatively low levels of sustainability and outreach due to its significantly rural clientele, estimated at 85 per cent.

It is probably safe to suggest that donor influence in NGO transformation in much of Sub-Saharan African is similar to the Ugandan experience. For example, in the Gambia, both donors and Northern Private Voluntary Organizations (PVOs) put pressure on NGOs to increase the scale of their operations and seek to achieve sustainability (Makoba, 2001). K-REP Bank is the largest MFI in Kenya and the first NGO in Sub-Saharan Africa to transform – from a 'project', to an NGO in 1993, and then to a commercial microfinance bank in 1999 (J-Intersect, 2005: 4). Though K-REP initiated its own microcredit programmes (modelled on the Grameen Bank), its successful transformation into a microfinance bank benefited greatly from its having begun as a USAID project providing grants, training, and technical assistance to other NGOs for microenterprise development projects (J-Intersect, 2005: 4): one could say that this initial role as a financial intermediary funded by USAID was critical to the success of its transformation. By the end of 2004 it was serving an estimated 51,600 clients. However, there are a few cases in Africa where the government – through legislation or its central bank policies – has compelled NGO MFIs to commercialize or transform into RFIs. The actions of the Ethiopian government in the late 1990s provide a good example. According to Getu (2007: 173–4), 'a new policy was promulgated by the Government of Ethiopia in 1996 [that] brought an end to the operation of unregulated microfinance programs by NGOs. Since then all the NGOs have been compelled to restructure their microfinance operations under separate entities registering them as regulated MFIs directly supervised by the National Bank of Ethiopia.'

In Africa, donor influence extends, beyond transforming NGO MFIs, to including a few commercial banks (private or state-owned) and involving them in *downscaling* services to low-income clients. Two commercial banks, one in Kenya and another in Zimbabwe, have sought to 'downscale services', relying heavily on DFID and USAID to pay for technical assistance and provide operating and loan capital (at least in the short-term). In 1997, the Commercial Bank of Zimbabwe (CBZ) was able to extend its financial services to micro-clients and small microenterprises as a result of support and funding from DFID. Bell et al. (2002: 4) describe the genesis of the microfinance programme of the Cooperative Bank of Kenya (CBK), also in 1997: '[although the bank] was prepared to meet most capital and recurrent expenditures and to provide the loan capital, it sought funding for the technical assistance that it needed, to develop new products and methodologies and to make the necessary institutional changes. DFID agreed to provide funding for this, and Bannock Consulting (of the UK) was contracted as the technical assistance provider … USAID agreed to pay for study tours as well as cover some capital expenditure' in 1998 in order to mitigate the CBK's financial crisis, created in part by the terrorist bombing of the adjacent US Embassy in Nairobi. Bell et al. report that in both cases of downscaling to the micro-credit niche, 'donor-funded technical assistance [and loan capital in the case of CBZ] has been crucial in helping overcome considerable obstacles, including resistance to the new microfinance culture from the mainstream bank staff' (Bell et al., 2002: 1).

As for the remaining Sub-Saharan picture, 'West Africa is dominated by credit cooperatives' while 'regulated non-bank financial institutions stand out in East Africa' and 'Southern Africa is mainly served by a large number of NGOs [and] some downscaled banks' (Mokaddem, 2009: 3–4). To sum up: regardless of whether transformations are triggered by donors, market competition or government initiatives, transformed 'NGO MFIs have two primary objectives: (1) to provide clients with a range of financial services beyond credit, including savings and transfer services; and (2) to increase access to capital, whether through commercial borrowings … deposits, raising equity, or all three' (Lauer, 2008: 1). The commercialization of MFIs in Latin America was fuelled by competition and the infusion of private sector investment. In Asia, the process has been driven primarily by government initiatives and donor support. And in Africa, donor pressure to transform MFIs into regulated financial institutions (RFIs) has been a critical factor. The Latin American commercialization experience could be considered evolutionary in nature and heavily influenced by the

Financial Systems approach. By contrast, transformed MFIs in both Asia and Africa appear to adhere to the Integrated approach: most of them still seek to pursue social objectives as well as financial. The Latin American microfinance sector is heavily commercialized, while in Asia and Africa, commercial (for profit) MFIs and regular (non-profit) NGO MFIs co-exist. In both Asia and Africa, a few commercial banks have 'downscaled' their operations to include the microcredit niche with donor support, while commercial bank downscaling activity in Latin America is widespread and relies primarily on debt or equity financing.

5.2 Commercialization and Sustainability: In Search of a Balance

Although the proponents of the 'commercialization thesis' consider it to be the ultimate path to sustainability,[6] there is a need to *decouple* commercialization from sustainability. As a leading practitioner of microfinance points out, the debate regarding MFI impact and sustainability affects MFIs occupying the *middle ground* – namely, *social enterprises*, which focus on the 'double bottom line', seeking to achieve financial and social objectives (Dunford, 1999). The other extremes are commercial MFIs (such as BancoSol in Bolivia) and traditional NGOs or social service providers. Hence, the central question facing microfinance enterprises with a 'double bottom line' is whether an MFI can 'sufficiently cover its costs and earn a return

---

6   Proponents see commercialization as allowing 'MFIs greater opportunity to fulfil their social objectives of expanding access of the poor to an array of demand-driven microfinance products and services on a sustainable basis' (Charitonenko and Campion, 2004: 2–3); sustainability which is used interchangeably by such proponents with commercialization is considered 'the only way to reach significant scale and impact far beyond what donor agencies can fund' (Kapper, 2007: 16); other proponents (Christen and Drake, 2001: 1) view commercialization as a market approach that 'implies principles such as sustainability, professionalism, and efficiency in the provision of financial services'.

on the money invested in it' while reaching out to a larger poor population (Babri and Vom Dorp, 2009: 22). In other words, 'can microfinance reach very large numbers of the very poor and still be sustainable and have important impacts?' (Dunford, 2006: 2). Over the years, the concept of 'sustainability' has evolved from recovering all recurrent operating costs of MFIs to 'covering all recurrent financial and operating costs ... including hidden costs of inflation and loan reserves' (Dunford, 1999: 3).

Sustainability implies that an MFI is able to cover all its costs while ensuring on-going financial and non-financial services to its poorest clients, or low-income ones, over a considerable period of time. The goal of sustainability is not to become totally subsidy-free, as 'that is neither necessary nor sufficient to achieve [an MFI's] true objectives ... a really good, sustainable social enterprise is not highly dependent on subsidies but also not necessarily subsidy-free' (Dunford, 1999: 3–4). In general, sustainability is often analysed at the level of the microfinance *institution* rather than at the *client* level. This often leads to a schism or disconnection between client views of sustainability and those of the MFI. For example, in a study of three rural microfinance institutions in Nepal, it was found that customers of the organizations studied 'never thought in terms of institutional sustainability when they obtained loans' (Acharya and Acharya, 2006: 119). According to the study:

> more than 80 per cent of the small farmers interviewed mentioned that they did not think about 'institutional' sustainability. For them, 'individual' sustainability came first rather than the institutional one. They believed in prosperity of individuals as the foundation of sustainability of a microfinance institution that resulted in a 'trickle-up' effect. However, almost all Executive Committee (EC) members [and MFI management and staff] were concerned about institutional sustainability. (Acharya and Acharya, 2006: 119)

Such views among clients can undermine institutional sustainability. The same study revealed that 'the lack of a sense of ownership toward the organization and apathy towards institutional sustainability were some of the reasons for high credit defaults amongst small farmers' (Acharya and Acharya, 2006: 124). Other experts argue that 'a focus on [institutional] sustainability leads to a compromise in the ability to reach out to the ones in the greatest need of financial assistance, hence a change in the original mission of microfinance which is to serve the poor' (Babri and Vom Dorp, 2009: 11). But MFIs that focus on sustainability *and* programme subsidization tend to keep targeting 'the extremely poor'; [they also] achieve ... depth of outreach and are efficient' (Babri and Vom Dorp, 2009: 37). Over the years, MFIs have increased their outreach to the poor and have demonstrated the potential profitability of the financial services they provide to low-income clients.

However, 'there is still a large unmet demand for microfinance and an estimated 400–500 million poor and low-income people worldwide still do not have access to microfinance' (Economic and Social Survey of Asia and the Pacific, 2005: 252). Hence the challenge of microfinance is 'how to extend the benefits of micro-level intervention to a larger and poorer population' in a sustainable manner (Economic and Social Survey of Asia and the Pacific, 2005: 251). Some microfinance experts believe that MFIs represent the opportunity to combine socially responsible investment with a capital return and this combination is regarded as something of a 'holy grail' in the business (Babri and Vom Dorp, 2009: 1; Dunford, 1999: 1–4).

Many experts believe that for MFIs to achieve financial sustainability and outreach, they require the following: (1) a supportive or regulatory environment; (2) a willingness to charge market interest rates, even on grants and soft loans; and (3) the ability to reduce costs, while improving productivity or efficiency (Meyer, 2007; Charitonenko and Campion, 2004). This means that MFIs undertaking such initiatives can achieve outreach and sustainability. Some experts still insist that 'regardless of the legal structure, achieving scale is critical to success, and from an institutional perspective, the key to developing a wide variety of services for a large number of clients lies in reducing the average transaction cost' (Christen and Drake, 2001: 12). High operating costs, especially for rural MFIs, make it difficult to achieve financial self-sufficiency (Ingves, 2005). In this situation, it is assumed that MFIs have three basic choices to lower such costs: (1) they can increase their breadth of operations; (2) they can raise interest rates and fees to borrowers; or (3) they can accept subsidies (Babri and Vom Dorp, 2009: 24). '[A] reduction in the costs of providing services, can result in simultaneous improvements in both financial and social performance, but many decisions entail a trade-off over time between them' (Copestake, 2007: 1724). In order to achieve scale, while reducing transaction costs, the MFIs have to take three more steps: (1) expand the financial services provided, increasing both access and outreach; (2) establish linkages or partnerships with financial institutions, such as credit unions or post banks; and (3) invest in technological innovations that seek to drive down costs for both clients and themselves (Christen and Drake, 2001: 13–14). Indeed, achieving scale while reducing costs is what institutional sustainability is all about.

Although most MFIs have a great desire to become sustainable over time, the reality is 'that only 10 per cent of MFIs are able to survive without subsidies' (Babri and Vom Dorp, 2009: 17). According to Barr (2005: 282), 'the Microfinance Exchange, which tracks performance for about 150 microfinance institutions, has found that [only] about 40 per cent of the institutions it tracks are financially self-sufficient'. Kapper (2007: 18) confirms that 'fewer than 100 MFIs claim self-sustainability', and, according to the United Nations Development Programme 'only a fourth of the funded micro-lending institutions are considered successful' (Babri and Vom Dorp, 2009: 18). Such evidence suggests that for the bulk of MFIs worldwide, sustainability remains an elusive goal. It is extremely challenging for rural MFIs like FOCCAS Uganda to reduce costs and increase outreach without substantial donor or government support in terms of grants, subsidies or soft loans. Extending help to the poor in rural areas is 'a particularly difficult challenge even for efficient MFIs because of the high costs involved in reaching dispersed populations and making small loans to farmers with risky enterprises' (Meyer, 2007: 4).

The debate concerning sustainability revolves, for many, around balancing the social and financial goals. Alternatively, the debate is about MFIs achieving scale or increasing outreach to low-income clients while reducing costs of delivering services to their clients. According to Babri and Vom Dorp (2009: 22), 'it is this double-sided benefit of poverty alleviation and profit-making that has spurred the sustainability debate.' Hence balancing sustainability and outreach, though difficult[7] is the ultimate promise of microfinance:

---

7   'According to the IMF (2005), the MFIs that have become self-sustainable tend to be
     larger and more efficient. They also tend not to target the very poor, 'as targeting the

Ten years ago [it was assumed by experts] that achieving both goals would simply be a matter of raising interest rates on loans. But today micro-lenders see that the key to managing the trade-offs has much to do with containing expenses as with raising revenues. To a large extent, this means thoughtfully managing human resources ... The July 2003 Microbanking Bulletin ... reports that MFIs reaching out mainly to poor clients incurred operational expenses that were, on average, about 60 per cent of the total loan amount given. Personnel expenses made up just under half of that. The proportionately high personnel costs arise because even small loans and deposits require much of the same paper work and oversight as larger transactions. (www.id21.org/2004)

Managing an integrated microcredit service delivery model (such as the *Credit with Education* model used by FOCCAS Uganda) to try to achieve financial sustainability poses an immense challenge. In particular, 'it seems especially difficult to adopt the business orientation without at the same time abandoning or compromising the social mission of the organization. Successful integrated-service delivery systems must find a balance between the pursuit of the financial bottom line and the social bottom line' (Dunford, 2001: 24). Because managements tend to be oriented toward financial performance (which is easily quantifiable or measured), while donors are inclined to fund either microcredit or education but not both, 'there has been a natural skew of management concern toward the financial bottom line and away from the social mission' (Dunford, 2001: 24). In other words, efforts to achieve sustainability in integrated microcredit-education programmes tend to create the potential for mission drift associated with commercialization. However, Pro Mujer in Bolivia 'has found a good, medium-cost compromise – integrated at the level of supervision, parallel at the level of field staff in contact with clients. The *will* of Pro Mujer to find grant support for this hybrid model is bolstered by the *will* to achieve self-reliance, eventually with their own program-generated revenues' (Dunford, 2001: 39, my emphasis). In general, 'programs near to achieving sustainability have only been able to do so by becoming more

---

less poor leads to increase in loan size and improved efficiency indicators, whereas MFIs focusing on the poorest tend to remain dependent on donor funds' (Wrenn, 2005: 13).

efficient, usually over a period of years' (Buss, 2008). In order to balance financial and social goals, MFIs need to have:

> appropriate loan sizes for clients matching their needs; realistic interest rates; savings as a prerequisite; regular, short and intermediate repayment periods and achieving scale ... If these measures to achieve sustainability are put in place, while focusing on the needs of the poorest, then both the social and financial objectives can be achieved. (Wrenn, 2005: 13)

Evidence shows that some MFIs not only serve large numbers of the poor, but are doing so while covering their costs fully (Dunford, 2006; Gonzalez-Vega, 1998). Large efficiently run NGO MFIs such as the famous Grameen Bank, ASA and BRAC in Bangladesh, have not transformed into RFIs; yet they have achieved both outreach and sustainability over several years (Dunford, 2006; Hishigsuren, 2006). However, there are several lesser known MFIs worldwide that have achieved both goals. For example, Kashf Foundation, the third largest MFI in Pakistan, is reported to have merged 'these two goals of financial sustainability and poverty alleviation without compromising either' (Katz, 2008). It is reported that Kashf Foundation today 'has 152 branches around the country [and] has dispersed more than $200 million to more than 300,000 families' (Kristof, 2010: 10). Furthermore, a study of 66 MFIs in Kenya, 'revealed that there were a few MFIs that had attained financial sustainability as a result of their sound financial controls and provision of quality portfolios' (K'Aol and Ochanda, 2000: 1–3). According to the same study, 'sustainability in many [MFIs] is making a significant dent in poverty to achieve massive scale in order to be profitable' (K'Aol and Ochanda, 2000: 8–9). It is important that programmes that fail to achieve sustainability within a reasonable time (often considered five to seven years) should not be abandoned by donors or the government. The rationale for supporting such MFIs is that 'microcredit programs, by definition, cannot be fully sustained because they require considerable capacity building among the poor, something not found when assessing the efficiency of formal lending institutions. As such, microcredit should be evaluated on the extent to which financial systems and their instruments reach the poor directly, increasing their participation in market processes and by this empowerment in political processes' (Buss, 2008: 11). K-REP, a Kenyan NGO MFI, that transformed into a commercial bank in 1999, is still committed to its social mission and serves 'a significant number of poor clients', estimated at 51,600 in 2004 (J-Intersect, 2005: 4). In spite of its transformation, K-REP has successfully sought to achieve a balance between expanding outreach and improving its financial performance.

In the 'sustainability-outreach' debate, as we have seen, welfarists (using the Integrated approach) have tended to focus on outreach, while the institutionalists (using the Financial Systems approach) have stressed sustainability and efficiency. However, 'recently ... representatives from both camps seem to have moved towards the centre, concluding that under certain conditions, sustainability and outreach may be compatible' (Hermes et al., 2008: 6). In fact, 'there is little strong evidence to suggest a conflict between improving MFI sustainability and reaching poorer clients with smaller loans' (Meyer, 2007: 3). The experience of large unregulated MFIs such as the Grameen Bank, BRAC and ASA, shows that they have achieved both sustainability and outreach without necessarily undergoing commercialization or transformation into RFIs. This implies that viable MFIs (whether large MFIs or RFIs) must incorporate 'the best practices' in their operations or adopt suitable institutional structures including linkages or partnerships.

Implemented correctly and consistently, commercialization may have the capacity to assist in the achievement of social mission, because it can help the RFI raise more funds (in terms of commercial loans, savings or equity) and increase the breadth and depth of outreach (Katz, 2008). In other words, commercialization can be seen as a way to help MFIs achieve financial sustainability and expand outreach. But the MFIs need to avert 'mission drift'. Unfortunately, the evidence indicates that more efficient MFIs focus less on poorer borrowers, and do indeed risk diluting their socially responsible roles (Hermes et al., 2008). An extensive study of twelve MFIs carried out in 49 countries found evidence of 'a trade-off between efficiency and outreach' (Hermes et al., 2008: 6). The same study showed that:

> MFIs that focus on providing loans to individuals perform better in terms of profitability. Yet, the fraction of poor borrowers and female borrowers in the loan portfolio of these MFIs is lower than for MFIs that focus on lending to groups. It also

suggests that individual-based MFIs, especially if they grow larger, focus increasingly on wealthier clients ... This mission drift does not occur as strongly for the group-based MFIs. (Hermes et al., 2008: 6)

While commercial MFIs focus on faster growth due to increased financial sustainability and efficiency, unregulated MFIs seeking sustainability and outreach, emphasize growth over time. According to Copestake:

> Many MFIs have emphasized the prime importance of serving more clients through growth. The cost of investing in new capacity has an adverse financial effect in the short-term, but this can be offset eventually by realization of economies of scale. Improved financial performance is also necessary for growth in order to mobilize resources; hence there may be a case for lowering *current* social performance to enhance *future* social performance. In contrast, other MFIs have opted for a slower growth strategy, putting greater emphasis on current depth of outreach and impact. Such decisions reflect variation in time horizons, but more importantly they reflect path-dependent judgments about how current performance is likely to affect future social performance opportunities. (Copestake, 2007: 1724)

MFIs seeking to grow too quickly may face challenges 'including losing the economies of scale necessary to serve poor entrepreneurs' (Buss, 2008: 13). This was the case with Corposol, a Colombian NGO. However, in the final analysis it seems that commercialization is undertaken to gain sustainability and outreach rapidly, while unregulated MFIs tend to achieve the same goals more gradually. In spite of progress towards sustainability, 'reaching financial sustainability and scale has proved elusive for many microfinance institutions, and even those that are now self-sustaining have required significant donor support' (Barr, 2005: 283).

5.3 Commercialization and Mission Drift: Myth or Reality?

Although commercialization tends to increase sustainability and outreach, the potential for an MFI to lose its sense of social mission may be strong. Proponents of commercialization of MFIs view the process as critical for providing enough capital to meet the financial needs of the majority of poor people (Copestake, 2007). On the other hand, critics of commercialization tend to associate it with the potential for or actual *mission drift*, as profit-oriented MFIs cater to the financial needs of wealthier or less poor clients. It is not entirely clear whether or not commercialization leads to a focus on less poor clients. The evidence from Latin America, which has the greatest experience of commercialization, seems to suggest that such mission drift is the exception rather than the norm. At the same time, potential or actual mission drift for RFIs cannot easily be discounted or denied.

In order to understand and explain mission drift, we need to use Hishigsuren's (2007) model of evaluating mission drift in microfinance. The model, based on the evaluation of ASA (Activists for Social Alternatives), a microfinance institution that serves women in rural India, assumes that the original goal of the NGO MFI is to alleviate poverty. Therefore, it considers any decline in focus on that goal or deviation to non-poor clients as evidence of mission drift. In addition, the model has developed the following three measures to determine if an MFI remains on course: (1) depth of poverty outreach – client income levels, interest rates, loan sizes, and other indicators; (2) quality of outreach – levels of satisfaction with services and products; and (3) scope of outreach – types of services offered, both financial and non-financial (Hishigsuren, 2007: 207 and 217). According to this model, mission drift can be evaluated by comparing the changes in an NGO *before* and *after* commercialization or scaling-up (Hishigsuren, 2007: 204).

The findings of the study indicate that ASA, as a category of MFI, 'has not drifted from its poverty alleviation mission significantly when the drift is measured in terms of depth, quality and scope of outreach' (Hishigsuren, 2007: 256–7). However, the evidence indicates that 'the area most affected by the scaling-up process is quality of reach'. In particular, 'the caseload of [Field Officers] has almost doubled with ... about one half the time as before scaling-up [for working] with individual members' (Hishigsuren, 2007: 257). In the case of ASA, the study concludes that 'mission drift happens not because of deliberate decisions by management or the board; rather because of the challenges posed by the scaling-up process' (Hishigsuren, 2007: 257). For Copestake (2007: 1734), mission drift means that 'ex-post changes in stated preferences ... fit unplanned performance outcomes.'

He attributes this to situations 'where MFIs' goal setting, performance assessment, and management systems are weak' (Copestake, 2007: 1734). According to Babri and Vom Dorp (2009: 26), 'empirical evidence suggests that the more we rely on economic rationality, the more we compromise *social return*. [This means] that a focus on financial sustainability increases the tendency for microfinance organizations to move upwards on the poverty scale, serving the market on the top of the iceberg, [that is to say] the richest of the poor.' Using the same model to compare the NGO PRODEM with BancoSol in Bolivia revealed 'that BancoSol does in fact exhibit some mission drift tendencies' (Barzelay, 2007). In spite of its rhetoric of continuing to serve poor clients, BancoSol 'has decided to enter a more up-scale market'. Senior managers argue that this involves the addition of new markets, not distraction from the original focus of helping the poor' (http://222.scoop.co.nz/ 2008: 3), but it is reported that '20 per cent of [BancoSol's] clients are in fact not poor and the remaining 80 per cent are not exclusively under the poverty line' (http://Link.scoop. co.nz/2008:3).

The experiences of PRODEM and BancoSol show that the rapid growth associated with commercialization may allow a financial institution to reach more clients and therefore generate greater returns, but it also tends to encourage banks to drift from their goal of poverty alleviation for those who need microfinance the most (http:scoop.co.nz/2008:3). Most studies of commercialization in Latin America contend that the process has not contributed to mission drift because the original target population was less poor (urban poor entrepreneurs) and that larger loan sizes could be due to several factors such as choice of strategy, period of entry into the market or the maturation of both the target group and loan portfolio (Christen, 2000).

According to several studies of Latin American pioneer MFIs that transformed, their target clients were often small businesses and urban-based poor entrepreneurs and not poorer micro-borrowers in rural areas, as in Africa or South Asia (Berger et al., 2006; Christen and Drake, 2002; Drake and Rhyne, 2002; Christen, 2000). Transformed MFIs continued to cater for the same client base without going up-market. Hence, no mission drift can be said to have occurred. Furthermore, the studies claim that the increase in both interest rates and average loan sizes are not indicators of mission drift 'because the client base remained poor households ... [and] the rising loan sizes ... a result of the client base of established MFIs graduating to larger loans' (Hogarth, 2009: 6). Larger loans may also be a result of the 'generational factor' – 'the extent to which a microfinance institution was initially part of the pioneering group or first generation of microcredit NGOs, or whether it is part of the new entrants into the sector' (Christen, 2000: 32).

In the case of pioneer NGOs and MFIs that transformed, Christen (2000: 33) sums up, 'there was no mission drift since their initial target was not the poorest of the poor, but small enterprise development'. In situations involving large differences between the average loan balances of commercial and unregulated MFIs, this 'may simply reflect the fact that two groups started out to serve quite different populations and decided on different strategic paths for obtaining funding from the outset' (Christen, 2000: 33–4). Finally, the average loan balance of RFIs may be attributed to the maturity of the loan portfolio and the clients. This is primarily due to the incremental lending to mature clients over time.

It seems that in the case of Latin America, transformed MFIs did not necessarily drive microfinance institutions up-market as most of them have continued to serve the original target client group of small, urban-based entrepreneurs. Indeed, the mixed results of the Latin American experience cautions against *blanket assertions* of mission drift attributed to commercialization worldwide. In South Asia, especially in Bangladesh and Sri Lanka, commercialization is perceived negatively because of concerns about exploitation of the poor (Charitonenko and Rahman, 2002; Charitonenko and De Silva, 2002). The fears of exploitation relate to concerns over the MFIs charging high interest rates to their poorer clients. The issue of whether interest rates are lowered or increased as a result of commercialization is explored in the next section of this chapter. In Indonesia, the transformed BRI serving millions of clients, is perceived as creating the potential for mission drift because it is increasingly targeting peri-urban and rural clients with regular incomes (Economic and Social Survey of Asia and the Pacific, 2005). However, it should be noted that BRI finances its operations from savings and 'it does not aim at, or assist, the very poorest potential borrowers' (Uphoff et al, 1998: 200). In India, a transformed and regulated financial institution, SHARE, 'has increased the number of its borrowers more than ten-fold in five years' (Economic and Social Survey of Asia and the Pacific, 2005: 261), but there is still concern that it faces the problem of mission drift. Evidence of commercial MFIs in Indonesia and Bolivia seems to show 'that self-sufficiency positively affects outreach. However, the [same] empirical evidence indicates the breadth of outreach at the expense of depth of outreach' (Babri and Vom Dorp, 2009: 32). While 'the evidence on the breadth of outreach is clear' (Fernando, 2004: 7), that on the depth of outreach tends to be ambiguous and controversial as its failure is associated with diluting the social mission.

In Africa, where a few MFIs have been transformed into RFIs, there is still very considerable concern about mission drift. The commercialization of MFIs in Africa, which started in the late 1990s and early 2000s has struck 'fear within the industry that NGOs that embrace the commercialization option are likely to experience mission drift' (Getu, 2007: 170). In reality, the few African MFIs that have transformed seem to indicate that the outcry over this is perhaps misplaced. The Centenary Rural Development Bank (CERUDEB) in Uganda continues to provide individual loan products to thousands of rural farm-based enterprises and households. It is reported that: 'the main reasons clients use CERUDEB's financial services are the low barriers to entry, including a minimum savings deposit balance of US$6.00 and a minimum loan amount of US$30.00. In addition to business loans, CERUDEB has instituted an innovative small-holder agricultural loan product, which is based on projected level of agricultural production, has a flexible repayment schedule and takes into account off-farm income' (Charitonenko and Campion, 2004: 8–9).

In Kenya, K-REP Bank, which transformed from an NGO into a commercial microfinance bank in 1999 and was serving 51,600 clients in 2004, 'demonstrates that it is possible to be commercially viable and serve a significant number of poor clients' (J-Intersect Research Review, 2005: 5). K-REP has tried to achieve a balance between expanding outreach and improving financial sustainability. Its continued commitment to its social mission in spite of its transformation shows that 'being a commercial micro-finance institution is no cause [after all] for mission drift' (Getu, 2007: 169). Some MFIs in Uganda, including the remaining three transformed ones or

MDIs, are concerned that the requirement to bring in other shareholders might lead to social mission being overridden by 'the business approach' (Tumusiime-Mutebile, 2010: 15), but the governor of the Bank of Uganda (the supervisory agency) does not see a problem. Though there is indeed ownership dilution (the maximum shareholding allowed by the MDI Act 2003 is 30 per cent), the bank has, according to the governor, 'taken note that an upward review of the period within which new entrants have to comply with the 30 per cent limit may provide adequate time to identify and attract socially minded investors' (Tumusiime-Mutebile, 2010: 15).

Getu (2007: 175–6) identifies major areas where commercialization could lead to mission drift and discusses measures to take against it. The areas of concern within an MFI include: (1) ownership structure; (2) management focus on profitability; (3) technology focus; and (4) outreach. As the ownership of commercial MFIs tends to be mixed, private investors in particular are likely to 'be driven by personal gain and ... could be profit-maximizers' (Getu, 2007: 175). A focus on dividends and profits may be reinforced by senior management 'committed to a single bottom line approach such as profitability, sustainability, or size (scale up)' (Getu, 2007: 175). Although technological innovations for service delivery are useful in reducing costs and improving productivity, 'the focus on technological perfection is likely to serve as another area of possible mission drift since non-technological aspects will tend to be neglected' (Getu, 2007: 175).

Finally, as commercial MFIs become more preoccupied with reaching a larger population (both targeted and untargeted), 'there is the danger that [they] will become more number-driven and end up focusing on the quantity and not the quality of their clients' (Getu, 2007: 175–6). Getu (2007: 170–1) uses the example of the Opportunity International Bank of Malawi (OIBM) to argue that mission drift can be prevented after MFI transformation.[8] OIBM transformed into a commercial bank in 2003. It is:

8   Opportunity International, an American Christian-based PVO, 'aims to serve about 100 million borrowers, savers and family members by 2015 and mobilize about US$1 billion by 2010. It currently runs twelve microfinance (commercial) banks in Africa, Asia and Eastern Europe and plans to establish two new ones per annum by 2010 bringing the total to eighteen. Ten will be in Africa (Getu, 2007: 170–1).

a savings-led microfinance bank with the mission to empower the poor through access to credit, deposit and insurance services. It aims to reduce the financial risks faced by the poor, to bring information into communities that reduce transaction costs and to provide cost-effective services which are valued by its clients. It puts focus on respect, security, reliability and customer delight. It is also committed to achieving outreach, quality and impact and to building a robust and sustainable organization. (Getu, 2007: 171)

The OIBM not only sounds and behaves like an NGO committed to a social mission, while taking a business approach, but also provides group and individual loan products for different target groups and businesses. The individual loan products target micro-entrepreneurs (such as market vendors), small and medium-sized businesses, groups or associations (such as the Malawi Council for the Handicapped), and also large businesses. According to Getu (2007: 176), 'commercialization doesn't necessarily lead to a mission drift and ... with the right checks and balances, it can rather serve as a means of realizing the desired mission: *transformation*.'

In order to prevent mission drift in OIBM after transformation, Opportunity International instituted several initiatives including: (1) engaging social investors concerned about pursuit of the social mission; (2) ensuring that senior management (all 'seasoned Christian professionals') were committed to the 'double bottom line'; and (3) employing an action-reflection approach, similar to the *Progress Tracking* discussed in Chapter 4, to make sure that all stakeholders, social investors, management, staff and clients were appraised of the agreed transformation path and adhered to it (Getu, 2007: 178).

Review of performance in African commercial MFIs reveals that commitment to the *'double bottom line'* and an *ownership structure* that encourages social investors to be engaged can, and does, minimize or prevent mission drift. Experiences of commercialization in Latin America, where pioneer, transforming MFIs expanded their target client groups, suggest that concern about mission drift can be real and justified. However, MFIs in Asia and Africa have been determined to keep pursuing a 'double bottom line', and 'mission drift has not become a reality in most cases' (Hishig-suren, 2006: 39). Furthermore, 'most transformed MFIs have been able to [increase] their outreach – their scale and scope of operations – mainly because of greater access to resources' (Hishigsuren, 2006: 39). At the same time, there are mechanisms to minimize or prevent the occurrence of mission drift before, during and after transformation (Getu, 2007). Such mechanisms should be seriously explored and considered by stakeholders committed to achieving the social and financial goals of transformed MFIs.

5.4 The Future of Commercialization

> We need to hold our [microfinance] industry to the standards of building assets and wealth for the poor, and not be found guilty of practices that strip assets and wealth from the poor. We need to move toward positive actions that balance out and restrain the negative actions that happen when private interests enter into what started as a public-spirited effort to develop sustainable ways to serve the poor. (Chuck Waterfield, CEO, MFI Solutions, 2008: 47)

Commercial MFIs represent a rare opportunity to combine socially responsible investment with profitability, the combination considered the 'holy grail' of microfinance (Babri and von Dorp, 2009; Dunford 1999). Proponents of commercialization consider it to be either inevitable, irreversible or the only way to achieve sustainability and exponential outreach or growth. This view conveys a win-win proposition for microfinance. Other proponents want to see 'a future where microfinance is almost completely interwoven into the fabric of a country's financial infrastructure' (Ballantyne, 2009: 12). Advocates of mainstreaming microfinance into the traditional financial sector, believe that 'microfinance will only realize its potential if it is integrated into a country's mainstream financial system' (Copestake, 2007: 1721; Kapper, 2007: 38). To the critics, such mainstreaming could undermine the very idea of microfinance for the poor, who have always been unserved or under-served by traditional financial institutions.

For Hishigsuren (2006: 40), the fact that, worldwide, only 43 MFIs had transformed by 2006 'raises the question why more MFIs are not transforming'. The experience of transformed MFIs certainly suggests that institutional transformation is difficult to achieve. Transformed or commercialized MFIs face a number of challenges including: (1) determining a suitable governance and ownership structure; (2) raising adequate capital; and (3) having to go on charging high interest rates in spite of market competition. Commercial MFIs have a different governance structure from the non-commercial, determined by ownership of shares or equity. Although transformation and ownership bring greater competencies to microfinance, *'balancing shareholders' demands* for client outreach and profitability can stress the traditional MFI structure so greatly that many of its core staff, including the founders, frequently find themselves marginalized in the reformed institution' (Drake and Rhyne, 2002: 13; Christen, 2001: 11–12). Increased private ownership may bring about 'a reduced concern with reaching down as far as possible into poor segments of the population' (Drake and Rhyne, 2002: 14; Christen and Drake, 2001: 12), *thereby* causing mission drift. In extreme situations, the hybrid model that pursues the 'double bottom line' may be problematic too. This happens when 'the need to generate returns for investors overwhelms the social mission ... [or] the business falters altogether and cannot support the nonprofit' (Strom, 2010: B7). It is not surprising that newly transformed MFIs, still heavily influenced by mission, often fear or distrust private capital and demands to be profit-oriented.

Conversely, private capital is often uncomfortable with sharing ownership with 'socially-oriented' owners, particularly those not familiar with the discipline and orientation of risk capital' (De Sousa-Shields, 2007: 20). In reality, 'transformation has only attracted a small amount of "true" private sector ownership' (Christen and Drake, 2001: 12). Instead, public development agencies and non-profit organizations remain the largest investors in most transformed MFIs. In Africa, where even successful commercial MFIs often struggle to attract private capital, the AfriCap Fund does invest in commercially-oriented microfinance institutions. Since 2000, this fund has made eleven major investments, coming to a total of $10.4 million (De Sousa-Shields, 2007: 20). Generally, 'private funds financed by profit-maximizing investors will ... take less risk and expect higher returns than IFIs or MIVs [i.e. microfinance investment vehicles]. Therefore, International Financial Institutions or IFIs and private funds with socially-motivated capital are best placed to invest in riskier MFIs' (Kapper, 2007: 33).

The good news is that 'the overwhelming majority of microfinance investors are motivated by social objectives and do not approach microfinance with a pure profit motive, but rather with the dual goal to foster social advancement among the marginalized while also obtaining a profit that may range from below-market to fully risk-adjusted returns' (IAMFI, 2008: 1). Vinod Khosla, the billionaire venture capitalist, has invested in SKS microfinance, which lends to poor women in India. He was recently quoted as saying he plans to plough back SKS's recent IPO of $117 million into other ventures that aim to fight poverty, while still trying to make a profit (Bajaj: 2010: B1). The investors in commercial MFIs tend to have different expectations of social impact. 'Some investors believe that the social outreach aspect of microfinance is sufficient to infer social benefits and they don't need further proof. Others want some sort of metrics – but measured at the MFI, not the client level for greater efficiency. Still others feel that social metrics unnecessarily distract management and that scarce resources are better spent on product development, client outreach and loan portfolio administration' (IAMFI, 2008: 2).[9]

As previously stated, the two most important reasons why NGO MFIs transform are: (1) to provide clients with a range of financial services beyond credit, including savings and transfer services; and (2) to increase access to capital, through commercial borrowings and/or deposits and raising equity (Lauer, 2008: 1). The transition to private debt or equity capital for transformed MFIs 'tends to be slow and difficult as many MFIs lack the management capacity to attract and absorb private capital' (De Sousa-Shields and King, 2005: 42). In Kenya, Hishigsuren (2006: 13) relates, 'K-REP began seeking investors [within the country] but banks were not interested due to a lack of understanding of microfinance, thinking it would not be profitable.

---

9   Beth Rhyne, VP ACCION (MFI Solutions, 2008: 29) and author of 'How Do Mixed Ownership Boards Manage the Double Bottom Line?', suggests there are tools to do this; that social performance tools should be set up to measure specific social performance objectives and measure whether they are achieving them. Rhyne admits that these tools – i.e. social performance measurement and consumer protection codes or principles – 'are good tools, but they are only as strong as the will to use them or the legal requirement.'

After the issue received media attention, banks expressed an interest but by then foreign investors had been identified.' In Uganda, microfinance actors and international donor agencies are concerned about inadequate deposits and a former programme manager for the Department for International Development (DFID) Financial Sector Deepening Project, Paul Rippey, has expressed scepticism over the market's ability to absorb all of the new MDI entrants (De Sousa-Shields and King, 2005: 18–19). As the transformed MDIs in Uganda have learned with difficulty, 'deposit funding is typically slower to materialize and more costly than MFIs originally plan': it can take many years to reach ideal deposit-to-debt ratios and cost structures (De Sousa-Shields and King, 2005: 28).

Hence, the challenge facing newly transformed MFIs 'is to grow deposits to the point where they become the main funding source for all transformed and transforming MFIs' (De Sousa-Shields and King, 2005: 42). However, 'if Rippey [of DFID] is right, competition for deposits, especially in urban markets will become fierce in the next years, which he asserts, will be a good thing for consumers but not necessarily for deposit-starved MFIs' (De Sousa-Shields and King, 2005: 19). Uganda Microfinance Limited (UML), one of the four MFIs that transformed into MDIs in 2003, has been successful in attracting external investments. In particular, the Equity Bank of Kenya (in which Helios EB International has massive investments) has acquired 100 per cent of the UML's share capital. It is reported that Equity which acquired UML 'posted an impressive performance in 2007, announcing a pre-tax profit of Shs 2.4 billion, a 116 per cent increase up from Shs 1.1 billion in the same period the previous year (Olita, 2008).

While the transformed institutions in Latin America 'seem to have benefited from specialized equity funds' (BancoSol in Bolivia, 34 per cent; Mibanco in Peru, 26 per cent), 'those in Africa and Asia have retained a significant ownership by their founding NGOs' (Hishigsuren, 2006: 24–5). And in the case of CARD Bank in the Philippines, the clients own about 33 per cent of the shares. Client ownership 'not only encourages poor clients to build an asset base and potentially increase their income, but also contributes to the positive financial performance of the institution' (Hishigsuren, 2006: 25). As a result of increased commercialization and over-reliance on interest revenue generated to fuel profitability and outreach, some commercial MFIs are serving the interests of private investors at the expense of the borrowers (Yildirim, 2008). The case of Compartamos in Mexico, before and after the profitable sale of the Initial Public Offers (IPOs), demonstrates this development. It is reported that 'on April 20, 2007, the Mexican microfinance institution Banco Compartamos completed an initial public offering (IPO) selling 30 per cent ownership of the bank. The existing investors received $450 million, valuing the entire institution at some $1.4 billion. An intense discussion, focused largely in the United States ... ensued' (Microcredit Summit E-News, July 2007: 1).

For some proponents of commercialization, Compartamos represents the evolution of microfinance to the next level, from 'a small player in the financial world to that of an essential tool in global finance. Its significance in developing countries is increasing and it is attracting more outside investment' (Ballantyne, 2009: 7). To critics, this is not a social enterprise with a 'double bottom line'. The critics see no difference between what Compartamos has done and straight usury – application of the practices money lenders have been doing for centuries and which compelled Muhammad Yunus to start Grameen Bank. As one critic observes, the future of microfinance going down this path will be 'progressively and rapidly blurring the lines between microfinance and money lending' (MFI Solutions, 2008: 47). Professor Muhammad Yunus, the founder of the Grameen Bank and the 2006 Nobel Peace Laureate, strongly disapproves of Compartamos' profitable IPO sale and is quoted as saying:

> I am shocked by the news about the Compartamos IPO. Microcredit should be about helping the poor to get out of poverty by protecting them from the money lenders, not creating new ones. A true microcredit organization must keep its interest rate as close to the cost-of-funds as possible. Compartamos' business model, and the message it is projecting in the global capital markets, is not consistent with microcredit. There is no justification for interest rates in the range of 100 per cent. ... Some are saying that the IPO will give a significant boost to the 'credibility' of microfinance in global capital markets. But that is my fear, because it is the wrong kind of 'credibility'. It is leading microcredit in the money lenders' direction. The only justification for making tremendous profit would be to let the borrowers enjoy it, not external profit-driven investors ... When socially responsible investors and the general public learn what is going on at Compartamos, there will very likely be a backlash against microfinance. The field may find it difficult to recover if corrections are not made. (Microcredit Summit E-News, July 2007; MFI Solutions, 2008: 38)

Recently, Yunus has found himself on the defensive because of what appear to be 'politically motivated' accusations that one of his nonprofit companies adulterated vitamin-fortified yogurt, and that he himself had mishandled donor funds from the Norwegian Government (even though the same government cleared him of wrongdoing or misuse of funds) (Polgreen, 2011: 10). He seems to have antagonized the political elite in Bangladesh when, in 2007, he declared the country's politics to be riddled with corruption and floated a short-lived political party of his own. And so, when Ms Hasina Sheikh of the Awami League came to power as Prime Minister in 2008, she sought to eliminate him as a political rival. These allegations threaten to undermine Professor Yunus' major achievements. His Grameen Bank (founded in 1976) now serves 8.3 million women borrowers and has given out US$10 million in loans. Government efforts to oust Professor Yunus from the bank he founded is a major concern to 'microfinance experts [who] worry that a government takeover of Grameen Bank may turn it into a tool of political patronage and destroy it' (Polgreen, 2011: 10). At the same time, Yunus' supporters are upset that the legacy he has built over the years, culminating in his being awarded the 2006 Nobel Peace Prize, may be irreversibly tarnished.

Similarly, Greg Mortensen, the high profile author of *Three Cups of Tea* and founder of the Central Asia Institute – an NGO that has built schools for girls in Afghanistan – has been accused of various offences: 'misstating how he got started building schools; lying about a dramatic kidnapping; exaggerating how many schools he has built; and using his charity organization ... as his personal ATM. The attorney general of Montana, where his charity is based, has opened an inquiry into the allegations' (Kristof, 2011: A21). Unfortunately, whether such allegations are true or not, they are bound to leave supporters of microfinance worldwide disillusioned and cynical.

Concern about Compartamos' IPO saga has extended even to some ardent supporters of commercialization. For example, Schmidt (2008: 26), who once asserted that any 'moral' criticism of the commercialization approach was 'misguided' from both an economic and an ethical perspective, has admitted that Compartamos' policy of charging 100 per cent interest and of using the IPO to secure funds has gone too far. He has acknowledged that the high interest rates and the estimated high yield on equity of about $100 per year between 2000 and 2007, appear to be 'a flagrant exploitation of the customers, which in any event seems to constitute an ethical problem'.

Although Compartamos was not the first commercial MFI to issue shares on the public stock exchange,[10] the return on investment of these earlier pioneers did not yield as high a return as Compartamos took (MFI Solutions, 2008: 5). The outcry against Compartamos has been two-fold. First, Compartamos charged very high interest rates, well above market rates (an effective interest rate of 105 per cent while the rate of inflation was under 10 per cent). As a result, it became very profitable, generating 'an annual rate of return (ROE) over 50 per cent' (MFI Solutions, 2008: 8). More importantly, 'as [Compartamos] reached profitability, their interest rates did not come down. They continued to keep them high and generate high profits' (MFI Solutions, 2008: 8). Hence the concern was that Compartamos was making huge super-profits from grossly overcharging its estimated 600,000 poor clients. The second reason for the outcry against Compartamos' profitable IPO has been to do with the extraordinarily high return on its $6 million equity investment (from various investors such as IFC, ACCION Gateway Fund and other social investors) between 2000 and 2006. 'Connected with an IPO is thus an obligation which the MFI in question and its management undertake to ensure that the shareholders receive the returns which they expect, give and take the odd fluctuation' (Schmidt, 2008: 23). The high rate of return on equity has been attributed to the high interest rates charged to clients and the perception that Compartamos is both well-managed and profitable. As a result, Compartamos' IPO selling 30 per cent ownership of the bank to commercial investors and hedge fund managers fetched $450 million for existing investors and put the value of the MFI at some $1.4 billion.

---

10   Prior to Compartamos' IPO, other commercial MFIs such as BRI (2003) and the
      Equity Bank in Kenya (2006, on the Nairobi Stock Exchange) had issued IPOs –
      but their return on investment was not as high as that of Compartamos in 2007.

Hence, the criticism that high interest rates were charged to poorer borrowers to provide enhanced profits for rich investors. In addition, critics argue that the belief that market competition would keep interest rates of commercial MFIs down is misplaced. In the case of Compartamos, interest rates were high before *and* after the IPO, in spite of the competition and the low or declining rate of inflation. The experience of MFI market competition in Bolivia, Uganda, and Bangladesh shows that interest rates have either declined gradually, increased or remained steady over the years. Indeed, 'the different experiences of these countries suggests that lower interest rates are not the inevitable result of market development, but are more likely to result when certain conditions are present: [there] must be sufficiently large providers in the market, with sufficient incentive and sufficient ability to reduce their rates' (CGAP-FOCUS Note, 2006: 2). It is reported that:

> in Bolivia, rates dropped only after the pioneering MFIs reached profitability. Rate cuts were also linked to the emergence of new funding vehicles that created the liquidity for rapid growth market leaders. In Uganda, the recently implemented MDI law may similarly allow larger MFIs to attract lower-cost deposits to fund their lending growth. In Bangladesh, profitable larger MFIs may have the financial capacity to absorb lower rates, but because there is no strong customer demand, MFIs do not have the incentive to reduce rates. (CGAP-FOCUS Note, 2006: 13)

In Bangladesh too, 'where microfinance is considered competitive, interest rates on microloans have remained stubbornly high' (CGAP – FOCUS Note, 2006: 1). And in the case of Uganda, 'with the lowest market penetration of the three countries and a large number of small firms and MDIs that are not yet in a position to attract lower-cost deposits, interest rates are still high. Despite banking-sector reforms and the licensing of the four new commercial banks, high interest rates are major constraints' (AFDB/OECD, 2008: 601). According to a CGAP-FOCUS Note (2006: 6) 'all Ugandan MFIs ... expect substantial reduction in microcredit rates over the next five years, from an average effective rate of around 50 per cent ... to below 40 per cent' but the interest rates will still remain high for low-income clients.

It is expected that commercial and non-commercial MFIs will continue to coexist in the medium and long terms. As noted previously, a World Bank study of 346 of the world's leading MFIs, found that 'only 10 per cent of the MFIs consist of commercial microfinance banks' (Ballantyne, 2009: 4), while 90 per cent consist of NGOs and non-profit MFIs. There is therefore a dual system and the development of both approaches should be watched. According to Labie (2005: 5), 'underestimating what [the] commercial approach can bring to microfinance would be a major mistake as it might be the best chance to eventually face actual demand. At the same time, over-estimating it by advocating that all microfinance organizations should evolve towards commercial schemes would also be a mistake because there are many things that we are still unable to do in microfinance.' Perhaps one of the many things we can still do with microfinance, is to view it 'as a platform, not a product; one that relies on high volumes, not high margins, and that uses limits on private benefit, holistic performance standards, and third-party certification to help MFIs meet both their bottom lines' (Counts, 2008: 1).

Now that the failure of both states and markets in Africa to achieve sustainable development has been discussed, the next chapter proposes a triple partnership as a potential solution based on the Autonomous Development Fund model which engages the state, non-governmental sectors and the support of donor agencies in the development process. The chapter also considers some of the most important criticisms raised against this model.

CHAPTER SIX

The Triple Partnership for Development in Africa

> Sub-Saharan Africa (SSA) has failed to achieve rapid and sustained economic growth ... Without a fundamental change in the policies and behaviour of African governments, donor countries and international agencies, the growth crisis in SSA will continue. (Sachs, 1999: 157)

6.0 Introduction

This chapter discusses the creation of a Triple Partnership for Development in Africa. In order to achieve sustainable development,[1] the developmental state, the non-governmental sector and supporting donor agencies have to work in close partnership (UN Economic and Social Commission for Asia and the Pacific, 2001: 2); and in African countries with a viable market, the private sector may become part of the proposed partnership. In spite of differences inherent in such a partnership, it allows 'actors to combine their capacities, expertise, resources, networks, ... adds value for each of them, and ... allow[s] them to engage in areas and issues in which they would or could not engage on their own' (Africa Progress Report, 2011:

---

1 Sustainable Development (SD) implies promoting development that seeks to alleviate poverty and protect the environment as well as conserve natural resources. For a detailed analysis of sustainable development and sustainable livelihoods (SL), see Hoon and Hyden (2001); and Tisdell and Zhunge (1999). According to the United Nations Development Programme, there are five aspects to sustainable human development which affect the lives of the poor and vulnerable: (1) empowerment; (2) cooperation; (3) equity; (4) sustainability; and (5) security (Speth, 1997: 4).

56). Increasingly, business involvement in development activities occurs because of the convergence between business interests and development objectives. In particular, 'as businesses realize the commercial opportunities and benefits involved, they are ... willing to complement development efforts of African governments and international donors' (Africa Progress Report, 2011: 56).

Evidence from successful rural development programmes in Africa and other developing countries indicates that reforms which have contributed greatly to the improvement of people's lives have come from the state, NGOs, the private sector, international donors and leading universities (Uphoff et al., 1998: 9). More importantly, the same evidence suggests that successful development programmes have been insulated from political interference or have kept politics at arm's length. This has been achieved in both authoritarian and democratic states that possess a strong developmental orientation.

As noted earlier, a 'developmental state' in this study is conceived as an active (or proactive) state pursuing a development agenda in collaboration with other important stakeholders such as donors, non-governmental organizations and microfinance institutions (Gumede, 2011). Such a developmental state has two important components. According to Mkandawire, 'in terms of ideology, a developmental state is ... [one] that conceives its "mission" as that of ensuring economic development ... Such a state establishes as its principle of legitimacy its ability to promote sustained development ... The elite must be able to establish an "ideological hegemony", so that its developmental project becomes ... a "hegemonic" project to which key actors in the nation adhere voluntarily. The state-structure side ... of the developmental state emphasizes capacity to implement economic policies ... effectively' (Mkandawire, 2001: 290). In other words, 'a developmental state is about state involvement in the economy and society, but not by a state-dominated economic developmental model' (Economic Report on Africa, 2011: 111).

We will now explore the possibility of establishing an Autonomous Development Fund (ADF) model, as proposed by Hyden (1995, 1998, 2005 and 2008). We will look into how it could be implemented in selected African countries, to serve as a new vehicle for the potential collaboration of the state, NGOs and donors in the development process. The proposed programme would initially start in a few African countries that are committed to genuine economic reform and would complement, rather than supplement, ongoing government, NGO and donor development programmes and initiatives. It is important to note that traditional approaches to development assistance in Africa, such as SAPS and PRSPs, have largely failed to bring about the desired economic development and poverty reduction (Ellerman, 2002).

Most African countries are not expected to achieve their Millennium Development Goals (MDGs) by 2015 and are characterized by wide gaps of poverty and inequality. In particular, Sub-Saharan Africa has about one third of the world's poor. While the share of the poor 'in the continent's population is declining, their absolute numbers have increased from 268 million to 306 million over the last decade' (Africa Progress Report, 2011: 28). To reverse this situation, 'new forms of collaboration between the state and society ... need to be cultivated, involving rural people and their organizations, the business sector and a variety of civil society actors' (IFAD Rural Poverty Report 2011, 2010: 16). For example, there is need for 'innovative forms of collaboration, in which governments play effective roles as facilitators, catalysts and mediators; the private sector, NGOs and donors are significantly engaged' (IFAD Rural Poverty Report 2011, 2010: 22). This inevitably calls for new forms of partnership that transcend 'the typical, sectoral, program-based approaches that have been adopted in many developing countries' (IFAD Rural Poverty Report 2011, 2010: 230).[2] According to Ellerman (2008: 251), the central question in the *helper-doer* (or donor-recipient) relationship behind development assistance revolves around making the right choice of approach between 'the direct approach based on power and authority to improve the behaviour of the doers and the indirect approach based on methods aiming to respect and enhance the autonomy of doers.'

---

2   The new approach may call for 'a culture of innovation and learning by all stakeholders, and a willingness to part ways with generic blue prints and large-scale categorizations' (see IFAD Rural Poverty Report 2011, 2010: 230–1).

Development-oriented NGOs and microfinance institutions (such as the Grameen Bank) are considered good examples of autonomy-respecting development assistance (Ellerman, 2008 and 2002). This is because such programmes put the interests of their customers or clients at the centre of the development process. As one observer puts it, 'the gap between aid and development will close only when aid is made accountable to its intended beneficiaries. Institutionalizing accountability to the poor in development agencies requires allowing, even encouraging, the dispossessed to participate in planning and decision-making' (Durning, 1988: 3). And, as Geo-Joja and Mangum (1999: 97) point out, 'a reformulation of aid strategy so as to achieve basic human needs rather than grandiose maximization of the GNP growth rate could reanimate the flagging support of donors for what began as the primordial tool of international assistance – humanitarian capital formation for economic development dedicated to the well-being of the entire population.' The proposed Autonomous Development Fund model subsumes most elements of autonomy-respecting development assistance.

6.1 Context for Development Assistance in Africa

In spite of significant development aid provided to Africa over the past three decades, most Sub-Saharan African countries have failed to achieve economic development and poverty reduction and often they do not deliver basic services such as education, healthcare and clean water at all effectively. As we have argued in previous chapters, factors explaining why development efforts have failed on the continent include widespread corruption, economic mismanagement, patronage and lack of accountability, insufficient capital and inadequate human and institutional capacity to implement agreed priorities in an effective way. However, at the core of Africa's economic and political crisis is the failure of African political leadership. It has provided neither effective governance nor sound economic management

(Mills, 2010; Hyden, 2008; Meredith, 2005). There are two lessons to be learnt from this. First, past experience indicates that once development funds are controlled by African governments, '[the funds] easily become means of dispensing political patronage. [Indeed] they often end up serving the interests of the political leaders who control them' (Development Dialogue, 1995: 5). Secondly, 'past experience with foreign aid … [shows that] it works best when prospective beneficiaries have a stake in the venture; when it is adapted to the particular circumstances of the situation in which it is being dispensed; and, when it makes people feel enthusiastic and ready to cooperate to achieve a common objective' (Hyden, 1998: 3).

Critics of development aid consider it to be both ineffective and counterproductive; others think it has been stolen or wasted. And Moyo (2009) in her controversial book, *Dead Aid*, wants aid to Africa ended altogether. A few critics, blaming both donors and African governments, claim that aid has increased dependence on external sources, while decreasing accountability to the African people (Hyden, 2008). Although donor controlled funds 'may be efficiently managed, [they] are typically removed from the realities of the recipient country and perceived as donor institutions' (Development Dialogue, 1995: 5).

In spite of such criticisms, supporters of aid to Africa maintain it has been effective (Africa Progress Report, 2010; the Commission for Africa Report, 2005). In particular, proponents of aid claim there have been significant improvements, at least in the way aid is coordinated and dispensed. For example, they argue that innovations like direct budget support (DBS), Cash on Delivery (COD), and sector-wide funding arrangements (SWAPs) have managed to improve and even maximize the effectiveness of aid. These innovations, together with public service reforms (such as the creation of executive agencies outside traditional government ministries) are expected to improve both the effectiveness and impact of aid.

6.2 The Proposed Autonomous Development Fund (ADF) Model

The proposed Autonomous Development Fund (ADF) model[3] is a tripartite approach to development involving the government, donor agencies and the non-government sector. In addition to ensuring that aid is neither controlled by the donors nor recipient governments, the model seeks to achieve the twin goals of 'greater aid effectiveness and increased local accountability in the concerned African countries' (Development Dialogue, 1995: 6). According to Hyden (1998: 1), the proposed ADF model would serve 'as an intermediary between the donors ... and the operative recipients [NGOs and African governments], thereby promoting greater local responsibility and accountability and motivating Africans to take important steps toward improved governance'. Furthermore, even if 'there is no guarantee that corruption and other possible malpractices would completely disappear with the creation of these Autonomous Funds ... they do stand a much greater chance of reducing [these evils] than those institutional arrangements that prevail or have been tried in the past' (Hyden, 2008: 270). Indeed, the ADF model is seen as representing a new way of thinking about dispensing foreign aid to Africa.[4] More importantly, there

3   The Autonomous Development Fund (ADF), though associated with Goran Hyden (1995, 1998, 2005 and 2008), 'is an African initiative, originally taken up by the African Association of Public Administration and Management (AAPAM) as a way of encouraging African governments to think of ways to give them more bargaining space with donors' (see Development Dialogue, An Introduction, 1995: 4–5). Also, see Goran Hyden (2008: 268) where he acknowledges that 'some years ago, the Public Administration and Management (AAPM) bought together an "expert consultation" of representatives from African governments, NGOs, and the donor community including the World Bank; it made provisions for what the group called autonomous development funds.'

4   Goran Hyden (1998: 3–5), discusses four assumptions that constitute the rational for this new approach: (1) the effectiveness of foreign aid depends on how it is dispersed; (2) a trustful relationship between donor and recipient is a precondition for good use of foreign aid; (3) donors need to be less selfish or nationalistic in their approach to foreign aid; and (4) funding must be available at both the central and local government levels.

is emerging consensus that in order to achieve sustainable development, 'aid must be drastically revamped in order to make a difference' (Koehn and Ojo, 1999: 2). The two most important features of the Autonomous Development Fund model are:

a) consolidation of external aid from diverse donors that now flows in uncoordinated fashion ... directly to government departments, or to NGOs, and its redirection into an Autonomous National Development Fund [and],
b) the Development Fund would encourage non-partisan competition among public and nongovernmental organizations for project funding based upon promising and sustainable proposals.
(Koehn and Ojo, 1999: 5)

According to Hyden, the principal objectives of the ADF model would be to:

- provide funding on a competitive basis to organizations in and outside government;
- serve as a catalytic mechanism for mobilizing and allocating funds within sectors identified as priority areas in government policy;
- ensure resource allocation based on professional criteria;
- encourage a demand-driven process of development;
- stimulate local capacity-building; and
- promote donor coordination within African countries based on local institutional priorities.
(Hyden, 2008: 268 and 2005: 46)

The ADF model proposed here differs from previous development funds implemented by donor agencies and recipient African governments, because the ADF 'is a public but politically independent institution; caters to both government and civil society; is a funding, not an operational entity; aggregates finances from many sources; brings donors and recipients together in new ways; and is national in scope of operation' (Hyden, 1998: 5–6).

Previous development funds pioneered by the international donor community and implemented by African governments have been under the control of the Office of the President or the Ministry of Planning and Development (Hyden, 2005: 46). As a result, the funds have only too easily become 'slush funds' for powerful political figures' (Hyden, 2008: 269). To avoid such unwanted political control or influence, the proposed ADF model would seek to ensure four basic prerequisites. Hyden sets them out as follows:

1. shared governance between government, civil society and donor agencies;
2. board members all serving in their individual capacity;
3. funds have a national, but sector-specific mandate; and,
4. funds as public institutions are accountable to the national legislature. (Hyden, 2008: 269 and Hyden, 2005: 47)

It is expected that even though the ADF would be a public institution accountable to the legislature and other stakeholders, it would be insulated from politics or government interference. However, critics contend that it is not possible to insulate such an entity from either politics or corruption. The sceptics' concerns and criticisms of the model are considered later.

In his extension of the ADF Model to the operations stage, Koehn (1999: 6–7) describes how an indigenous foundation consistent with Hyden's basic principles and objectives might be 'organized, managed, and positioned to attach foreign aid to competitive proposals.' According to Koehn, the five main principles needed to guide the operation of the ADF model are:

1. development-funding priorities are responsive to needs identified from below rather than from above or dictated by donors;
2. implementing institutions are organized and administered in a manner that encourages managers to innovate, to incorporate valuable development-management lessons into day-to-day operations, and to build cumulative operational experience into the project cycle;
3. operating costs are managed responsibly by rewarding cost-effective procedures and management strategies;

4. financial operations adhere to professional standards of accountability; and,
5. eligibility criteria, application procedures, and evaluation criteria are transparent and easily understood; compliance is relatively uncomplicated.

(Koehn, 1999: 38).

To succeed in the current political context, the autonomous fund as a public institution must be accountable to the legislature and other stakeholders, while insulating itself from politics or government interference. Evidence from autonomous development funds in the Philippines shows that the most important factor in their effectiveness was 'the maintenance of the funds' autonomy and objectivity and the protection of their boards and staff from partisan political pressures' (Gonzales, 1995: 53). Hence, it is critical that 'both donors and African governments ... rethink their relations to respective clients; [and] donors vis-à-vis other organizations in society' (Hyden, 1998: 7). For the ADF to maintain both autonomy and independence, it has to be national in scope and accessible to all stakeholders. It should also have a representative board of trustees whose members have national (and even international) reputations of integrity and honesty (Koehn, 1999: 44).

In his opening speech at the 1995 Kampala (Uganda) ADF Workshop, President Museveni acknowledged that the ADF model represented new thinking about dispensing foreign aid to Africa. According to the President: 'the new thinking [about dispensing foreign aid] is that, instead of foreign aid being merely an outcome of political bargaining between donors and recipient institutions, it should be marketed through legally and politically independent funds incorporated in the recipient country. These intermediaries would eliminate many of the structural bottlenecks that presently cause foreign aid to be ineffective or misused' (Museveni, 1995: 7).

In the conclusion to his address, the President endorsed the creation of the ADF model, saying:

There is a need to overhaul the foreign aid system to make aid [a] more effective tool of development. Aid to Africa should be directed to building independent institutions which give Africans a greater choice and control over the incoming resources.

In this perspective lies the transformation of the whole foreign aid system from one which is primarily based on political bargaining to one which builds on the principle of marketing aid among competitive bidders. (Museveni, 1995: 9)

At the rhetorical level, speaking as head of state of an African government, President Museveni is on record as having endorsed the ADF model as potentially a non-partisan fund for socioeconomic development on the continent. The greatest challenge is to ensure that African governments possess both the commitment and political will to accept the new thinking of the aid regime, and reduce patronage and corruption accordingly. It is unclear whether or not this can be achieved.

Hyden argues that donors have been reluctant to provide aid to African countries because they have 'suggested or documented cases of corruption, perceived lack of commitment among recipient government officials, [and] increased pressures to show results' (Hyden, 1995: 37). The ADF model assumes that all stakeholders will have a say in how the aid is managed and utilized. Although the dispersal of foreign aid is to be arranged on a competitive basis (using known and approved criteria), proposals from both experienced and inexperienced national and local organizations will be considered. Hence, the process will be inclusive rather than exclusive. This will enable both potential and prospective organizations in all public, private and NGO sectors to participate. Organizations hoping to receive grants, soft loans, or a mix of the two will be able to apply individually or through partnerships. What is critical to this is that eligible applicants possess social capital and the capacity to sustain the operations after the award ends (Koehn, 1999: 42). Those without social capital or implementation capacity should be assisted to acquire these resources. According to Koehn (1999: 58), 'by expanding the range of stakeholders that are empowered by the national development effort, the [ADF] is positioned to enhance domestic support for and commitment to increased self-reliance.'

Critics sceptical of the ADF model point out several things. They claim that it would not be possible to insulate the fund from politics or to reduce corruption; that donors are unlikely to increase aid beyond current levels; that an ADF would marginalize the role of central government in a state's economic activity; and that Africa lacks both human and institutional capacity to utilize aid effectively. Ojo (1998) raises some of the most important criticisms of Hyden's ADF model in a discussion on modification of a National Development Fund. The criticisms are three in number. First, he claims that the model fails in its competitive argument when it recommends allocating aid in some areas of development (mainly social) and not others (not on infrastructure, for example). Furthermore, he thinks that permitting local government access to the funds means there will be less central government control over the economy. His criticism that the proposed ADF model exempts large scale infrastructural development projects is a valid and important one. He is also correct in arguing that 'the sheer scale and complexity of infrastructural projects provide greater opportunities and avenues to engage in corruption and to exhibit ineptitude and inefficiency' (Ojo, 1998: 20). However, the criticism from Shivji (2005) and Ojo (1998) that the model would reduce the role of the state in economic development more than SAPs or PRSPs have already done is mistaken. This tripartite approach to dispensing aid to Africa not only brings the state back in (through the front door) but could 'restore indigenous control over the selection of priority development projects ... and internal responsibility for development outcomes' (Koehn and Ojo, 1999: 5).

The second criticism Ojo (1998) raises against the ADF model is that it limits government-to-government aid, thereby reducing present aid to Africa, which is already inadequate. The model envisaged by Hyden (1998) does *not* reduce or replace such aid; rather aid through ADF is considered complementary to ongoing aid to African governments and NGOs. As Hyden (1998: 9) aptly observes, 'the funds should not be seen as diverting finances from the government. Their role is to complement the state budget and help raise more money for development programs and projects.' Furthermore, Hyden points out that 'without having to abandon the preference for budget support, [donors could] negotiate with their African counterparts to set aside a certain amount for deposit into such autonomous development funds' (Hyden, 2008: 269). However, it is conceivable that, in the long run, once the funds become successful, they could attract more external assistance from the donor agencies looking for positive results and aid impact. This would be a good thing for the African continent and its people.

The third and final criticism of the ADF model from Ojo (1998) is that donors are unlikely to increase aid even if the fund were to demonstrate better use of it. He claims this is because all donors give aid to promote or enhance their own national (economic or strategic) interests. No doubt there is some truth in this, but donors are also concerned about showing the tax-payers in their own countries the results of effective aid in Africa. Although donors currently provide development aid to both African governments and the non-governmental sector, most donors are now channelling more of their funding through NGOs because they consider them to be more effective than governments. Through the ADF model, governments and NGOs with donor support are expected to maximize the impact of development assistance. One would expect such a situation to garner more external development assistance. It is possible, even probable, that the creation of the ADF model could serve as a catalyst for rich countries to increase and expedite pledges of aid they have made over the past couple of years. Donor attitudes and interests change, but more importantly, good performing African countries could make a powerful case for adequate and ideal aid. However, if the fund model is successful and no additional aid is forthcoming, African countries could quite correctly call the *donor bluff*. In any case, donors cannot desire development any more than African countries themselves. Hence, the tripartite approach which is embedded in the ADF model calls for a *triple partnership* based on shared interests, mutual trust and commitment to sustainable development. It is potentially a win-win situation.

The most important modification Ojo (1998) makes to the basic ADF model presented by Hyden (1998) is his proposal that donors should bypass the central government and earmark funds for local government and grassroots groups. This modification seems contradictory given his basic claim that the ADF model reflects 'the new western orthodoxy of rolling back the state from directly productive activities and control of decision-making, of keeping the state out of direct development activities and confining it to the realm of infrastructures' (Ojo, 1998: 29). The proposed autonomous development funds would provide support to local and central governments alike. In contrast to the corporatist model that links state authority structures to interests of civil society (Powell, 2008), the proposed ADF model would represent the interests of of state parties, NGOs and donors, and be under their control.

6.3 Institutional Reform in Africa

Recent and ongoing reforms in African countries provide the *building blocks* (or *'road map'*) for a developmental state to emerge and for the eventual establishment of autonomous development funds on the continent. In particular, the New Public Management (NPM) approach to institutional reform has 'begun encouraging a stricter division between the political and managerial spheres on the assumption that development activities in African countries suffer from too little professional input when putting policy into practice' (Hyden, 2008: 265). Overall, this idea has contributed to the creation of contractually independent executive agencies, such as revenue and road authorities, which carry out their functions outside regular government administration (Hyden, 2008: 265). Such agencies seek to reduce patronage and political influence, while increasing professionalism and efficiency. In contrast to executive agencies, public enterprises (or parastatals) in Africa – though created outside government ministries or departments to spearhead economic development – have failed to achieve their objectives. This is because they have been heavily politicized and have served primarily as important vehicles for patronage (Makoba, 1998). Though quasi-autonomous in theory, board members and senior management of public enterprises tend to be political appointees who readily respond to political demands rather than to the operational or performance needs of their organizations (Crandall, 2010). Hence, parastatal organizations have not been insulated from politics or government interference in the same way as executive agencies or the proposed Autonomous Development Fund would be.

The experience of the Executive Agency model in Africa and Latin America, established with the support of donors in the 1980s and the 1990s, could easily provide a 'road map' for the creation of the proposed ADF model. The most important features of the Executive Agency model appear to overlap with those of the ADF model. It seeks to increase both institutional effectiveness and efficiency in the following ways:

i)   as a single purpose agency, it can focus its efforts on a single task;
ii) as an autonomous organization, it can manage its affairs in a business-
     like way, free of political interference in day-to-day operations; and,
iii) being outside the civil service proper, it can execute its own human
     resources strategy – recruiting, or retraining (or dismissing) and moti-
     vating staff.
(Crandall, 2010: 6)

Hence, executive agencies are able to make the government more professional and efficient, because 'each executive agency has sufficient autonomy
within the parameters of specific policies set by the government [to] take its
own initiatives, making those bodies both innovative and flexible in their
operations' (Hyden, 2008: 267). Though initially involved in tax revenue
collection, executive agencies could easily be extended to cover the core
sectors of social and economic development. In addition, countries that
already have an equivalent of the ombudsman or inspector/auditor general
of government need to empower these bodies to prosecute the criminals
or wrong-doers within regimes as well. Such bodies are required to balance the investigative authority they possess with the power to prosecute,
otherwise their hands are tied.

Fourteen countries in Sub-Saharan Africa have established autonomous revenue authorities (ARAs). These countries have moved 'tax collection out of the Ministry of Finance into a separate entity' (Fjeldstad and
Moore, 2009: 2). Both donors and the African countries involved saw the
ARA as a mechanism 'for increasing tax revenues, and thus increasing the
authority of the state' (Fjeldstad and Moore, 2009: 3). They are not interested in reducing the role of the state in fiscal activity, as critics of these
mechanisms claim.

The Uganda Revenue Authority (URA), established in 1991, was one of
the first ARAs in Africa. It is reported that '[the URA] results were impressive in early years, reflected by strong revenue growth in real terms that
levelled off by the late 1990s. [Since then], many of the previous administration and taxpayer compliance problems [have] gradually returned, including serious problems of corruption and inefficiency' (Crandall, 2010: 11).
Reasons for the URA's declining tax revenues since the late 1990s include
an over-narrow tax base, tax evasion or a culture of tax non-payment, with

widespread corruption at different levels of the tax revenue administration. For example in 2002, there were 'unsubstantiated' allegations of corruption involving the URA's first and longest-serving Commissioner General (1991 to 2000) (Mutumba and Osike, 2002). More recently, 'Transparency International ranked the Uganda Revenue Authority as the second most corrupt tax body in East Africa' (Ssewanyana et al., 2010: 18). Though they are called autonomous revenue authorities, the reality is that most African ARAs (including the URA) are semi-autonomous bodies that depend on annual government budget appropriations and hence, tend to be under direct financial control of governments. More importantly, all members, the Chair of the Board, and senior management are appointed by the President or the Minister of Finance and Planning. As a result of such appointments, political control and interference often intrudes on operational decision-making. For example, in the case of the URA, the Governor of the Bank of Uganda or the Secretary to the Treasury (both NRM government appointees) normally serve as board members with power to give policy direction to the URA and to oversee its management (the Governor, Bank of Uganda, 2001: 3–4). In addition, in the nineteen years of the URA's existence, there have been four Commissioner Generals (equivalent to CEOs) – three of them Ugandans and one foreign expatriate national – who have all been appointees of the President of Uganda. It seems that the creation of the URA has helped the NRM Government address the problems of human capacity, compensation, incentives and technological innovation more efficiently. However, the problems of patronage and corruption have not been resolved.

Autonomous Development Funds in Africa have been supported by both donors and African governments in the same way as the executive agencies considered earlier were. At the moment, these Development Funds appear to be at different stages of evolution (Hyden, 2008). In Tanzania, the Cultural Development Trust Fund (Mfuko wa Utamaduni Tanzania) is operational while in Uganda and Zambia the Funds are at an exploratory stage. Indeed, the 1995 Kampala Experts Report recommended a gradual approach to the establishment of the Autonomous Development Fund 'because it allows for careful attention to political, legal, managerial and financial as well as other issues. [Furthermore], there is need ... to create or build confidence to ensure the funds' survival' (Chileshe, 1997: 25–6).

The Tanzania Cultural Development Trust Fund (TCDTF) was established by an Act of Parliament in 1999 as an autonomous fund for promoting cultural development throughout the country. It has an independent board of nine persons representing all major stakeholders and has been able to attract donor support as well as mobilize funds locally for the cultural sector in the country. The Cultural Development Fund 'has responsibly allocated grants not only to activities and artists based in the main city of Dar es Salaam, but also to the twenty regions of the country. Thus, it has had a catalytic effect while serving as a model for how money can be used in ways that enhance the principles of good governance' (Hyden, 2008: 271). In a 2004 contract between the Tanzania Cultural Trust Fund and the Norwegian Ministry of Foreign Affairs (MFA), the Cultural Development Fund received nearly 4.5 million Norwegian kroners to finance programme activities for the planned period 2005–7. As part of its obligations, the Trust Fund was required to 'ensure that program funds are properly accounted for and keep available for immediate inspection all accounting records, systems and all relevant documentation' (MFA and Tanzania Culture Trust Fund Contract, 2004: 2). As regards corruption or fraudulent practices, the contract made it clear that:

> MFA will cancel this contract or portion of this contract and have the right to demand the cancellation of any contract financed under this contract with immediate effect if it determines that corrupt or fraudulent practices were engaged in by representatives of Tanzania Culture Trust Fund or of a beneficiary of the aid funds during procurement or during the execution of the contract without the Trust Fund having taken timely and appropriate action satisfactory to MFA to remedy the situation. (MFA and Tanzania Culture Trust Fund Contract, 2004: 11)

Sixteen years after the 1995 Kampala ADF workshop to discuss the viability of implementing the ADF model on the continent, Uganda, the host of this crucial conference, has yet to establish its own Autonomous Fund. This is particularly surprising given President Museveni's endorsement of the idea and the way his then Minister of Finance and Economic Planning characterized the workshop as 'exceptionally serious, giving his assurance of Uganda's readiness to be used as a model for the implementation of the follow-up actions ... necessary to institutionalize the independent funds'

(Development Dialogue, 1995: 5). The Ugandan case shows that until African leaders and their people realize it is their responsibility to improve the current political and economic situation, nothing significant will happen. In particular, African leaders will not only need to embrace the new thinking about dispensing foreign aid, they will also need to have the commitment and political will to experiment with Autonomous Development Funds. Furthermore, African leaders will need the discipline and fortitude to seek to reduce patronage and corruption and genuinely to pursue a policy-driven development agenda.

In Zambia, efforts to implement Autonomous Development Funds have revolved mainly around using existing public and private financial institutions as intermediaries for the ADF funds (Chileshe, 1997; Changa Management Services Report, 1997). According to a consultancy report prepared for the National Economic Advisory Council on the establishment of Zambia's ADF:

> The ADF will not lend directly to end users, but it will channel its loans through intermediaries that can follow the ADF mission and objectives. This approach is considered to be cost-effective, and is likely to ensure that the bulk of ADF resources actually go to developmental expenditure rather than to administrative costs. Accordingly, it was decided to commission a study to identify and make some preliminary assessment of potential intermediaries for the ADF. (Changa Management Services Report, 1997: 3)

Based on this report, the Development Bank of Zambia (DBZ), which provides long-term financing to all sectors of the economy, could perform the role of financial intermediary for the ADF. Use of existing institutions, whether public or private, may not be a viable option as these tend to be vulnerable to intrusive politics and corruption, two major challenges Autonomous Development Funds seek to avoid at any cost.

Evidence shows that both existing public and private financial institutions in Zambia have performed very poorly. It is reported that those established by the government are 'bedevilled' by a mass of problems: 'poor management; inadequate availability of funds for lending; political interference in the operation of the institutions themselves; questionable inability of selected projects; low recovery rates; inadequate supervision and monitoring of beneficiary projects; and high administration and operational costs' (Chileshe, 1997: 12). Those established by the private sector do no better: they are 'encumbered by: poor management result-ing in mismanagement of the institutions themselves; low recovery rates; dependence on external sources of funding; neglect of savings mobiliza-tion from members; and low per capita incomes and hence, low savings' (Chileshe, 1997: 12 again). Reliance on pre-existing public institutions to serve as intermediaries to autonomous development funds – ones that are not executive agencies – is a non-starter that should be discarded alto-gether, as these institutions are unlikely to change the status quo or usher in the desired performance. However, it is possible for existing local and national institutions to compete for ADF funds, as suggested in the pro-posed ADF model.

Although Zambia has gone further than Uganda in exploring the crea-tion of Autonomous Development Funds, neither country has an opera-tional ADF as in Tanzania. There is an urgent need for African governments and donors as well as powerful national and international NGOs to push for the establishment of Autonomous Development Funds in selected African countries on either a pilot or experimental basis. The success of such programmes could then be used to persuade reluctant or uncommit-ted African governments and donors to participate in this new develop-ment enterprise. Without such concerted efforts, it will take much longer to establish viable Autonomous Development Funds on the continent. Africa cannot wait for the ADF model, untried and undemonstrated, to make all stakeholders 'feel enthusiastic and ready to cooperate to achieve a common objective' (Hyden, 1995: 37). The countries of the continent have to *make* this idea both attractive and operational by example – and as a matter of urgency.

In addition to institutional reforms aimed at creating executive agencies or Autonomous Development Funds, there are other changes in the public sector designed to improve the extent of professionalism and efficiency. We have argued that pre-existing public institutions (with the exception of executive agencies) should not serve as intermediaries for the Autonomous Development Funds, but Mackey (1999) contends that reforming Man-agement Development Institutes could be critical in providing technical and professional training for the managers required to run Autonomous Funds. Although this idea sounds a good one, as some pre-existing public institutions could be used to reinforce the functioning of Autonomous Funds, the danger is that most of these bodies are either highly politicized or are not capable of performing the new and challenging tasks required under the ADF model. However, Management Development Institutes, like other pre-existing public institutions could be allowed to compete for monies disbursed by Autonomous Funds. To succeed, they may have to realign their objectives and link them to actual performance or results.

There is undoubtedly a great need to establish strong and effective public institutions that are both performance-oriented and capable of achieving sustainable development in Sub-Saharan Africa (AfCoP Casebook, 2010: 2). For such public institutions to achieve results – financial institutions included – they will need to focus on five major areas: improving both governance and management; monitoring and evaluating their performance; enhancing accountability and partnerships; planning and budgeting; and building statistical capacity (AfCoP Casebook, 2010: 3). Focusing on these five key areas would 'ensure that managers are using evidence to make decisions and development stakeholders are able to keep track of progress. It [would ensure] that governments shift from delivering outputs to generating real outcomes' (AfCoP Casebook, 2010: 3). Case studies on managing results within the African context have revealed that ownership, or 'buy-in', of development programmes by all stakeholders is critical to programme success. According to these case studies:

> leaders and high level managers advocated the will for change at the top level of the public administration, often with the support of elected political office holders. Their programs then trickled down through participatory processes and capacity building training. Staff on the ground made sure that targets defined by top managers applied to their contexts and were therefore better able to measure the results ... Local civil servants must also understand why they are asked to deliver and report on achievements ... Committing staff to personal objectives and core competencies also proved to be successful incentives to increase performance once initial capacities are built. (AfCoP Casebook, 2010: 3)

Noel et al. (1999) propose the use of a development-cooperative model
rather than development assistance. They define the development-cooperative model as 'a process by which institutions (public, private and non-
governmental), their members and their clientele work together to achieve
individual and shared objectives' (Noel et al., 1999: 140). The model is based
on the assumption that institutions of higher learning (the universities) are
best suited for bridging the gap between top-down (state) development
assistance and bottom-up NGOs' assistance strategies, which are currently
dominant. The development-cooperative model being piloted in Africa,
and in several transitional societies of the former Soviet Union, focuses on
collaborative performance (or results-based) partnerships that seek to:

1. access and leverage resources from various key stakeholders;
2. access and use complementary expertise (while building additional
   human and institutional capacity);
3. achieve synergy among multiple development objectives;
4. expand geographic and client range;
5. promote sustainable results; and
6. improve coordination among partners from centralized to local
   levels.
   (Noel et al., 1999: 140–1)

In Malawi and Mali, such collaborative partnerships have been successfully
implemented within sectors of government or academic institutions. While
US land-grant universities 'are experienced in working with voluntary
and nongovernmental organizations' because of their outreach mission
(Noel et al., 1999: 154), their African counterparts have no such experience,
as they tend to concentrate on teaching and research. This suggests that
African universities may not be the ideal intermediaries to bridge the gap
between the state and NGOs in the development process. Furthermore,
reliance on government ministries or government-controlled universities
in Africa to create and utilize a development-cooperative model may not
work because of the inherent problems of political interference, corruption,
and inefficiency. It seems that pre-existing institutions, whether government institutions or government-controlled universities, present the risk

of corruption or continued use of patronage. Hence, such institutions should not serve as intermediaries for Autonomous Funds. Rather, they could be end-users of such funds.

Finally, Sachs (1999) presents what he calls the New Partnership for Growth in Africa as an alternative to the ADF model. The centrepiece of this model is the high and sustained growth rate projected – in excess of 5 per cent per year. The model has three components as follows:

1. A commitment by selected African governments to adopt and implement ... comprehensive, growth-oriented economic reforms that open the economy to international trade, remove the public sector from areas of the economy that can be served by the private sector, and focus the government's attention on the key public goods – education, health and infrastructure;

2. Initiative from the United States to work with other major donors to end aid to Africa as we know it [initially through deep debt relief and short-term budget support]; and,

3. Enhanced U.S. and international support for key scientific and technological investments in participating countries.
(Sachs, 1999: 157–8).

At the core of Sachs' (1999) New Partnership for Growth in Africa is a disguised, but intensified form of neoliberal policy of the kind that has failed miserably, as we have shown in previous chapters. It is because of such failure that Autonomous Development Funds have been proposed in the first place. Although Sachs wants the United States to lead this effort, current budget and debt problems and the strategic interests it has around the globe seem to preclude the US from playing such a role in Africa. As we have discussed elsewhere in this study, a focus on high growth rates alone would inevitably lead to increased poverty and inequality, as the example of Uganda since the mid 1990s clearly demonstrates. Evidence shows that high rates of economic growth do 'not automatically lead to sustainable human development and the elimination of poverty' (Speth, 1997: 3). Furthermore, more foreign aid may not necessarily reduce the level of poverty either. Arimah (2004: 411) points out that an increase in

aid per capita does not necessarily 'correspond to a reduction in the proportion of a country's population living below the national poverty line.
[This is because] foreign aid is not adequately channelled to poor countries
where [it is] most needed, but to strategic allies, and as such, may not be
an antidote for poverty.'

Finally, unlike the Autonomous Funds, the proposed New Partnership
for Growth in Africa would, it claims, 'supplement [or perhaps replace]
the efforts of the governments of these countries so that within a decade,
high and sustained rates of economic growth will be well-established and
all extraordinary sources of foreign aid can cease' (Sachs, 1999: 159). While
Autonomous Funds have a chance in the long term to end aid as we know
it, the New Partnership for Growth in Africa is unlikely to garner sufficient
donor funds to create sustainable development and thus make future aid
unnecessary, as it claims. In the final analysis, the proposal is unrealistic
since it is a disguised version of failed neoliberal policies like the Structural
Adjustment Programs tried out in the 1980s and 1990s, and the current
Poverty Reduction Strategy Papers.

6.4 The African Developmental State and Sustainable Development: Bringing the State Back In

For African states to promote economic and social transformation effectively, they require five major elements: (1) development-driven leadership
and a developmentalist coalition; (2) strong and transformative public
institutions; (3) an overarching development strategy; (4) increased investment in research and development; and (5) new and progressive social
policies (Economic Report on Africa, 2011: 106). As the case of Botswana
demonstrates, a capable and committed leadership that believes in promoting economic and social transformation is critical. Such political leadership has to assemble and work with a powerful technical team that puts
the development agenda above everything else. As Tony Blair, the former

British Prime Minister aptly observes, 'Africa's problems have been caused as much by a lack of capacity to govern as a lack of aid' (http://www.africangovernance.org/).

Because of competing class and ethnic interests, putting together a developmental coalition may be difficult. Hence, there is a need to avoid 'a one-size-fits-all' approach and allow each country to develop its own developmental coalition and developmental priorities. The African Peer Review Mechanism (APRM) under the New Partnership for Africa's Development (NEPAD) provides a governance platform for the state and the people to discuss, negotiate and agree on a development agenda and coalition through country self-assessment and peer review. NEPAD, launched in 2001 to promote growth and reduce poverty on the continent, permits African countries (individually and collectively) to determine their own destiny and the international community to complement such efforts. Its major problem is the perception that it was created by the African elite and donors to the exclusion of ordinary people and their civil society organizations.

Beyond a committed and visionary leadership, there is a need to build strong public institutions and to base recruitment on merit rather than on political patronage or ethnic and religious considerations. In addition, such institutions must be insulated from political interference. In particular, all public institutions, including financial institutions such as the Central Bank, the Tax Revenue Authority and the Ministries of Planning and Finance have to be re-established, revived or strengthened with the aim of ensuring effective coordination and implementation of development programmes and projects. Overall, development policy may vary from one African country to another; so temptations of imposing a 'one-size-fits-all' policy should be resisted. For example, African countries where subsistence agriculture is dominant should focus on creating cooperatives and community-based organizations to improve the well-being of subsistence farmers. In other cases, the focus should be on the promotion of agribusiness and agro-based exports to increase both rural productivity and incomes through the creation of employment opportunities.

In today's knowledge-driven global economy, African countries should seek to increase investment in research and development through universities and other tertiary institutions. Increased production and productivity due to innovation, specialized skills and scientific knowledge would make African countries competitive in the global economy while contributing to GDP and employment.

Finally, social policies in Africa need to be created, revised or strengthened. Such social policies should include measures to increase income support (like the credit or cash payments to the poor in Mexico). And they should aim 'gradually to reduce income inequality and ensure access to the basic social goals of education, healthcare and decent livelihoods for people' (Economic Report on Africa, 2011: 110).

As indicated above, for African countries to achieve sustainable development, they need a political leadership committed to national development and to strengthening and deepening the institutional reforms taking place in the public sector. The goal of such public sector reform has been to increase both the human and institutional capacity to implement policies effectively and efficiently (Gramajo, 2006). To achieve that goal, public institutions are required with competent professionals and with the autonomy and authority to implement development priorities. Furthermore, executive agencies need to be expanded and insulated from politics, while pilot and experimental Autonomous Funds are transformed into fully operational bodies, as in the case of the Tanzania Cultural Development Trust Fund. In addition, the state should proactively pursue a broad and collaborative development strategy 'in which [their] governments play effective roles as facilitators, catalysers, and mediators; and the private sector, NGOs and donors are significantly engaged' (Rural Poverty Report 2011, 2010: 22). Such a broad approach to development should target both smallholder (or subsistence) agriculture and the non-farm economy. Although variations are to be expected, due to differences in political and economic circumstances, such an approach should entail the following steps: (1) improving the overall environment of rural areas to provide more employment and self-employment opportunities for the poor and youth; (2) advancing individual capabilities of subsistence farmers and improving their overall risk management capacity; and (3) strengthening the collective capacities of rural people through 'bottom-up' organizations such as microfinance institutions, SACCOS or community-based organizations (Rural Poverty Report 2011, 2010).

Attaining these objectives requires new investments and partnerships involving the state, NGOs, the private sector and the international donor community. This calls for the creation of public-private-NGO sector partnerships that offer smallholders support to develop new market opportunities. For example, in Uganda, IFAD has promoted and supported the development of the oil palm sector. In this partnership:

> IFAD co-financed the Vegetable Oil Development Project, which was designed to reduce Uganda's reliance on imported vegetable oils while also increasing smallholders' income by expanding their involvement in this sector. Under the project, the Government signed a direct foreign investment agreement with BIDCO, a large private investor, which covered the construction of an oil palm refinery and the development of oil palm plantations and supporting infrastructure. BIDCO brought to the partnership technical expertise and investment capital, while IFAD supported smallholders to contribute their land and labour to the partnership. (Rural Poverty Report 2011, 2010: 141)

In the case of the oil palm sector, the donor (IFAD), the government of Uganda and BIDCO (a private investor) have worked in partnership to create and improve marketing and employment opportunities for smallholder oil palm producers. The initiative has included the creation of the Kalangala Oil Palm Growers Trust which provides its members with access to extension services and loans. The issue of state involvement in such partnerships is 'no longer ... *whether state policies or investments may be needed to reduce the risk environment that smallholder farmers face; rather the question is how interventions can be made in a way that pursues national policy priorities in the most effective, least costly and most sustainable manner*' (Rural Poverty Report, 2011, 2010: 228). Cheru and Calais (2010: 237) propose that the African state be reassigned 'a proactive role in providing strategic guidance on many fronts – from the way in which productive resources are organized to the mobilization of financial and human resources – in order to transform African economies, with the ultimate goal of eradicating poverty and creating the conditions for a just and democratic social order.' According to a recent Economic Commission for Africa Report, 'achieving the desired degree of diversification and transformation [i.e., economic and social development] in Africa requires the state to assume and play a pivotal role in the development process' (ECA Report, 2011: Foreword).

The Africa Governance Initiative (AGI), founded three years ago by Tony Blair, relies on the use of an embedded team of experts in Sierra Leone, Rwanda and Liberia, to build trust and deliver meaningful social change. Tony Blair is quoted as saying:

> Modern government is not about traditional civil service, it is about getting things done. It is about effecting change ... Our teams are not fly-in, fly-out consultants. They have to be embedded in the system. That is how you build trust. All of these countries have got masses of reports lying on the shelf telling them what they need to do. I keep saying the 'what' is not hard to work out ... the question is the 'how'. One of AGI's first pieces of advice to African leaders is to prioritise. In all these countries, we say if you have 100 priorities you will get nothing done, but if you have a limited number of objectives that is different. (http://www.africagovernance.org/)

Thus, the role of the state in economic activity needs to be re-oriented or re-configured, not reduced (Speth, 1997). In other words, we need to *mend, not end* state involvement in economic development: the real need is to bring the state back into the development process as a *smarter* developmental state. Such a state would be ideologically committed to economic development and would seek to deploy its bureaucratic and political resources to the task of economic development (Taylor, 2003). Furthermore, the political elite controlling the state would derive, or seek to derive, political legitimacy from economic performance. As Fowler (1999: 52) has aptly observed, 'African regimes will have to revise their ideas about their sources of legitimacy and their role and right to decide on and control social development processes. [In addition], this will require the creation of mechanisms for negotiating with the NGO community and donor agencies – mechanisms which seldom exist at present.' As such, the regimes could be democratic, quasi-democratic or authoritarian. Asian developmental states were authoritarian – as is China now – but they still achieved phenomenal economic growth in the 1980s. In Africa, Botswana and Mauritius are developmental states that are democratic as well. Hence, the performance of developmental states, whether authoritarian or demo-cratic, is a product of social engineering undertaken by political actors working with a technical team embedded in strong public institutions.

The East Asian developmental state not only derives its legitimacy from economic development, but is both capable of, and strongly committed to, rapid growth. This is 'a societal project defined by the elite and intended to transform or benefit all society' (Makoba, 1998: 26). Although African states lack the human and institutional capacity to pursue policies similar to those executed by Asian developmental states, they are in a position to acquire such capabilities through successful institutional reform. And in the words of Ellerman (2002: 3), the ultimate goal for developing countries, including those in Sub-Saharan Africa, is 'to learn how to learn'. They must become learning societies, as the East Asian 'tigers' did.

Botswana (an exceptional case in Sub-Saharan Africa) has managed to sustain both democracy and economic development since its independence in the late 1960s. The most important factors behind this achievement have been: (1) a unified political elite committed to development; (2) massive diamond revenues used for the public good; and (3) strong public institutions insulated from politics (Von Soest, 2009; Sebudubudu and Lotshwao, 2008; Taylor, 2003; Samatar and Samatar, 2002 and Owusu and Samatar, 1997). The political leadership in Botswana has remained committed to both its democratic and economic ideals. In addition, the leadership has possessed 'the [political] will to direct and ensure that National Development Plans are executed' (Sebudubudu and Lotshwao, 2008: 6). Above all, in the public service arena, the focus has been on technical expertise and competency rather than political expediency. Samatar and Samatar (2002: 43) believe this has been achieved by having skilled technocrats and by guarding their authority, so that they have control over both planning and budgeting. They point to two major factors: '(1) insulating the policy-making process from society-centred groups; [and] (2) protecting the technocratic cadre's ability to plan, budget, and monitor programme implementation. It [has] also [been empowered to enforce] fiscal discipline while remaining free, for the most part, from political influence.' Overall, then, the Botswana public service has been underpinned by professional competence and insulated from politics or government interference – a situation strikingly absent in other Sub-Saharan African countries.

Under the proposed ADF model it is possible to limit or restrict corruption, patronage and clientelism while improving competency, professionalism and efficiency in core social and economic development sectors. In such a context, the 'smart' developmental state cannot afford not to take a central coordinating role for the public, private and NGO sectors (Taylor, 2003). As a result, the ADF model has the potential to provide the 'retreating African state', damaged by SAPs and PRSPs, with another chance to return to the centre of the development process. The same model may also serve as a counter-force to partisan, and often divisive, parochial politics associated with competition for power in quasi-democratic multi-party political contexts (Hoon and Hyden, 2001). Far from diminishing government activity in the economy and increasing donor control of the development process, the ADF model could reinvigorate the state.

6.5 Donor Support of the New Development Efforts

It is important to realize that sustainable human development cannot occur in the absence of good governance – 'the exercise of political, economic and administrative authority in the management of a country's affairs at all levels' (Speth, 1997: 2). According to Speth (1997: 3), the former UNDP Administrator, 'good governance includes the state, but transcends it by taking in the private sector and civil society ... Because each [of the three actors] has weaknesses and strengths, a major objective of [UNDP's] support for good governance is to promote constructive interaction among all three.' The state – in particular the developmental state – should take the lead in the triple partnership for development, while international development agencies (for both bilateral and multilateral assistance) are expected to facilitate the coordination of development aid in Africa. Currently, donors provide development assistance to both governments and the non-governmental sector. However, it is believed they channel more of their funding through NGOs/MFIs because they consider these organizations to be more effective than governments. Governments are often seen as being both corrupt and inept. The ongoing public sector reform in Sub-Saharan Africa together with the creation of proposed Autonomous Development Funds is expected to reverse this situation in both the medium and long terms.

The creation of the ADF model, has the potential to serve as a catalyst for rich countries to increase and expedite the dispensing of aid to Africa, including aid pledged by ODA countries. Since 2005, both the G8 and the European Union (EU) have pledged to increase the level of their development aid to Africa, and in 2010 the EU renewed its commitment to increase aid so as to reach a target of 0.7 per cent of Gross National Income by 2015. In spite of these pledges, the total aid received so far is still inadequate. This is due to the 2008 global economic crisis and also to concerns about widespread corruption and lack of capacity in African countries to absorb additional aid. Already donor-driven innovations such as direct budget support (DBS), Cash on Delivery (COD), and sector-wide funding arrangements (SWAPs) have dramatically improved the coordination and disbursement of aid. However, such innovations have so far failed to maximize the impact of aid on the poor or to prevent patronage and corruption. Combined public sector reforms and the creation of Autonomous Funds would go a long way to ensure effective implementation of development priorities, reduce the level of corruption and increase transparency and accountability. Aid effectiveness and impact on the poor and vulnerable groups would greatly improve. Also, 'donor agencies ... will have to move away from unrealistic expectations that NGOs will be self-financing. Such an acceptance has critical implications for their funding commitments, strategies and contracting practices' (Fowler, 1999: 67).

6.6 NGOs and MFIs as Partners in Development

Because NGOs, and especially MFIs, tend to be cost-effective and to target the poor, they have been receiving significant aid from donors. In some instances, donor agencies have collaborated with NGOs and MFIs to pursue development projects and delivery of services such as health and education. However, since NGOs and MFIs on their own cannot bring about sustainable development, they need to partner with states and donors to achieve this goal.

The NGOs are important in the development process because they provide 'an opportunity for cooperation and collective action that helps not only individuals but also society at large' (Hyden, 1995: 44). NGOs and MFIs seek to improve poor peoples' livelihoods and to promote long-term economic development. In Sub-Saharan Africa, where states and markets have neither achieved development nor effectively delivered basic services such as education and health, NGOs and MFIs have stepped in really quite effectively to fill the void created. However, even if it is true that 'civil society has accomplished things that the state [or market] has failed to do', the assumption that it is a matter of *either/or* is mistaken. 'The two should be treated as interlinked' (Hyden et al., 2004: 74). At the same time, NGOs and MFIs, like donors and governments, need to rethink their strategies and roles under the new development paradigm. In particular, 'NGOs must: (1) reappraise their long-term strategies and role within the continent; (2) take on board the political implications of being potentially the major suppliers of social services in the country; (3) renegotiate their position with [governments]; (4) question some of the myths about their own sustainability as actors in Africa's development; and (5) recognize that in global terms their resources are negligible in relation to the forces that cause and maintain poverty' (Fowler, 1999: 65).

Increasingly, country poverty reduction strategy programmes or national development plans include NGOs and MFIs in national efforts to achieve growth and poverty reduction. However, both governments and donors need to treat NGOs as true partners or equals in the development process (Hyden, 1995: 44). Such partnerships may exist from time to time in different African countries, but they need to be consistent and to last. In Uganda, initially, both donors and the government provided strong support to NGOs and MFIs as part of the country's overall strategy to increase growth and reduce poverty. It is reported, for example, that the initial success of microfinance in Uganda was due to significant donor funding, skilled human resources, active government support, and intensive collaboration among the major stakeholders in the country. However, this positive collaboration and relationship with government and donors changed after 2007 as donors reduced grant funding and government redirected its funding to political SACCOS in order to garner popular political support in various districts throughout the country. Yet available evidence indicates that for MFIs and SACCOS to succeed, they need to insulate themselves from direct government involvement in their operations and decision-making.

It is expected that with the creation of Autonomous Development Funds, the Ugandan government would be able to restore its relationship with NGOs and MFIs and treat them as equal development partners. Also, the government could continue to support SACCOS without abandoning support for NGOs and MFIs. Finally, under the ADF model, linkage banking undertaken by Postbank Uganda to provide rural finance to the northern areas could be strengthened and extended through all Uganda.

6.7 The Proposed ADF Model at Work

For the proposed ADF model to serve both government institutions and the non-governmental sector, it has to operate through various windows to permit maximum flexibility and greater access to the poor and eligible vulnerable groups. Such windows might include the following:

Window I to cater for proposals where there is no immediate return on investment such as training and education programmes;

Window II, to address the needs of those many groups that fail to obtain credit from regular banks and credit institutions because they are too poor. Project requests from these sources may be funded on a 'soft loan' basis in order to give them a chance of succeeding; and

Window III, to operate with regular commercial interest loans to organizations like regulated and unregulated MFIs that are capable of handling these.

Furthermore, the ADF model would ensure that most foreign and domestic development funds and resources get channelled to both governments and NGOs in an efficient and transparent manner. In this way, the ADF would serve as a focal point for both contact and interaction among the three major actors in the development process – the state, NGOs and donors. By seeking to promote shared governance and control over the development process, the ADF would bring together major stakeholders in a newer and more productive way than has ever been managed previously. At the same time, it would ensure the accountability of these actors to the national legislature, and ultimately to the people. Although dispersing foreign aid through ADFs would be competitive, use of known and approved criteria for fund allocations would ensure a high degree of inclusiveness when serving government and non-government institutions alike.

It is expected that the proposed ADF model would create 'the conditions under which all sectors [public, private and civil society] and individual organizations within them, can compete on an even basis and stimulate each other to greater achievements and synergies' (Hyden, 1995: 49). Partnerships involving the state, NGOs and donors, if carefully pursued and effectively coordinated, can help to build capacity, leverage more aid and achieve important development results. In this way, such 'partnerships can clearly complement, expand and improve government-led development efforts' (Africa Progress Report, 2011: 7). There is no doubt that given the right political leadership, focused development plans, NGO participation and donor support, African countries can make significant advances even under tough conditions.

6.8 Summary

The fact 'that governmental, nongovernmental, and private (for-profit) institutions all have limitations for promoting development does not make each irrelevant. Rather, it means that none can be relied upon as an exclusive channel for bettering ... livelihoods and quality of life' (Uphoff et al., 1998: 7). Hence, the best strategy to achieve sustainable development is one that engages government, the non-governmental sector and donor agencies around national development priorities. Under the proposed Autonomous Funds, involvement on a competitive basis would be extended to the private sector as well. Both executive agencies and experimental or pilot Autonomous Development Funds in Africa have the support of governments, donors and *expert consultants* or scholars. Such a consensus is necessary if these mechanisms are to be *mainstreamed* and piloted in targeted African countries with a genuine desire and commitment to undertake fundamental economic reform. A new policy-driven development agenda in Sub-Saharan African countries will require new thinking from all stakeholders in the development debate.

Under current Poverty Reduction Strategy Papers, African countries with donor support are already involved in some form of joint planning and implementation of various development programmes and priorities. However, there is a need to identify and reinforce areas of *mutual cooperation* among the three major developmental actors to create a true *triple partnership*. Some of the greatest challenges likely to face the new thinking and the creation of Autonomous Development Funds are: (1) how, as a public institution, the ADF can guarantee its autonomy from both the state and society; (2) how it can ensure that its role in development is complementary to that of the government, rather than supplementary; (3) how to boost donors' willingness to increase aid from the current levels; and (4) how to obtain the commitment and political will of African governments to accept the new thinking of the aid regime and to implement fundamental economic reforms. As previously stated, governments, donors, and NGOs will *all* have to undergo rethinking about their strategies and roles in the development process.

Thoughtful planning is essential. It is important to remember that such partnerships are not a panacea to development challenges that face African countries. For example, 'if not coordinated with existing initiatives and closely aligned to national development frameworks, partnerships can complicate, dilute and even undermine other development efforts. They can also lead to harmful competition for resources and unnecessary duplication of effort' (Africa Progress Report, 2011: 56).

The final chapter provides a comprehensive overview and synthesis of this study and gives a summary and conclusions.

CHAPTER SEVEN

Summary and Conclusions

This study has explored an alternative strategy for development in Africa – one that goes beyond the current market- or state-led strategies. In spite of massive development aid for the past three decades, most Sub-Saharan African countries, including Uganda, have failed to achieve economic development, alleviate poverty or deliver basic services such as education, health or clean water in an effective way. Development efforts have failed due to a whole range of factors. These include widespread corruption, economic mismanagement, patronage and lack of accountability, insufficient capital, and inadequate human and institutional capacity for implementing agreed priorities properly. However, at the core of Africa's economic and political crisis is the failure of its leadership to provide effective governance and sound economic management. All these difficulties, combined with the failure of the neoclassical policies of the 1980s and 1990s, have forced us to think again about approaches to African development. The triple partnership approach proposed in the previous chapter seeks to engage the state, the non-governmental sector and donor agencies in a coordinated development effort. And the Autonomous Development Fund (ADF) model, analysed in the same chapter, is expected to serve as a vehicle for the three-way collaboration of these major actors in the development process.

As the African state has retreated or become marginalized in economic activity and service delivery, due to the Structural Adjustment Programs imposed by the World Bank and the IMF, the role of non-governmental organizations and microfinance institutions has become central. In particular, development-oriented NGOs and MFIs have stepped in to fill the vacuum created as a result of government inadequacies. Both NGOs and MFIs cater primarily for the poor and other marginalized segments of the population. Donors have continued to provide development assistance to both governments and the non-governmental sector. However, as explained in Chapter One, donors are increasingly channelling more aid to NGOs and MFIs. This is because they consider them to be more effective in using aid than governments are. The situation cries out for governments, donors and NGOs to work together so they can maximize the impact of such development assistance.

Critics of aid to Africa argue that it is ineffective and even counter-productive. Others think it has been stolen or wasted through various forms of corruption. And recently, Moyo (2009) in her controversial book, *Dead Aid*, has argued that aid to Africa should be ended altogether. In spite of such criticisms, it appears there have been significant improvements in how aid is coordinated and dispensed. Donor-driven innovative mecha-nisms, such as direct budget support (DBS), Cash on Delivery (COD), and sector-wide funding arrangements (SWAPs), have sought to improve and maximize effectiveness. These, together with public service reforms such as the creation of executive agencies operating outside the administration, are expected to increase the impact aid has. However, for this to succeed it is important to end government corruption and patronage and for states to develop their capacity to implement agreed development priorities.

At the level of the whole African continent, the New Partnership for African Development (NEPAD) looks at development as a process of empowerment and self-reliance. NEPAD requires African leaders and their people to determine their own destiny, but with international support. The successful implementation of NEPAD programmes and policies at national level will depend on the commitment and political will of individual African leaders. The proposed public-private-donor partnerships under NEPAD are expected to extend beyond aid to include foreign direct investment. For instance, the proposed Investment Climate Facility (ICF) is expected to improve Africa's investment climate a great deal by coordinating both donor and private sector investment. As we discuss later in this chapter, the new thinking about development requires a strong partnership, involv-ing the state, donors, NGOs, and even the private sector. In addition to providing infrastructure, an enabling policy and the legal environment, African states should be brought back into the development process – and this time in closer collaboration with the partners just mentioned. Such a partnership, as we saw in Chapter Six, requires a 'smarter', developmental state and strong public institutions insulated from politics but operating within the legal framework. It also requires redefinition of the roles and strategies of donors and NGOs and their relationship to the state, so they fit into the new pattern.

In Uganda (the country of our case study), major policies undertaken from the late 1980s to the present have been based on the neoliberal paradigm. These policies, which include the Structural Adjustment Program (SAP) and successors such as the Poverty Eradication Action Plan (PEAP) and the Poverty Reduction Strategy Papers (PRSPs), have contributed some positive results, largely at the macroeconomic level. However, as we discussed in Chapter Two, these policies have not led to significant poverty reduction or improved the well-being of most Ugandans. Implementation of the various poverty reduction/alleviation programmes was tried without significant NGO/MFI participation. This is, in part, because the NRM Government believes in the critical role of the private sector as the engine of growth and development. At the same time, donors, who have had great influence over the dispensing of aid, have relied on conditions or contracts to compel the government to make budget allocations to particular sectors – for example, the social sector.

As a result, there has been little cooperation among major stakeholders in Uganda. Furthermore, despite the government's political rhetoric about the importance of the rural agricultural sector, there have not been significant budgetary allocations to it, even though this vital sector serves four out of five households in the country. In general, the peasant sector has been relegated to being a holding sector: the present aim is to ensure rural welfare and employment until modernization and commercialization of agriculture takes place. Under the Plan for Modernization of Agriculture (PMA), the government has identified three categories of farmers: subsistence, semi-commercial (or medium) and commercial. It is the semi-commercial and commercial farmers who have received the bulk of government funding and agricultural extension services provided through the National Agricultural Advisory Services (NAADS). These two categories of farmers tend to have strong political connections and exploit such networks for their advantage. Subsistence farmers, who have no political influence or connections, have been neglected and deprived of any government support.

Although Uganda's current National Development Plan (2010–15) proposes the creation of Public-Private Partnerships (PPPs) in targeted or flagship industries within manufacturing and the export-oriented sector, it seems unlikely that the plan will be extended to cover the agricultural sector or agri-business. Above all, the country's Industrial Parks Policy, undertaken through the Uganda Investment Authority (UIA), is not linked organically to investments in agro-processing or manufacturing and export-oriented sectors. The launching of political SACCOS in 2007 under the Prosperity for All (PFA) programme, with a mandate to deliver government-supported rural credit, highlights the overriding political considerations of the NRM Government in its approach to the rural sector. Currently, there are concerns – even fears – that the government's direct involvement in SACCOS may undermine their performance in the same way as *Entandikwa* was undermined by political interference in the mid 1990s.

Uganda's expected windfall in oil revenues, if wisely and properly utilized, could provide urgently needed funds to fuel the country's economic development and prosperity. However, there is considerable scepticism about how the oil revenue will be spent, given that there is no law governing its allocation and there is widespread corruption at all levels of the government. It is not clear how the government will avoid the dreaded *oil curse* (or '*Dutch disease*') endemic to resource-rich countries, especially ones in Sub-Saharan Africa.

While Uganda seems to have performed reasonably well in terms of policy formulation and innovation, it has not fared as well in terms of policy implementation. This is largely due to problems of human and institutional capacity, to patronage and lack of accountability, and to the absence of political commitment or will. To achieve sustainable development, Uganda (like other African countries) will not only need more aid and increased trade and investment, but also a strong partnership involving the government, NGOs and donors. This is the case because these major actors cannot bring about the desired development on their own, whether in Uganda or in other African countries.

Although NGOs and MFIs seek to improve poor peoples' livelihoods and promote long-term economic development directly, on the whole they have been used to fill a 'development gap' created by failed states or nascent markets in Sub-Saharan Africa. Increasingly, country Poverty Reduction Strategy Papers or national development plans have been including NGOs and MFIs in national efforts. This is largely because of their record: impact studies show that microfinance services really do (or can) help reduce poverty, contribute to food security and empower clients, especially poor women. Despite this, governments tend to treat NGOs and MFIs as junior partners in the development process; they do not see them as *equals*. Under the proposed Autonomous Fund model discussed in the previous chapter, NGOs and MFIs will be considered part of a triple partnership with the government and donors.

Within Sub-Saharan Africa, Uganda is one of a few countries to incorporate development-oriented NGOs and MFIs as part of its poverty reduction strategy (under both the Poverty Reduction Strategy Papers and its successor, the National Development Plan for 2010–15). At least until 2007, both donors and the government saw NGOs and MFIs as critical in the country's efforts to promote growth and reduce poverty. The initial success of microfinance in Uganda is attributed to significant donor funding, skilled human resources, active government support and collaboration from the major stakeholders. However, this collaboration was largely between donors and the non-governmental sector. In particular, donor coordination via the Private Sector Donor Sub-Group (PSDSG) has had the greatest impact on the development of the Ugandan microfinance industry.

The government of Uganda and the donors active there initially provided strong support to NGOs and MFIs as part of their overall development strategy for increasing growth and reducing poverty. All this changed from 2007, when donors reduced their support and the government redirected its funding to politically-oriented SACCOS. After this, donor funding to MFIs in Uganda shifted from grants and soft loans to commercial loans and leveraging of access to credit lines through commercial banks. This funding structure proved cumbersome, especially for unregulated MFIs and NGOs, such as FOCCAS Uganda, which had an extensive rural outreach: it was forced to liquidate in 2007 as a result (Rozas, 2009). Evidence clearly shows that for MFIs or SACCOS to succeed they need to insulate themselves from direct government involvement in their decision-making and operations. Despite the collaborative efforts, donors and government did not have or develop a coherent strategy for rural credit outreach in the country. However, since donor, government and NGO collaboration has been tried before in Uganda, it is hoped that with the new thinking, such collaboration may be further intensified. In particular, the proposed ADF model (considered in the previous chapter) is expected to improve the three-way collaboration on the basis of mutual interest and shared development goals and priorities.

Without continued donor and government support, a few unregulated MFIs will remain successful, but somewhat marginal to the development effort. On the other hand, the three remaining transformed MDIs may be fully integrated into the mainstream financial sector, but still face inadequate deposits and potential mission drift. The proposed ADF model may serve to reverse this outcome, as it would provide funds to both the regulated and unregulated MFIs, but on a competitive basis. Furthermore, innovations such as *linkage banking* of unregulated MFIs with formal financial institutions would greatly reduce risks and costs of delivering financial services to poor customers. Post Bank Uganda has pioneered several linkage banking initiatives – but with mixed results so far. Overall, the Ugandan government, with the support of donors and in collaboration with the microfinance sector should develop a strong pro-poor financial services strategy rather than rely on ad hoc populist initiatives such as the political SACCOS created under the Prosperity for All programme.

Although microfinance is a popular and powerful strategy for promoting development and poverty reduction worldwide, it still has a very long way to go if it is to cover the millions of un-served and under-served poor in developing countries – and especially those in Sub-Saharan Africa. And, despite its importance and rapid growth, microfinance alone is not a panacea (or 'magic bullet') for ending poverty in the world. Overall, there is conflicting evidence regarding the impact of microfinance on economic development and poverty reduction.

As discussed in Chapter Four, there are three major reasons for difficulty in assessing the impact of microfinance on client livelihoods. First, it is a problem to know what to measure and how to measure it. This is compounded by the 'double bottom line' of financial and social goals. While there is consensus in the industry about measuring financial impact, there is disagreement on how to measure *social* impact. Second, there is a tendency to confuse performance indicators with indicators of impact assessment. Performance indicators, such as outreach, repayment rates or client satisfaction, are not identical to measures of impact, such as income generation, poverty reduction, client consumption and empowerment. Third, a problem arises from emerging integrated or embedded approaches such as *ImpAct* or *Progress Tracking* which seek to *prove and improve* the effectiveness of microfinance simultaneously. These emerging approaches attempt to link performance to impact or outcomes. This is based on the assumption that performance is concerned with improving the delivery of services, while impact assessment deals with proving the effectiveness of services provided to poor customers. And while the focus of perform-ance is on the institutions (the MFI), impact is concerned primarily with customers or their well-being. These *practitioner-oriented* approaches also seek to accommodate donor and practitioner interests and priorities, which until recently have appeared to be divergent. It is possible for effective MFI performance to lead to positive results or outcomes, but the two concepts should neither be equated nor confused, as is often the case.

While *ImpAct* and *Progress Tracking* are considered internal learning tools for microfinance management, aimed at improving service and at tracking impact, there are four major approaches designed to assess impact at the micro, meso, and macro levels. These include: (1) the Household approach (or 'narrow approach'); (2) the Wider Impacts perspective which includes both participants and non-participants; (3) the Benefits Proc-ess approach; and (4) the Livelihoods Framework. For example, propo-nents of *wider impacts* perspective believe microfinance will play a critical role in achieving the UN Millennium Development Goals (MDGs) and argue, indeed, that it has already done so in Bangladesh, a country with a mature and substantial microfinance presence. As far as the overall impact of microfinance on poverty reduction is concerned, the results are *mixed*. However, despite challenges faced by impact studies of microfinance, a few empirical studies, focusing on increases in household incomes and consumption smoothing, have demonstrated significant rates of poverty reduction among clients.

The largest and most important study to date has been on the impact of microfinance on the participants of the Grameen Bank, and was undertaken by Khandker (2005). The study found increased income and consumption for both participants and non-participants. Non-participants benefited as a result of the growth in the local economy. These findings suggest that an increase in a client's income is sufficient to show poverty reduction. Hence, they seem to support the assumptions of the Wider Impacts perspective.

Critics of income-consumption-poverty studies claim such studies fail to account for underlying causes of poverty or powerlessness among microfinance clients. They also assert that the poverty situation in Bangladesh has not improved dramatically in spite of the large scale outreach to the poor in that country. Hence, there is a need to consider alternative approaches to income and consumption that look at changes in behaviour or assets of participants before and after programme participation. In particular, poverty-centred MFIs or 'microfinance plus' (such as Freedom from Hunger's *Credit with Education Program*) track changes in income and consumption as well as changes in behaviour or assets of participants. Both Freedom from Hunger (FFH) and Opportunity International (OI) offer financial and comprehensive educational services. Furthermore, they track and monitor how clients use their loans, at the same time providing training and educational services to clients – a policy which tends to increase the human capital of clients and their children. In addition to focusing on behaviour changes in education and health, poverty-oriented MFIs often track clients' assets as an alternative to income and consumption. The asset assessment approach considers the amount of land owned by clients, availability of livestock, or the presence of physical assets such as pots and pans in client households. Change in assets is considered a reliable indicator of improvements in economic conditions and real reduction in vulnerability to shocks or risks. However, it is an expensive approach. To reduce costs associated with this approach, clients can be selected and surveyed, as in the case of the Grameen Bank, or clients can be permitted to do the assessment of their assets themselves – though this reduces the accuracy of results.

In most cases, studies that evaluate the impact of microfinance and point to improvements cannot conclusively demonstrate if such improvements are a result of programme impact or of client attributes. The problems of impact attribution are complicated by lack of data and use of methodologies that fail to isolate the effect of programme participation. As a result, studies that track changes in income, consumption or asset accumulation face too many plausible explanations outside the frame of programme impact. On the other hand, studies that compare participants and non-participants face the twin problems of clients' self-selection and programme placement bias. To address these methodological challenges, Dunford (2006) suggests the creation of a *randomized control trial* design. This would ensure that a new client or a new programme site is unlikely to differ statistically from the corresponding control due to self-selection or programme placement biases.

Proponents of commercialization of microfinance – microfinance using a business approach – argue that it is the only way to achieve both sustainability and outreach, or scale. In addition, they assume that once MFI sustainability is achieved, donor funds can be leveraged to reach even more un-served and under-served clients. By contrast, critics of commercialization view the process as undermining microfinance's commitment to serve the poor, as this may lead to 'mission drift' (in other words, moving up market and abandoning the poor). Despite the growth of MFIs worldwide, a recent World Bank Report (2009) shows that only 10 per cent of MFIs consist of commercial microfinance banks. This means that 90 per cent of MFIs are unregulated. Hence, the co-existence of regulated and unregulated MFIs in the medium and long-terms is a reality. Furthermore, large unregulated MFIs, such as the Grameen Bank, BRAC, and ASA in Bangladesh, have continued to increase outreach and achieve sustainability without transforming into Regulated Financial Institutions. This means that commercialization is a necessary, but not sufficient, condition for achieving sustainability and outreach.

In Latin America, commercialization has been both gradual and multifaceted. The most powerful motive for commercialization there has been the desire of MFIs to grow exponentially while using loans or borrowed funds from the private sector. The microfinance landscape has been characterized by the profit motive and intense competition (in contrast to Asia and Africa). More importantly, the target population in Latin America includes not-so-poor *micro-entrepreneurs* along with the genuine poor. In

Asia, commercialization has been driven by both donors and governments and it has been largely selective or targeted. In some Asian countries, private commercial or development banks have either facilitated the commercialization of MFIs or have expanded bank activities to serve down-market niches (though to a lesser extent than in Latin America). Overall, government has been very instrumental in Indonesia and the Philippines, while largely unsupportive or hostile in Bangladesh and Sri Lanka, respectively. In Sub-Saharan Africa, including Uganda, commercialization has been primarily donor-driven for two major reasons. First, most if not all NGOs and MFIs are dependent on donors for funding and technical assistance. Second, costs of transformation, regulation and internal development of MFIs tend to be extremely high, requiring more donor funds. In Uganda, the influence of donors and Bank of Uganda technocrats was critical to the transformation of the only four NGO MFIs into MDIs in 2003. Since then, no more transformations have occurred due to the prohibitively high costs of making this change. In a few other African countries, like Ethiopia, governments, through legislation or their central bank policies, have compelled NGO MFIs to transform into RFIs. Very few commercial banks in Sub-Saharan Africa either operate microloans or have *downscaled* services to low-income clients. And the few that have made such offers have relied on donor funding and technical assistance. As discussed in Chapter Five, the commercialization of microfinance in Latin America has been fuelled by private sector investment and competition. In Asia, the process has been driven by government initiatives and donor support. And in Sub-Saharan Africa, donor pressure to transform MFIs into RFIs has been the most critical factor.

The goal of all MFIs is to achieve sustainability, so they can cover all their costs while providing services to their clients over considerable periods of time. This applies to both regulated and unregulated MFIs. But in reality, only a few MFIs ever achieve sustainability: evidence worldwide suggests that this remains an elusive goal. And the few that do achieve sustainability may be regulated or unregulated MFIs – it makes no difference. While commercialization enables MFIs to achieve sustainability and outreach rapidly, large unregulated but efficiently managed MFIs, such as the Grameen Bank, do achieve the same goals, but more gradually.

As mentioned, critics of commercialization associate it with mission drift. However, evidence from Latin America shows that mission drift is the exception rather than the norm. This is because the original target population there, consisting of urban poor and small business entrepreneurs, was less indigent than those targeted in other areas. In South Asia, concerns over commercialization and mission drift centre round a fear of exploiting poor clients (rather than abandoning them) through the charging of high interest rates. In Africa – which has a few MFIs that have transformed into RFIs (or MDIs in Uganda) – there is greater concern over mission drift in terms of abandoning poor clients. In reality, this has not yet happened. For example, CERUDEB, the only microfinance bank in Uganda, still provides micro-loans to subsistence farmers, and K-REP in Kenya continues to be financially sustainable while expanding outreach to its poor clients. Overall, the experience of African RFIs shows that commitment to the *'double bottom line'* and an *ownership structure* that allows social investors to be engaged can, and does, minimize or prevent mission drift. Also, the development of differentiated products and the targeting of different clients in terms of their socioeconomic status can help prevent it. This was the case with the Opportunity International Bank of Malawi. The threat of mission drift is real, but there is no need to be too preoccupied with it, as it is not the greatest challenge facing transformed MFIs. In Uganda, the greatest challenge comes from insufficient deposits and a lack of access to private investment, both local and foreign. Meanwhile, there are mechanisms discussed in Chapter Five that help to minimize or prevent mission drift before, during and after transformation (Getu, 2007).

Commercial MFIs represent a rare opportunity to combine socially responsible investment with profitability (the 'holy grail' of microfinance). The question is how to achieve this. Since, to date, transformation has attracted more public banks/agencies and social investors than private debt or equity investment, the chances of commercial MFIs continuing to achieve the 'double bottom line' are still great. Worldwide, the transformation of MFIs into RFIs will continue to be gradual and circumspect. In general, private debt or equity capital is hard to secure, partly because of lack of management capacity to attract or absorb private capital. And in some Sub-Saharan African countries, such as Uganda, there are inadequate deposits to finance growth and expansion of the services provided by MDIs. Since the cost of transformation is prohibitively high, most MFIs and their Boards and founders are not motivated to commercialize.

Assumptions that market competition keeps interest rates of commercial MFIs low seems to be misplaced. Evidence from Bolivia, Uganda, and Bangladesh suggests that interest rates have declined slowly, increased or remained the same. Indeed, some commercial MFIs seem to rely heavily on interest revenue to fuel profitability and outreach. However, over-reliance on interest revenue may blur the line between microfinance and *money lending* – as the case of Compartamos in Mexico demonstrated with the sale of its high value IPO in 2007. Compartamos not only charged excessive interest rates to its 600,000 clients (in spite of the low rate of inflation), but made an extraordinarily high rate of return on its equity investment as a result of its profitable IPO. This has raised accusations that poor clients were exploited to benefit rich initial equity investors. However, as stated previously, the reality is that commercial and non-commercial MFIs will continue to co-exist in the medium and long-terms.

The abysmal performances of the state and the market in promoting economic development in Sub-Saharan Africa calls for the state, NGOs and donors as well as the private sector to embrace the new thinking that urges all these stakeholders to work together in the development process. It is clear that none of these stakeholders, on their own, can bring about the desired development. The establishment of Autonomous Development Funds (ADFs) in Sub-Saharan Africa would serve as a new vehicle for promoting a close partnership among states, NGOs and donors. It would complement rather than supplement on-going efforts from any of these. It would also, almost certainly, reduce patronage and corruption – two major problems that hinder the development process in Sub-Saharan African countries.

The two most important features of the ADF model are: (1) consolidation of external aid and its redirection through a national autonomous development fund; and (2) encouragement of non-partisan competition among public agencies and NGOs for project funding based on promising and sustainable proposals. To minimize political control or influence, the ADF model would ensure that:

- governance is shared among all stakeholders;
- board members and the chairperson are independent of the stakeholders (serving in their individual capacities);
- funds have a national scope, even if they operate in specific sectors; and
- funds as public institutions are accountable to the national legislature.

Critics sceptical of the ADF model make several objections. They claim it is not possible to insulate the fund from politics or corruption. They also believe that donors are unlikely to increase aid beyond current levels, and fear that the scheme would marginalize the role of the central government in economic activity. They think that Africa lacks both the human and the institutional capacity to utilize aid effectively.

In spite of the criticisms, the ADF model would be a vast improvement on the current situation on the continent. The ADF concept, combined with current public sector reforms such as the creation of executive agencies, would increase professionalism and efficiency as well as reduce corruption and patronage. Through the ADF model, African governments and donor support are expected to maximize the impact of development assistance. One would expect such a situation to attract more external aid. Indeed, as we argued in the previous chapter, the success of Autonomous Funds could serve as the catalyst for rich countries to increase and expedite the overseas development assistance pledged since 2000. Rather than marginalize the role of the state in economic activity (as is the case currently with SAPs and PRSPs), the ADF model is likely to bring the state back in, to lead the development process. Finally, the ADF model holds out the greatest hope for African countries to increase capital and improve both their human and institutional capacity to utilize aid more effectively.

Recent and on-going public sector reforms (such as the creation of independent executive agencies) in Sub-Saharan Africa provide the *building blocks* – or the *road map* – for the establishment of developmental states as well as Autonomous Development Funds. The goal of such public sector reforms has been to reduce patronage and political influence, while increasing professionalism and efficiency. In particular, the most important features of the executive agencies seem to overlap with those of Autonomous

Funds. The executive agencies also seek to increase institutional effectiveness and efficiency, while insulating decision-making and operations from political interference. Though created and operated as semi-autonomous bodies, Autonomous Revenue Authorities (ARAs) in Sub-Saharan Africa (including the Uganda Revenue Authority or URA) rely heavily on government budget appropriations and the chairs and members of their boards as well as senior management tend to be political appointees. Hence, ARAs in Africa are neither autonomous nor insulated from political control or influence. Autonomous Funds could be established in such a way as to avoid this problem.

As discussed in the previous chapter, Autonomous Development Funds in Africa are at different stages of evolution or conception. In Tanzania, the Cultural Development Trust Fund is operational, while in Uganda and Zambia, Funds are at an exploratory stage. The Cultural Development Fund in Tanzania has an independent board of nine persons representing all major stakeholders and has attracted donor and local funds. The Cultural Fund has successfully served as a model of how funds can be used in ways that benefit their clients and that enhance the principles of good governance. The successful implementation of Development Funds in Sub-Saharan Africa will require African leaders to embrace the new thinking about dispensing development aid. Such leaders will need the political will and discipline to reduce patronage and corruption and genuinely pursue a policy-driven development agenda. This will take time, but will eventually have to be done. There is no viable alternative if Africa is to have a successful future.

In Zambia, efforts to implement Autonomous Funds have revolved mainly around using existing public and private financial institutions as intermediaries. However, as we have argued in Chapter Six, the use of existing institutions is not a good idea, as these tend to be vulnerable to intrusive politics and corruption (the twin challenges that the ADF model seeks to avoid or undermine). It is, however, possible for existing local and national institutions to compete for ADF funds and hence become *end users* rather than *intermediaries*. There is an urgent need for African countries and donors, as well as powerful national and international NGOs, to advocate the establishment of Autonomous Funds in selected African countries on either a pilot or experimental basis. This is vital, as the success of such programmes could be used to persuade reluctant or uncommitted African governments and donors to participate in this new development enterprise. Without such efforts, it will take much longer to establish viable autonomous development funds on the continent. And time is not on the side of millions of marginalized African people.

In addition to institutional reforms aimed at creating executive agencies or Autonomous Development Funds, there are other changes in the public sector designed to improve the extent of institutional professionalism and efficiency. For example, Mackey (1999) contends that reforming Management Development Institutions in Africa could be critical for providing the technical and professional training for the managers required to run autonomous funds. Although this idea sounds a good one, the inherent danger is that most of these institutions (for example the Uganda Management Institute and the Kenya Institute of Administration) are either highly politicized or incapable of performing the new and challenging tasks required under the ADF model. However, as we have argued previously, such Management Development Institutions, like other pre-existing institutions, public and private, would be allowed to compete for monies dispersed by Autonomous Funds.

Noel et al. (1999) propose the use of a development-cooperative model rather than development assistance. The model is based on the assumption that institutions of higher learning (the universities) are best suited to bridge the gap between top-down state policies and the bottom-up NGO development assistance strategies that are currently dominant. In Africa, Malawi and Mali have successfully established such collaborative partnerships within sectors of government or academic institutions.

Unlike land grant universities in the United States, which have an outreach mission and possess experience in cooperative initiatives, African universities are ill suited for bridging the gap between the state and NGOs. More importantly, reliance on government ministries or government-controlled African universities to create and utilize a development-cooperative model could bring in problems of political interference, corruption and inefficiency. Use of pre-existing institutions in Africa always carries that risk. Again, such institutions could be end users of Autonomous Funds rather than intermediaries.

For African countries to achieve sustainable development, they need to strengthen and deepen the ongoing institutional reforms in the public sector. At the same time, executive agencies need to be expanded beyond tax revenue collection and road transportation to cover social and development sectors. And they must be insulated from politics. On the other hand, pilot and experimental Autonomous Development Funds should be created or transformed into operational bodies, as happened with the Tanzania Cultural Development Trust Fund. The state is expected to take a leading role in the tripartite partnership. It should proactively pursue a broad and collaborative development strategy, with a focus on transforming smallholder (subsistence) agriculture and the non-farm economy, using NGOs, MFIs and community-based organizations. This means that the state's role in economic activity needs to be reconfigured, not reduced (Speth, 1997). The 'smarter' developmental state would be ideologically committed to development, and its elite would seek to derive their political legitimacy primarily from economic performance. Such regimes could be democratic, quasi-democratic, or even authoritarian, provided they deliver economic performance and safeguard basic human rights.

Although most African states lack the human and institutional capacity to pursue and implement their policy priorities effectively, they are poised to acquire such capabilities through successful institutional reform. This would change their behaviour towards development, corruption and patronage. Furthermore, African leaders could learn lessons from their counterparts in Botswana where, since independence in the late 1960s, the leadership has been committed to achieving both democracy and economic development through the creation of strong public institutions insulated from politics.

Under the proposed ADF model, African countries have the chance to restrict corruption, patronage and *clientelism* while, at the same time, improving competency, professionalism and efficiency in core social and economic development sectors. The ADF model has the potential to provide the *retreating African state* (damaged by SAPs and PRSPs) another opportunity to return to the centre of the development process. Critics of the model, who claim it will reduce or diminish government involvement in the economy and allow donor control of the development process, are mistaken.

While the African state is expected to take the lead in the proposed triple partnership for development, donors are expected to facilitate the coordination and dispensing of development aid in Africa. Increasingly, country poverty reduction strategy programmes or national development plans include NGOs and MFIs in efforts to achieve growth and poverty reduction. However, under the new tripartite approach both governments and donors should treat NGOs as true partners or *equals* in the development process (Hyden, 1995). And the partnership with NGOs should both be consistent and lasting, rather than temporary or short-lived.

To serve both government institutions and the non-governmental sector well, the proposed ADF model may have to operate through various windows, or a tiered system, to allow maximum flexibility and increased access to its resources by the poor. This would ensure that public, private, and civil society organizations all compete for funds, but on a level playing field.

On their own, none of these stakeholders – government, NGOs, donors, and even the private sector – can achieve economic development. Hence, the best strategy to achieve sustainable development is one that engages all these stakeholders around national development priorities. Inevitably, a new policy-driven development agenda in Sub-Saharan Africa, such as the one proposed here, will demand fresh thinking amongst all stakeholders in the development debate. Perhaps more importantly, it will require a proactive and visionary political leadership. Ultimately, the three main developmental actors have to identify and reinforce areas of mutual cooperation in order to create a true and working *triple partnership*. To achieve this, the three stakeholders in the development process will have to undertake a reappraisal of their strategies and a redefinition of their roles. And if this happens, it will bring about Africa's rebirth, or what Thabo Mbeki, former South African President, called the 'African Renaissance' (Mbeki, 2001: 178).

Bibliography

ACCION (2007). 'Guidelines to Achieve Social Performance'. *Insight* No. 24.

Acemoglu, D. and Johnson, S. (2006). 'Disease and Development: The Effect of Life Expectancy on Economic Growth'. *NBER Working Paper No. 12269.*

Acharya, Y.P. and Acharya, U. (2006). 'Sustainability of Microfinance Institution from Small Farmers' Perspective: A Case of Rural Nepal', *International Review of Business Research Papers*, 2 (2), 117–26.

Adnan, A. (2004a). 'Effects of Agricultural Credit and Microfinance on Expenditure Patterns in Yemen'. PhD Thesis submitted to the Graduate School of Graduate Studies, Universiti Putra Malaysia, May 2004.

Adnan, A. (2004b). 'The Small Skill Credit Awareness and Decision-Making Among the Rural Women in Yemen'. A working paper.

Adedeji, A., Teriba, O. and Bugembe, P. (eds) (1991). *The Challenge of African Economic Recovery and Development.* London: Frank Cass.

AfCoP Casebook (2010). 'Managing for Development Results: A Focus on Africa'. <http://www.afcop-mfdr.org> accessed 24 February 2011.

African Development Bank and World Bank (2011). 'Leveraging Migration for Africa: Remittances, Skills, and Investments'. <http://www.africa.eu-partnership.org> accessed 11 July 2011.

Africa Economic Outlook (2008). Uganda. AfDB/OECD.

Africa Governance Initiative (2011). <http://www.africagovernance.org> accessed 3 July 2011.

Africa Growth Initiative (2011). 'Foresight: The Continent's Greatest Challenges and Opportunities for 2011'. Brookings Institution, January 2011.

Africa Progress Panel (2010). Africa Progress Report 2010, Geneva, Switzerland.

Africa Progress Panel (2011). Africa Progress Report 2011. Geneva, Switzerland.

Aghion, A.B. and Murdoch, J. (2005). *The Economics of Microfinance.* Cambridge, Massachusetts: MIT Press.

Aghion, P., Howitt, P. and Mayer-Foulkes, D. (2004). 'The Effect of Financial Development on Convergence: Theory and Evidence', *The Quarterly Journal of Economics*, 120 (1), 173–222.

Allen, H. (2008). 'Questions to Hugh Allen on Village Savings and Loan Associations (VSLAs)'. <http://www.microfinancegateway.org> accessed 24 February 2010.

Apter, D.E. and Rosberg, C.G. (eds) (1994). *Political Development and the New Realism in Sub-Saharan Africa*. Charlottesville and London: University Press of Virginia.

Arimah, B.C. (2004). 'Poverty Reduction and Human Development in Africa', *Journal of Human Development*. 5 (3), 399–415.

Armendariz, B. and Morduch, J. (2010). *The Economics of Microfinance*. Cambridge, Massachusetts: The MIT Press.

Arnold, S.H. and Nitecki, A. (eds) (1990). Culture and Development in Africa. Trenton, N.J.: Africa World Press.

Arun, T., Imai, K. and Sinha, F. (2006). 'Does the Microfinance Reduce Poverty in India? Propensity Score Matching based on a National-Level Household Data'. Institute for Development Policy and Management, University of Manchester, Working Paper, No. 17.

Ashe, J. (2007). 'Saving for Change: A Savings-Led, Asset Building, Sustainable Strategy for Providing Basic Financial Services to the Rural Poor'. Oxfam America, June 2007.

Asian Development Bank Institute (2004). 'Characteristics of Microfinance in Asia and Latin America'. <http://www.abdi.org/discussion-paper> accessed 9 March 2010.

A (Uganda) Civil Society Perspective. (2009). 'Unlocking Uganda's Development Potential'. <http://www.ngoforum.or.ug> accessed 9 March 2010.

Babri, M. and Von Dorp, M. (2009). 'The Commercialization Debate: A Contextual Study of Microfinance in India'. Master's Thesis submitted to Umea University School of Business Education, October 2009.

Bagala, A. (2009). 'Fake SACCOS Fail Prosperity for All Programme'. <http://www.monitor.co.ug> accessed 14 March 2009.

Bajaj, V. (2010). 'In Capitalism, Sun's Co-founder Sees a Pathway to Help the Poor'. *The New York Times Business Day*, 6 October, B1 and B4.

Bakewell, O. (2007). 'Keeping Them in Their Place: The Ambivalent Relationship Between Development and Migration in Africa'. *International Migration Institute (IMI), University of Oxford, Working Paper No. 8*.

Ballantyne, M. (2009). 'Microfinance: Entering a New Era' <http://www.knol.google.com> accessed 9 March 2010.

Banerjee, A. and Esther, D. (2004). 'Do Firms Want to Borrow More? Testing Credit Constraints Using a Directed Lending Program'. CEPR Discussion Papers, No. 4681.

Bangura, A.K. (2009). 'A Time Series Analysis of the African Growth and Opportunity Act: Testing the Efficacy of Transnationalism', *Journal of Third World Studies*, XXVI (2), 31–50.

Bareebe, G. (2011). 'Walk-to-Work Campaign Continues'. <http://www.monitor. co.ug/news/national> accessed 5 May 2011.

Barigaba, J. (2009). 'Uganda Development Plan Enters Key Stage'. <http://www. theeastafrican.co.ke/news> accessed 11 November 2009.

Barnes, C., Gaite, G. and Kibombo, R. (2001). 'The Impact of Three Microfinance Programs in Uganda', AIMS, Brief No. 30.

Barnes, C. and Sebstad, J. (2000). 'Guidelines for Microfinance Impact Assessments'. Discussion paper for the CGAP 3 Virtual Meeting, 18–19 October 1999.

Barr, M.S. (2005). 'Microfinance and Financial Development', *Michigan Journal of International Law*, 26 (271), 271–96.

Basu, B., Blavy, R. and Yulek, M. (2004). 'Microfinance in Africa: Experience and Lessons from Selected African Countries'. International Monetary Fund Working Paper, WP/04/174.

Bates, R.H. (1981). *Markets and States in Tropical Africa: The Political Basis of Agricultural Policies*. Berkeley: University of California Press.

Baum, A. and Lake, D.A. (2003). 'The Political Economy of Growth: Democracy and Human Capital'. *American Journal of Political Science*, 47 (2), 333–47.

Bazaara. N. (2001). *Structural Adjustment Participatory Review Initiative*. Center for Basic Research. Kampala, Uganda.

Bbumba, S.N.M. (2009). Budget Speech Financial Year 2009/10. Delivered to the Ugandan Parliament by Minister of Finance, Planning and Economic Development. 11 June 2010.

Bebbington, A.J. and Bebbington, D.H. (2001). 'Development Alternatives: Practice, Dilemmas and Theory', *Area*, 33 (1), 7–17.

Bebbington, A. and Farrington, J. (1993). 'Governments, NGOs and Agricultural Development: Perspectives on Changing Inter-Organizational Relationships'. *The Journal of Development Studies*, 29 (2), 199–219.

Bell, R., Harper, A. and Mandivenga, P. (2002). 'Can Commercial Banks Do Microfinance? Lessons from the Commercial Bank of Zimbabwe and the Co-operative Bank of Kenya', *Small Enterprise Development Journal (SED)*, 13 (4), 35–46.

Benin, S. et al. (2008). 'What is New Under the Restructured NAADS?' <http:// www.naads.or.ug> accessed 24 February 2010.

Berberoglu, B. (ed) (2010). *Globalization in the 21st Century: Labor, Capital, and the State on a World Scale*. New York: Palgrave Macmillan.

Berger, M., Goldmark, L. and Miller-Sanabria, T. (eds) (2006). *An Inside View of Latin American Microfinance*. Washington DC: Inter-American Development Bank.

Bolton, G. (2008). *Africa Doesn't Matter*. New York: Arcade Publishing.

Brett, E.A. (1998). 'Responding to Poverty in Uganda: Structures, Policies and Prospects', *Journal of International Affairs*, 52 (1), 313–37.

Brown, C. (2009). 'Democracy's Friend or Foe? The Effects of Recent IMF Condition-ality in Latin America', *International Political Science Review*, 30 (4), 431–57.

Brown, S.S. (2011). 'Toward a Theory of Transnational Transfers'. Book chapter pre-pared for a volume on transnational transfers and global development.

Buss, T.F. (2005). 'Microcredit in Sub-Saharan Africa', *Journal of Microfinance*, 4 (1), 1–11.

Buss, T.F. (2008). 'Microenterprise in International Perspective: An Overview of the Issues'. <http://www.spaef.com> accessed 28 February 2010.

Butagira, T. (2011). 'Museveni Wants Constitution Amended'. *Daily Monitor*, 11 May, 1. <http://www.monitor.co.ug/news/national> accessed 11 May 2011.

Butagira, T., Wandera, D., Wanumbwa, R. and Bareebe, G. (2011). 'Museveni Agrees to Meet Besigye' 28 April, 2011. *Daily Monitor* <http://www.monitor.co.ug/news/national> accessed 28 April 2011.

Campion, A. (2001). 'Challenges to Microfinance Commercialization', *Journal of Microfinance*. 4 (2), 57–65.

Carlton, A., Manndorff, H., Obara, A., Reiter, W. and Rhyne, E. (2001). 'Microfinance in Uganda'. Prepared for the Austrian Ministry of Foreign Affairs, Department of Development Cooperation, Wien, Austria, 17 December 2001.

Cartwright, J., Khandker, S.R. and Pitt, M.M. (2006). 'Empowering Women with Microfinance: Evidence from Bangladesh', *Economic Development and Cultural Change*, 54 (4), 791–831.

CGAP. (2006). 'Competition and Microcredit Interest Rates'. *Focus Note 5*, No. 33, February 2006.

Changa Management Services. (1997). 'Report on Potential Intermediaries for Autono-mous Development Fund'. Report prepared for the Zambian National Economic Advisory Council.

Charitonenko, S. (2003). 'Commercialization of Microfinance: The Philippines'. Manila, Philippines, Asian Development Bank.

Charitonenko, S. and Campion, A. (2004). 'Expanding Commerical Microfinance in Rural Areas: Constraints and Opportunities'. Paper prepared for an international conference on Best Practices.

Charitonenko, S. and DeSilva, D. (2002). 'Commercialization of Microfinance: Sri Lanka'. Manila, Philippines, Asian Development Bank.

Charitonenko, S. and Rahman, S.M. (2002). 'Commercialization of Microfinance: Bangladesh'. Manila, Philippines: Asian Development Bank.

Cheru, F. and Obi, C. (eds) (2010). *The Rise of China and India in Africa*. London: Zed Books.

Cheston, S. and Kuhn, L. (2002). *Empowering Women through Microfinance*. A UNIFEM Publication.

Chhotray, V. and Hulme, D. (2009). 'Contrasting visions for aid and governance in the 21st century: White House Millennium Challenge Account and DFID Drivers of Change', *World Development*, 37 (1), 36–49.

Christen, R.P. (2000). 'Commercialization and Mission Drift: The Transformation of Microfinance in Latin America'. Paper prepared for CGAP, 22 December 2000.

Cjokesje. K. (1997). 'Autonomous Development Funding: The Zambian Experience'. Paper presented at a workshop on establishing an Autonomous Development Fund in Africa. Arusha, Tanzania, 24–26 February 1997.

Clinton, W. (2007). *Giving: How Each of Us Can Change the World*. New York: Alfred A. Knopf.

Cohen, M. and Sebstad, J. (1999). 'Microfinance Impact Evaluation: Going Down Market'. Paper prepared for the World Bank Conference on Evaluation and Poverty Reduction, 14–15 June 1999.

Coleman, E. (2002). 'Microfinance in Northeast Thailand: Who Benefits and How Much?'. ERD Paper Series No. 9. Asian Development Bank.

Collier, P. (2007). 'Uganda Launches Country Economic Memorandum'. <http://web.worldbank.org> accessed 24 February 2010.

Commission for Africa Report. (2005) <http://www.commissionforafrica.org> accessed 10 November 2010.

Commission of the European Communities. (2005). 'EU Strategy for Africa: Towards a Euro-African Pact to Accelerate Africa's Development'. Brussels, Belgium.

Copestake, J. (2006). 'Mainstreaming Microfinance: Social Performance Management or Mission Drift?'. An updated working paper.

Copestake, J. (2007). 'Mainstreaming Microfinance: Social Performance Management or Mission Drift?', *World Development*, 35 (10), 1721–38.

Costello, D. (2010). 'Can Microlending Save Haiti?'. *The New York Times*, 14 November, 1 and 6.

Counts, A. (2004). 'Microfinance and the Global Development Challenge'. <http://www.usinfo.state.gove> accessed 19 August 2008.

Counts, A. (2008). 'Reimagining Microfinance'. *Stanford Social Innovation Review*, 6 (1), 46–53 <http://www.ssireview.org> 10 February 2010.

Crabb, P.R. (2007). 'The Success of Microfinance: What Really Sustains This Poverty Relief Effort?' Working paper. Northwest Nazarene University, School of Business.

Craig, D. and Porter, D. (2003). 'Poverty Reduction Strategy Papers: A New Convergence', *World Development*, 31 (1), 33–59.

Crandall, W. (2010). 'Revenue Administration: Autonomy in Tax Administration and the Revenue Authority Model'. Technical Notes and Manuals, International Monetary Fund, June 2010.

Cull, R. Demirgue-Kunt, A. and Morduch, J. (2007). 'Financial Performance and Outreach: A Global Analysis of Leading Microbanks', *Economic Journal of the Royal Economic Society*, 117 (517), 107–33.

Cull, R. Demirgue-Kunt, A. and Morduch, J. (2008). *Microfinance Meets the Market*. New York University Wagner Graduate School, May 2008.

Daley-Harris, S. and Awimbo, A. (eds) (2006). *More Pathways Out of Poverty*. Bloomfield, Connecticut: Kumarian Press.

Datar, S.M., Epstein, M.J. and Yuthas, K. (2008). 'In Microfinance, Clients Must Come First'. *Stanford Social Innovation Review*, 6 (1), 38–45.

DeCapua, J. (2011). 'Ugandan Government Asked to Probe Security Force Violence'. <http://www.printthis.clickability.com> accessed 9 May 2011.

Deininger, K. and Okidi, J. (2003). 'Growth and Poverty Reduction in Uganda, 1999–2000: Panel Data Evidence', *Development Policy Review*, 21 (4), 481–509.

Delegation of the European Commission to Uganda. 'EU-Uganda, A Sustainable Trade Relationship'. <http://www.deluga.ec.europa.eu> accessed 14 February 2010.

DeLorenzo, M. (2007). 'China's Footprint in Africa is Expanding. What Will be the Actual Extent of China's Role on the Continent?' <http://www.aei.org> accessed 10 August 2010.

DeMel, S., Gutierrez-Nieto, B., Serrano-Cinca, C. and Marmolinero, C. (2007). 'Microfinance Institutions'. <http://www.isb.uzh.ch> accessed 10 February 2010.

Deng, L.A. (1998). *Rethinking African Development: Toward A Framework for Social Integration and Ecological Harmony*. Trenton, New Jersey: Africa World Press.

Deshpande, R., Pickens, M. and Messan, H. (2006). 'Uganda: Country-Level Savings Assessment'. A C-GAP Savings Initiative, April 2006.

DeSousa-Shields, M. (2007). 'Evaluation of Africap Microfinance Fund'. Micro Report No. 84, prepared for USAID, September 2007.

DeSousa-Shields, M. and King, B. (2005). 'MFI Financing Strategies and the Transition to Private Capital'. Micro Report No. 32, prepared for USAID, June 2005.

DFID/FSDU (2007). 'Study of the Effects of the Regulations for Microfinance Deposit Taking Institutions on the Microfinance Sector in Uganda', accessed 26 February 2010.

Dicklich, S. (1998b). *The Elusive Promise of NGOs in Africa: Lessons from Uganda*. New York: St. Martin's Press.

Dijkstra, A.G. and Van Dorge, J.K. (2001). 'What Does the "Show Case" Show? Evidence of and Lessons From Adjustment in Uganda', *World Development*. 29 (5), 841–63.

Dillon, S. (2010). 'Interview with Amartya Sen, Nobel Economist'. The New York Times, 20 June, A22.

DiRubbo, P. and Canali, G. (2008). 'A Comparative Study of E.U. and U.S. Trade Policies for Developing Countries: The Case of Agri-Food Products'. 12th Congress of the European Association of Agricultural Economists – EAAE 2008.

Doran, A. (2006). 'Private Sector Microfinance: From Poverty to Power'. <http://www.fpsp.org> accessed 10 February 2010.

Drake, D. and Rhyne, E. (eds) (2002). *The Commercialization of Microfinance: Balancing Business and Development*. Bloomfield, Connecticut: Kumarian Press.

Dunford, C. (2001). 'Building Better Lives: Sustainable Integration of Microfinance with Education in Health, Family Planning and HIV/AIDS Prevention for the Poorest Entrepreneurs'. A discussion paper commissioned by the Microcredit Summit Campaign.

Dunford, C. (2006). 'Evidence of Microfinance's Contribution to Achieving the Millennium Development Goals'. Prepared for Global Microcredit Summit, Halifax, Nova Scotia, Canada, 12–15 November 2006.

Dunford, C. (1999). 'The Holy Grail of Microfinance: Help the Poor and Sustainable?' Working Paper No. 5, Freedom from Hunger, Davis, California, 14 November 1999.

Dunford, C. (2005). 'Toward a Complete Progress Tracking System'. The SEEP Network Progress Note. No. 9, June 2005.

Durning, A.B. (1998). 'Action at the Grassroots: Fighting Poverty and Environmental Decline'. A Working Paper.

Duscha, M. (2008a). 'Microcapital Story: A Brief Survey on the Impact of Microfinance on Women'. Parts 1, 2, and 3 of a Series: *Targeting Women and its Effect on the Well-being of Poor Families*. <http://www.microcapital.org> accessed 8 December 2008.

Duscha, M. (2008b). 'Microcapital Story: Ugandan Government to Set Up Laws for Regulating its Microfinance Sector'. <http://www.microcapital.org> accessed 24 February 2010.

Easterly, W. (2003). 'Can Foreign Aid Buy Growth?' <http://www.dri.fas.nyu.edu/docs/10/11783> accessed 22 April 2011.

Easterly, W. and Reshef, A. (2010). 'African Export Successes: Surprises, Stylized Facts, and Explanations'. National Bureau of Economic Research (NBER) Working Papers Series, #16597. <http://www.nber.org/papers/w16597> accessed 22 April 2011.

Economic Commission for Africa (1989). 'African Alternative Framework to Structural Adjustment Programmes for Socio-Economic Recovery and Transformation (AAF-SAP)'. United Nations Economic Commission for Africa, Addis Ababa, Ethiopia.

Economic Commission for Africa (2011). 'Economic Report on Africa 2011: Governing Development in Africa – The Role of the State in Economic Transformation'. UNECA, Addis Ababa, Ethiopia, March 2011.

Economic Report on Africa (2011). 'Africa's Need for a Developmental State: Opportunities and Challenges'. <http://www.uneca.org/era2011>. Chapter 5, 95–114, accessed 11 May 2011.

Edigheji, O. (2005). 'A Democratic Developmental State in Africa? A Concept Paper'. Research Report No. 105, Center for Policy Studies, Johannesburg, South Africa, May 2005.

Edwards, M. and Hulme, D. (eds) (1997). *Beyond the Magic Bullet: NGO Performance and Accountability in the Post-Cold War World*. New York: St. Martin's Press.

Edwards, M. and Hulme, D. (1998). 'Too Close for Comfort? The Impact of Official Aid on Nongovernmental Organizations', *Current Issues in Comparative Education*, 1 (1), 6–28.

Edwards, M. and Hulme, D. (eds) (2001). *Beyond the Magic Bullet: NGO Performance and Accountability in the Post-Cold War World*. Sterling VA: Kumarian Press.

Eicher, C.K. and Staatz, J.M. (eds) (1984). *Agricultural Development in The Third World*. Baltimore and London: The Johns Hopkins University Press.

Eid, F. (2006). 'Recasting Job Creation Strategies in Developing Regions: A Role for Entrepreneurial Finance', *Journal of Entrepreneurship*, 15 (2), 115–43.

Ejigu, L. (2009). 'Performance Analysis of a Sample Microfinance Institutions of Ethiopia', *International NGO Journal*. 4 (5), 287–98.

Ekman, J. (2009). 'Political Participation and Regime Stability: A Framework for Analyzing Hybrid Regimes', *International Political Science Review*, 30 (1), 7–31.

Ellerman, D. (2008). *Helping People Help Themselves: From the World Bank to an Alternative Philosophy of Development Assistance*. Ann Arbor, Michigan: The University of Michigan Press.

Ellerman, D. (2002). 'Rethinking Development Assistance: An Approach Based on Autonomy – Respecting Assistance'. A working paper.

El Mansour Diop. (2001). 'New Partnership for Africa's Development', *Africa Quarterly*, 41 (4), 1–12.

Epstein, G. (2005). *Financialization and the World Economy*. Cheltenham, U.K. and Northampton, MA: Edward Elgar.

Fernando, N.A. (2004). 'Micro Success Story? Transformation of NGOs into Regulated Financial Institutions'. Speech delivered at the Regional Workshop on Commercialization of Microfinance, Bali, Indonesia, 25–27 May 2004.

Finan, G. (1972). *Not Much Time for the Third World*. London: Oswald Wolff Publishers.

FinScope Uganda (2007). 'Results of a National Survey on Access to Financial Services in Uganda'. Final report produced for DFID's Financial Sector Deepening Uganda Project, August, 2007.

Fiorillo, A. (2006). 'The Effects of Wholesale Lending to SACCOs in Uganda'. Final Report.

Fjeldstad, O.H. and Moore, M. (2009). 'Revenue Authorities and Public Authority in Sub-Saharan Africa', *Journal of Modern African Studies*, 47 (1) 1–18.

Gadzala, A. and Hanusch, M. (2010). 'African Perspectives on China – Africa: Gauging Popular Perceptions and Their Economic and Political Determinants'. Afro Barometer, Working Paper No. 117.

Gaile, G., Duursma, M. and Eturu, L. (1999). 'Centenary Rural Development Bank Ltd.: Microenterprise Impact Assessment'. Final Report, 28 June 1999.

Gertner, J. (2010). 'The Rise and Fall of the G.D.P.'. *The New York Times Magazine*, 16 May, 60–70.

Getu, M. (2007). 'Does Commercialization of Microfinance Programs Lead to Mission Drift?', *Transformation*, 24 (3 and 4), 169–79.

Goetz, A.M. and Gupta, R.S. (1996). 'Who Takes the Credit? Gender, Power and Control Over Loan Use in Rural Credit Programs in Bangladesh', *World Development*, 24 (1), 45–63.

Goldberg, N. (2005). '*Measuring the Impact of Microfinance: Taking Stock of What we Know*'. Grameen Foundation: USA Publication Series.

Golola, M. (2001). 'Decentralization, Local Bureaucracies and Service Delivery in Uganda'. Discussion Paper No. 2001/115.

Gonzalez, E.M. (1995). 'Autonomous Development Funds in the Philippines', *Development Dialogue* (2), 53–66.

Gonzalez-Vega, C. (1998). 'Microfinance: Broader Achievements and New Challenges'. Rural Finance Program, Ohio State University.

Goodwin-Groen, R., Bluett, T., and Latortue, A. (2004). 'Uganda Microfinance Sector Effectiveness Review'. C-GAP Report, October 2004.

Government of Uganda (2007). 'Five Year National Development Plan for Uganda: PEAP Revision Process 2007/08'. Top Management Retreat Proceedings Report, 10 September 2007.

Government of Uganda (2000). 'Medium-term Competitive Strategy for the Private Sector (2000–2005)'. Ministry of Finance, Planning and Economic Development, August 2000.

Government of Uganda (2000). 'Microfinance Institutions, Monitoring and Evaluation Survey Draft Report'. Ministry of Finance, Planning and Economic Development, March 2000.

Government of Uganda (2000). 'Plan for Modernisation of Agriculture: Eradicating Poverty in Uganda.' Ministry of Finance, Planning and Economic Development, August 2000.

Government of Uganda (2001). 'The Plan for Modernization of Agriculture (PMA).' Ministry of Finance, Planning and Economic Development, March 2001.

Government of Uganda (2003). 'Uganda's Progress in Attaining the PEAP Targets – in the Context of the Millennium Development Goals'. Background paper prepared by the Ministry of Finance, Planning and Economic Development.

Governor, Bank of Uganda (2001). Remarks by the Governor, Bank of Uganda, at the Uganda Revenue Authority Reception, 16 February 2001.

Gramajo, A.M. (2006). 'Where Did the Miracle Come From? Exploring Institutional Formation in Botswana', *Laissez-Faire*, 26, 45–54.

Green, E. (2010). 'Patronage, District Creation and Reform in Uganda', *Studies in Comparative International Development*, 45 (1), 83–103.

Gumede, V. (2011). 'Can Foreign Aid Buy Growth?' <http://www.thenewage.co.za> accessed 19 April 2011.

Gutierrez-Nieto, B. and Serrano-Cinca C. (2007). 'Factors Explaining the Rating of Microfinance Institutions', *Non-profit and Voluntary Sector Quarterly*, 36 (3), 439–64.

Gyezaho, E. (2009). 'Twenty-Three Years Later … Has Museveni Delivered the Fundamental Change?'. <http://www.monitor.co.ut> accessed 30 January 2009.

Hansen, H.B. and Twaddle, M. (eds) (1998b). *Developing Uganda*. Oxford: James Currey.

Hansen, H.B. and Twaddle, M. (eds) (1998a). *Uganda Now: Between Decay and Development*. London: James Curry.

Harper, C.L. and Leicht, K. (2007). *Exploring Social change: America and the World*. Upper Saddle River, New Jersey: Prentice Hall.

Hatch, J.K. and Frederick, L. (1998). 'Poverty Assessment by Microfinance Institutions: A Review of Current Practice'. Microenterprise Best Practices. <http://www.povertytoools/documents> accessed 10 August 2010.

Hartungi, R. (2007). 'Understanding the Success Factors of Microfinance Institutions in a Developing Country', *International Journal of Social Economics*, 34 (6), 388–410.

Heinbecker, P. (2011). 'The Future of the G20 and Its Place in Global Governance'. GIGI G20 Papers, No. 5, April 2011.

Hermes, N. and Lensik. R. (2007). 'The Empirics of Microfinance: What Do We Know?', *Economic Journal of the Royal Economic Society*, 117 (517), 1–10.

Hermes, N., Lensink, R. and Meesters, A. (2008). 'Outreach and Efficiency of Microfinance Institutions'. Center for International Banking, Insurance and Finance

(CIBIF), University of Groningen, the Netherlands and the University of Nottingham, UK.

Hillbom, E. (2008). 'Diamonds or Development? A Structural Assessment of Botswana's Forty Years of Success', *Journal of Modern African Studies*, 46 (2), 191–214.

Hishigsuren, G. (2007). 'Evaluating Mission Drift in Microfinance: Lessons for Programs with Social Mission', *Evaluation Review*, 31 (3), 203–60.

Hishigsuren, G. (2006). 'Transformation of Micro-finance Operations from NGO to Regulated MFI'. A working paper.

Hogarth, R. (2009). 'Microfinance Paper Wrap-up: Bangladesh' by Stephanie Charitonenko and S.M. Rahman. <http://www.microcapital.org> accessed 25 August 2010.

Hoon, P. and Hyden, G. (2001). 'Governance and Sustainable Livelihoods'. A working paper.

Howes, M. (1997). 'NGOs and the Development of Local Institutions: A Ugandan Case Study', *The Journal of Modern African Studies*, 35 (1), 17–35.

Hulme, D. and Moore, K. (2006). 'Why Has Microfinance Been a Policy Success in Bangladesh (and Beyond)? A working paper'. Institute for Development Policy and Management, University of Manchester, United Kingdom.

Hyden, G. (2008). *African Politics in Comparative Perspective*. New York: Cambridge University Press.

Hyden, G. (2006). 'Introduction and Overview to the Special Issues on Africa's Moral and Affective Economy', *African Studies Quarterly*, 9 (1 & 2), 1–8. <http://www.africa.ufl.edu/asq/> accessed 10 November 2010.

Hyden, G. (2005). 'Making Public Sector Management Work for Africa: Back to the Drawing Board'. Economic Research Working Paper No. 80. Prepared for the African Development Bank, November 2005.

Hyden, G. (1995a). 'Reforming Foreign Aid to African Development: A Proposal to Set Up Politically Autonomous Development Funds', *Development Dialogue* (2), 34–52.

Hyden, G. (1998). 'Reforming Foreign Aid to African Development: The Politically Autonomous Development Fund Model', *African Studies Quarterly*, 2 (2), 1–15.

Hyden, G. (1998). 'The Autonomous Development Fund Model: A Reply to Olatende Ojo'. <http://www.afarica.ufl.edu/asg/v2/v2i4a5.html> accessed 20 October 2010.

Hyden, G., Court, J. and Mease, K. (2004). *Making Sense of Governance: Empirical Evidence from Sixteen Developing Countries*. Boulder and London: Lynn Rienner Publishers.

Hyden, G., Okoth-Ogendo, H.W.O., and Oluwo, B. (eds) (2000). *African Perspectives on Governance*. Trenton, New Jersey: Africa World Press.

IAMFI (2008). 'The Commercialization of Microfinance: Fostering Industry Sustainability through Social Performance Indicators'. A position paper prepared by the International Association of Microfinance Investors (IAMFI), May 2008.

Id21 (2004). 'Realising the Potential of Microfinance'. *Insights*, 51. <http://www.id21. org> accessed 10 February 2010.

IFAD (2002). 'Rural Financial Services Programme Report and Recommendations of the President of Uganda'. Rome, Italy, 4–5 September 2002.

IFAD (2010). 'Rural Poverty Report 2011'. Rome, Italy, November 2010.

Ingves, S. (2005). 'Microfinance: A View from the Fund'. Paper prepared for the International Monetary Fund, 25 January 2005.

Jacobson, J.L. (1999). 'Uganda: The Provision of Microfinance in the Wake of Conflict'. *Microfinance and Development*. Johns Hopkins University, School of Advanced International Studies, May 1999.

J-Intersect Research Review. (2005). 'Microfinance for Profit'. <http://www.jintersect. com> accessed 19 April 2011.

John Paul II (1995). 'Post-Synodal Apostolic Exhortation ECCLESIA in Africa'. Yaounde, Cameroon, 14 September 1995.

Joughin, J. and Kjoer, A.M. (2009). 'The Politics of Agricultural Policy Reforms: The Case of Uganda'. A working paper.

Juuko, S. (2010). 'Uganda: URA Capacity in Spotlight'. <http://www.allafrica.com/ stories> accessed 29 November 2010.

Kabeer, N. (2001). 'Conflicts Over Credit: Re-evaluating the Empowerment Potential of Loans to Women in Rural Bangladesh', *World Development*, 29 (1), 63–84.

Kaikai, L. (2011). 'Museveni Defends Police Action on Protests'. <http://www.monitor.co.ug/news/national> accessed 3 May 2011.

Kairu, P. (2009). 'Uganda SACCOS Struggling with Poor Governance'. *The Monitor*, 31 December, 1.

Kamanyi, J. (2003). 'Development Assistance, Gender and Enterprise Development Impact Assessment: The Case of Uganda'. Poverty Reduction Strategy Paper prepared for the University of Manchester, UK Conference On Women in Sustainable Enterprise (WISE) Development, November 2003.

Kanyeihamba, G. (2011). 'Establish National Oil Council'. <http://www.monitor. co.ug/OpEd/commentary> accessed 17 April 2011.

K'aol, G.O. and Ochanda, R. (2000). 'Factors Influencing the Establishment of Microfinance Schemes in Kenya'. Nairobi: United States International University.

Kapper, A. (2007). 'Commercialization of Microfinance Institutions'. Finance and International Business, Paris Graduate School of Management, 24 June 2007.

Karlan, D. (2001). 'Microfinance Impact Assessments: The Perils of Using New Members as a Control Group'. A working paper.

Karlan, D. and Valivia, M. (2007). 'Teaching Entrepreneurship: Impact of Business Training on Microfinance Clients and Institutions'. Working Papers No. 107, Center for Global Development.

Kasirye, I. (2007). 'Rural Credit Markets in Uganda: Evidence from the 2005/6 National Household Survey'. Economic Policy Research Center, Makerere University, Kampala, Uganda.

Katz, R. (2008). 'The Commercialization of Microfinance: The Good, The Bad, and The Ugly'. <http://www.blogacumenfund.org> accessed 25 August 2010.

Khandker, S.R. (2005). 'Microfinance and Poverty: Evidence Using Panel Data from Bangladesh', *World Bank Economic Review*, 19 (2), 263–86.

Kibikyo, D.L. (2008). 'Assessing Privatization in Uganda'. PhD Dissertation, Department of International Development Studies (IDS), Roskilde University Center (RUC), Denmark.

Kilibo, C. and Schmidt, O. (2006). 'Anything but Credit? Financial Services "Going Micro". The Case of Uganda', Development and Cooperation, 33 (1), 21–3.

Kimenyi, M.S. (2009). 'Four Ways to Help Africa?' <http://www/brookings.edu/opinions> accessed 6 April 2010.

Kirsten, M. (2006). 'Linkages Between Formal and Informal Financial Institutions in Extending Financial Services to the Poor'. <http://www.dbsa.org/Research/Documents/Linkages> accessed 30 March 2006.

Kline, G. (2000). 'In Search of a New Development Paradigm', paper presented at the 18th Association of Third World Studies (ATWS) Conference, Denver, Colorado, October 2000, 19–21.

Koehn, P.H. and Ojo, O.J.B. (eds) (1999). *Making Aid Work: Innovative Approaches for Africa at the Turn of the Century*. Lanham: University Press of America.

Kristof, N. (2010). 'Here's a Woman Fighting Terrorism with Microloans'. *The New York Times Sunday Opinion*, 14 November, 10.

Kristof, N. (2011). 'Three Cups of Tea, Spilled'. *The New York Times*, Op-Ed, 21 April, A21.

Kristof, N. and WuDunn, S. (2009). *Half the Sky: Turning Operations in Opportunity for Women Worldwide*. New York: Alfred A. Knopf.

Kron, J. (2011). 'Opposition Leader Arrested in Uganda Protest'. *The New York Times*, 19 April, A10.

Kron, J. (2011). 'Protests in Uganda Build to Angry Clashes'. *The New York Times*, 30 April, A4.

Kron, J. (2011). 'Protests in Uganda Over Rising Prices Grow'. *The New York Times*, 22 April, A8.

Kron, J. (2011). 'Uganda Opposition Leader Wounded During Protest'. *The New York Times*, 15 April, A7.

Kulabako, F. (2009). 'Uganda's SACCOS to Get Funds Directly from Government'. <http://www.allafrica.com/stories> accessed 24 February 2010.

Labie, M. (2005). 'Microfinance: Making Profit for the Poor?' Paper written in support of a debate at the University of Antwerp, Brussels, 17 October 2005.

Lafourcade, A.L., Isern, J. Mwangi, P. and Brown, M. (2005). '*Overview of the Outreach and Financial Performance of Microfinance Institutions in Africa*'. Publication of the Microfinance Information Exchange (MIX).

Lanero, F. (2011). 'Hoot at Your Own Risk, Police Tell Protesters'. *Daily Monitor*, 23 May <http://www.monitor.co.ug/news/national> accessed 24 May 2011.

Lapenu, C. and Zeller, M. (2001). 'Distribution, Growth and Performance of Microfinance Institutions in Africa, Asia, and Latin America'. FCND Discussion Paper No. 114, June 2001.

Lauer, K. (2008). 'Transforming NGO MFIs: Critical Ownership Issues to Consider'. Prepared for CGAP, Paper 13, June 2008.

Lee, H.K. (2010). 'Microcapital Brief: Bypassing Microfinance Institutions, Uganda Savings and Credit Cooperatives (SACCOS) to Get Funds Directly from Government-Run Microfinance Support Center (MSC)'. <http://www.microcapital.org> accessed 24 January 2010.

Littlefield, E., Murduch, J. and Hashemi, S. (2003). 'Is Microfinance an Effective Strategy to Reach the Millenium Development Goals?'. A working paper.

Lokeris, P. (2009). 'Oil Speech by Minister of State for Mineral Development in Uganda'. <http://mediacentre.go.ug> accessed 11 January 2010.

Makara, S., Rakner, L. and Svasand, L. (2009). 'Turnaround: The National Resistance Movement and the Reintroduction of the Multi-party System in Uganda', *International Political Science Review*, 30 (2), 185–204.

Makoba, J.W. (1998). *Government Policy and Public Enterprise Performance in Sub-Saharan Africa: The Case Studies of Tanzania and Zambia, 1964–1984*. Lewiston: The Edwin Mellen Press.

Makoba, J.W. (2002). Nongovernmental Organizations (NGOs) and Third World Development: An Alternative Approach to Development', *Journal of Third World Studies*, XIX (1), 53–63.

Makoba, J.W. (1999). 'Rethinking current Explanations of Political changes in Sub-Saharan Africa', *Journal of Third World Studies*, XVI (2), 61–73.

Makoba, J.W. (1997). 'The Role of Africa's Culture in Economic Development', *Makerere Political Science Review*, 1 (2), 116–26.

Makoba, J.W. (2001). 'Toward the Commercialization of Microfinance Institutions: A Global Phenomenon', *Austrian Journal of Development Studies*, XVII (3 and 4), 353–63.

Maksudora, N. (2009). 'Contribution of Microfinance to Growth: Transmission Channel and the Ways to Test It'. Center for Economic Research and Graduate Education, Charles University, Prague, the Czech Republic.

Maldonado, J., Gonzalez-Vega, Y. and Vivianne, R. (2002). 'The Influence of Microfinance on Human Capital Formation: Evidence from Bolivia'. Paper presented at the Seventh Annual Meeting, Latin American and Caribbean Economics Association, October 2002.

Malinga, M. (2004). 'Uganda Microfinance Union: Impact Report', February 2004.

Management Systems International Report. (1995). '*Impacts of Microfinance*', submitted to USAID/Uganda, June 1995.

Matovu, D. (2006). 'Microfinance and Poverty Alleviation in Uganda: A Case Study of Uganda Finance Trust'. A Master's Thesis, School of Global Studies, Groteborgs University, Sweden.

Mattiano, G. (2006). 'The Rural Impact of Microfinance: Measuring Economic, Social and Spiritual Development in Kabale, Uganda'. MA Thesis submitted to the Graduate School of Arts and Sciences, Georgetown University, Washington DC, April 2006.

Mbaku, J.M. (2009). 'Governance, Wealth Creation, and Development in Africa: The Challenges and Prospects'. 4 (4) <http://www.web.africa.ufl.edu/asg> accessed 26 February 2010.

Mbeki, T. (2001). 'Speech of Thabo Mbeki', *Africa Quarterly*, 41 (1–2), 171–8.

McMichael, P. (ed.) (2010). *Contesting Development: Critical Struggles for Social Change*. New York and London: Routledge.

McMichael, P. (2008). *Development and Social Change: A Global Perspective*. Thousand Oaks, California: Pine Forge Press.

McNeil, Jr., D.G. (2010). 'Global Fight Against AIDS Falters as Pledges Fail to Reach Goal of $13 Billion'. *The New York Times*, 6 October, A10.

Mehta, S.C. (2002). 'Structural Adjustment in Africa: A Review Article', *Africa Quarterly*, 42 (1), 61–70.

Mengisteab, K. (1996). *Globalization and Autocentricity in Africa's Development in the 21st Century*. Trenton, New Jersey: Africa World Press.

Meredith, M. (2005). *The Fate of Africa: From the Hopes of Freedom to the Heart of Despair*. New York: Public Affairs.

Mersland, R. and Strom, R.O. (2007). 'Performance and Corporate Governance in Micro-finance Institutions'. A working paper.

Meyer, R.L. (2001). 'Microfinance, Poverty Alleviation, and Improving Food Security: Implications for India'. Rural Finance Program, Ohio State University, 31 December 2001.

Meyer, R.L. (2007). 'Microfinance Services for Agriculture: Opportunities and Challenges'. Paper presented at the International Conference on 'What Microfinance for Developing Countries' Agriculture?' Pierre Mendes France Conference Centre, Paris, 4–6 December 2007.

MFI Solutions (2008). 'The Implications of Increased Commercialization of the Microfinance Industry: What Can we Learn from the Discussions that Followed the Compartamos IPO?' <http://www.microfin.com> accessed 26 February, 2010.

Michel, S. and Beuret, M. (2009). *China Safari: On the Trail of Beijing's Expansion in Africa*. New York: Nation Books.

Micro Capital (2006). 'Ugandan President Attacks High Interest Rates of Microfinance Institutions'. <http://www/microcapitalmonitor.com> accessed 26 February 2010.

Micro Capital Institute (2004). 'The Commercialization of Microfinance in Latin America'. <http://www.microcapital.or> accessed 10 February 2010.

Micro-Credit Summit E-news (2007). 'Compartamos IPO: Microfinance Doing Good, or the Undoing of Microfinance?' <http://www.microcreditsummit.org/enews> accessed 26 February 2010.

Microfinance Institutions Database Survey Report. (2002). The Ministry of Finance, Planning and Economic Development, March 2002.

MicroRate (2004). 'Uganda Finance Trust Performance Rating' <http://www.microrate.com/> accessed 17 April 2011.

Mills, G. (2010). 'Why is Africa Poor?' Development Policy Briefing Paper No. 6, CATO Institute, Washington DC.

Mkandawire, T. (2001). 'Thinking About Developmental States in Africa', *Cambridge Journal of Economics*, 25 (3) 289–313.

MkNelly, B. (1992). 'Literature Review of the Likely Impact of the *Credit with Education* Strategy'. Freedom from Hunger, Davis, California, May 1992.

MkNelly, B., Watetip, C. and Lassen, C.A. (1996). 'Preliminary Evidence that Integrated Financial and Educational Services Can be Effective Against Hunger and Malnutrition'. Freedom from Hunger Research Paper No. 2, Freedom from Hunger, Davis, California.

Mohapatra, S., Ratha, D., and Silwal, A. (2010). 'Outlook for Remittances Flows 2011–12'. Migration and Development Brief #13, Migration and Remittances Unit, World Bank, Washington DC, 8 November 2010.

Mokaddem, L. (2009). 'Concept Note on Microfinance Scaling Up in Africa: Challenges Ahead and Way Forward'. African Development Bank, June 2009.

Moncrieffe, J.M. (2004). 'Beyond Categories: Power, Recognition and the Conditions for Equity'. Background paper prepared for the World Development Report 2006.

Moon, B.E. (2007). 'The Great Divide in Microfinance: Political Economy in Microcosm'. Paper, Department of International Relations, Lehigh University, 25 October 2007.

Morduch, J. (1999). 'The Microfinance Promise', *Journal of Economic Literature*, 37 (4), 1596–614.

Morduch, J. (1998). 'The Microfinance Schism'. Paper prepared for a meeting with CGAP, USAID, ACCION International and Harvard Institute for International Development, Cambridge, MA, Spring 1997.

Moyo, D. (2009). *Dead Aid*. New York: Farrar, Strauss and Giroux.

Mpuga, P. (2004). 'Demand for Credit in Rural Uganda: Who Cares for the Peasants?'. Paper presented at the Conference on Growth, Poverty Reduction and Human Development in Africa at the Center for the Study of African Economics, 21–22 March 2004.

Mufumba, I. (2010). 'Prosperity for All: Myths versus Realities'. <http://www.observer.ug> accessed on 24 February 2010.

Mugerwa, Y. and Imaka, I. (2011). 'Opposition MPs Walk Out as NRM Pass Jet Fighter Billions'. <http://.monitor.co.ug/news/national> accessed 28 April 2011.

Muhumuza, W. (2008). 'From Fundamental Change to No Change: The NRM and Democratization in Uganda', *Les Cashiers*, 2 (41), 21–42.

Mukasa, H. and Mukiibi, H. (2010). 'Bonna Bagaggawale Launched'. <http://www.newvision.co.ug> accessed 26 February 2010.

Mulondo, E. (2011). 'Catholic Bishops Call for Reason in Parliament'. Sunday Monitor, 12 June, <http://www.monitor.co.ug/news> accessed June 11, 2011.

Mulondo, E. and Wesaka, A. (2011). 'Lawyers Petition Chief Justice over Judicial Abuse'. *Daily Monitor 5 May* <http://www.monitor.co.ug/news/national> accessed 5 May 2011.

Museveni, Y.K. (1997). *Sowing the Mustard Seed: The Struggle for Freedom and Democracy in Uganda*. London and Oxford: Macmillan.

Museveni, Y.K. (2007). Speech on the official launch of 'Prosperity for All (PFA) Program'. <http://www.statehouse.go.ug/news> accessed 24 February 2010.

Museveni, Y.K. (2009). 'State of the Nation Address'. <http://www.statehouse.go.ug/news> accessed 8 September 2009.

Museveni, Y.K. (1995). 'The Role of Independent Funds for Social and Economic Development in Africa'. An opening address at the ADF Workshop, Kamala Uganda. *Development Dialogue* (2), 7–10.

Musoke, D. (1995). 'Entandikwa – Third Time Lucky?' <http://www.thefreelibrary.com> accessed 26 February 2010.

Mutumba, R. and Osike, F. (2002). 'I Don't Love Money: Rwakakakooko Addressing Reporters in Kampala Yesterday'. <http://www.mail-archieve.com/uganda.net> accessed 28 November 2010.

Mwaniki, R. (2006). 'Supporting SMEs Development and the Role of Microfinance in Africa'. IAFI Africa Trust, Nairobi, Kenya, November 2006.

Namazzi, E. (2010). Interview with Dr Specioza Wandira Kazibwe, the former Chairperson of the Ugandan Microfinance Support Center. *Daily Monitor*, 13 February, 1 and 6.

Nannyonjo, J. and Nsubuga, J. (2004). 'Recognising the Role of Microfinance Institutions in Uganda'. Bank of Uganda Working Paper.

Natilson, N. and Bruett, T.A. (2001). 'Financial Performance Monitoring: A Guide for Board Members of Microfinance Institutions'.

Naumann, E. (2009). 'AGOA at Nine: Some Reflections on the Act's Impact on Africa – U.S. Trade'. <http://programmes.comesa.int/attachments/article/235/09_comesa_Agoa_at_10_SACU_Naumann> accessed 3 May 2011.

Ndegwa, P. (1985). *Africa's Development Crisis and Related International Issues*. Nairobi: Heinemann Press.

Ngai, M.W. (2008). 'Uganda: Corruption Responsible for Poor Infrastructure (commentary)'. <http://www.afrika.no/noop> accessed 24 February 2010.

New York Times editorials. (1997). 'Micro-Loans for the Very Poor'. *The New York Times*, 16 February, A18.

New York Times editorials (2011). 'Saving the Doha Round'. *The New York Times*, 29 April, A24.

Nicholas, M. (2010). 'Corruption Threatens Uganda Oil Revenue – Opposition'. <http://uk.finance.yahoo.com/new> accessed 22 August 2010.

Nossiter, A. (2011). 'Burkina Faso Police Join in Popular Unrest'. *The New York Times*, 29 April, A16.

Nossiter, A. (2011). 'Guineans Revel in Prospect of First Free Vote After Era of Repression'. *The New York Times*, 27 June, 4, 8.

Nossiter, A. (2011). 'In Burkina Faso, Leader Keeps Cool Under Fire'. *The New York Times*, 10 May, A5.

Nossiter, A. (2011). 'Thousands Demand President's Ouster in Burkina Faso'. *The New York Times*, 1 May, 6.

Nymugasira, W. and Rowden, R. (2002). 'Poverty Reduction Strategies and Coherency of Loan Conditions'. Uganda National NGO Forum, Kampala.

Obasanjo, O. (2005). Speech as Chairman of the African Union, on the Occasion of Africa Day 2005, Paris. May 25, 2005.

O'Donnell, G.A., Schmitter, P.C., and Whitehead, L. (eds) (1986). Transitions from Authoritarian Rule: Prospects for Democracy. Baltimore: The Johns Hopkins Press.

Ojo. O. (1998). 'Rethinking Hyden's Development Fund Model: A Critique and Suggestions for Modification', *African Studies Quarterly*, 2 (2), 17–32.

Okello, O.A.C. (2009). 'Opposition Response to the Government Budget Statement FY 2009/10' presented by Okoman A.C. Okello, MP (FDC).

Olita, R. (2008). 'Equity Bank Shareholders Approve Uganda Microfinance Buyout'. <http://www.newvision.co.ug> accessed 16 February 2010.

Olupot, M. and Bekunda, C. (2010). 'Parliament Passes Bill to Tax Oil Revenues', *The New Vision*, 7 October, 1.

O'Neil, M. (2005). 'Microfinance Matters: A Practical Look at the Future'. United Nations Capital Development Fund, Issue No. 13, June 2005.

Owusu, F. and Samatar, A.I. (1997). 'Industrial Strategy and the African State: The Botswana Experience', *Canadian Journal of African Studies*, 31 (2), 268–99.

Panjaitan-Drioadisuryu, R.D.M. and Cloud, K. (1999). 'Gender, Self-employment and Microcredit Programs: An Indonesian Case Study', *The Quarterly Review of Economics and Finance*, 39 (5), 769–79.

Park, A. and Ren, C. (2001). 'Microfinance with Chinese Characteristics', *World Development*, 29 (1), 39–62.

Parliament of Uganda (2009). 'Report of the Parliamentary Budget Office on the Analysis of Government Fiscal Performance for Fiscal Year 2008/09'.

Pattnaik, J. (2008). 'A Critique of Neo-Liberal Development Alternatives', *Mainstream* XLVI (26), 1–5 <http://www.mainstreamweekly.net/Article757> accessed 28 March 2010.

Paul, S. and Israel, R.A. (1991). *Nongovernmental Organizations and the World Bank: Cooperation for Development*. Washington DC: The World Bank.

Petras, J. and Veltmeyer, H. (2001). *Globalization Unmasked: Imperialism in the 21st Century*. London: Zed Books.

Phillips, M. (2002). 'Politics of Poverty Cited at the World Bank'. *The Wall Street Journal*, 13 September 2002, A2.

Pitt, M.M. and Khandker, S.R. (1997). 'The Impact of Group-Based Credit Programs on Poor Households in Bangladesh: Does the Gender of the Participants Matter?' A Research Paper.

PlaNet Rating (2003). 'FOCCAS Uganda Global Rating'. <http://www.planetrating. org> accessed 24 April 2008.

Polgreen, L (2011). 'Microcredit Pioneer Faces An Inquiry in Bangladesh'. *The New York Times*, 30 January, 10.

Polgreen, L. and Bajaj, V. (2010). 'Microcredit is Imperiled in India by Defaults'. *The New York Times*, 18 November, A5, A8.

Poyo, J. and Young, R. (1999). 'Commercialization of Microfinance: A Framework for Latin America'. USAID Microsenterprises Best Practices Project. Washington DC: Development Alternatives Inc.

Provost, C. and Akinyemi, A. (2010). 'Europe and Africa: A Partnership of Equals?' *The Guardian*, 3 December 2010<http://www.guardian.co.uk/global-development/ poverty-matters> accessed 10 February 2010.

Rahman, S.M. (2004). 'Commercialization of Microfinance in Bangladesh Perspective'. <http://www.gdrc.org> accessed 26 February 2010.

Rapley, J. (2007). *Understanding Development: Theory and Practice in the Third World.* Boulder and London: Lynne Rienner Publishers.

Ratha, D. et al. (2011). *Leveraging Migration for Africa: Remittances, Skills, and Investments.* Washington DC: The World Bank.

Report of a Census of Financial Institutions in Uganda. (2006). The Ministry of Finance, Planning and Economic Development, June 2006.

Rhyne, E. and Busch, B. (2006). 'The Growth of Commercial Microfinance: 2004–2006: An Update to Characteristics of Equity Investments', Council of Microfinance Equity Funds (CMEF), September 2006.

Riddell, R.C. (1999). 'The End of Foreign Aid to Africa? Concerns about Donor Policies', *African Affairs*, 98 (392), 309–35.

Roberts, J.J. and Hite, A.B. (eds) (2007). *The Globalization and Development Reader: Perspectives on Development and Global Change.* Malden, Massachusetts: Blackwell.

Rozas, D. (2009). 'Throwing in the Towel: Lessons from MFI Liquidations [including FOCCAS Uganda]'. 20 September 2009. <http://www.microfinancegateway. org/p/site/m/template.rc/1.9.38716> accessed 4 May 2010.

Sachs, J.D. (2005). *The End of Poverty: Economic Possibilities for Our Time.* New York: Penguin Books.

Salamon, L. (1994). 'The Rise of the Non-Profit Sector', Foreign Affairs, 73 (4), 111–22.

Saleh, S. (2009). 'Savings Schemes: A Solution to Poverty'. <http://www.mediacenter. go.ug> accessed 14 March 2009.

Samatar, A.I. and Samatar, A.I. (eds) (2002). *The African State: Reconsiderations.* Portsmouth, New Hampshire: Heinemann Press.

Sanger, D. and Kramer, A.E. (2010). 'U.S. Lands Russia on Barring Arms to Iran, as Obama Speaks to U.N.'. *The New York Times*, 23 September, A11.

Schmidt, R.H. (2008). 'Microfinance, Commercialisation and Ethics'. Working Paper No. 194.

Scoop News (2008). 'Mission Drift in Microfinance Institutions'. <http://www.scoop.co.nz/stories> accessed 9 March 2010.

Sebstad, J., Neil, C. Barnes, C. and Chen, G. (1995). 'Assessing the Impacts of Microfinance Interventions: A Framework for Analysis'. USAID's Global Bureau/Office of Microenterprise Development, March 1995.

Sebudubudu, D. Lotshwa, O.K. (2008). 'Managing Resources and the Democratic Order: Lessons from Botswana'. University of Botswana. A working paper.

Semboja, J. and Therkildsen, O. (eds) (1995). Service Provision Under Stress in East Africa, Copenhagen, Denmark: Center Development Research.

Sen, A. (1999). *Development as Freedom*. Oxford: Oxford University Press.

Senghor, J.C. (2009). *'Going Public: How Africa's Integration Can Work for the Poor'*. London: Africa Research Institute.

Sengupta, R. and Aubuchon, C. (2008). 'The Microfinance Revolution: An Overview', *Review*, 90 (1), 9–30.

Sharma, M., Zeller, M., Henry, C., Lapenu, C. and Helms, B. (2000). 'Assessing the Relative Poverty Level of MFI Clients: Synthesis Report based on Four Case Studies', prepared for C-GAP, June 2000.

Shaw, T. and Mbabazi, P. (2004). 'Two Africas? Two Ugandas? An African Democratic Developmental State? Or Another Failed State?'. Centre for Foreign Policy Studies, Working Paper No. 125. <centreforforeignpolicystudies.dal.ca/pdf/fff-mbabazi.pdf> accessed 14 March 2011.

Shil, N.C. (2009). 'Microfinance for Poverty Alleviation: A Commercialized View', *International Journal of Economics and Finance*, 1 (2), 191–205.

Shivji, I.G. (2005). 'Revisiting the Debate on National Autonomous Development'. Faculty of Law, University of Dar es Salaam, Tanzania.

Shivji, I.G. (2007). *Silences in NGO Discourse: The Role and Future of NGOs in Africa*. Oxford: Fahamu.

Simanowitz, A. (2001). 'ImpAct: Improving Impact of Microfinace on Poverty'. A proposal submitted to the Ford Foundation, March 2001.

Simanowitz, A. (2008). 'The What, Why and How of Impact Assessments', <http://www.microfinancegateway.org> accessed 18 August 2010.

Smith, D. (2009). 'Change Beckons for Billionth African'. *The Guardian* 28 December 2009 <http://www.guardian.co.uk/world> accessed 26 February 2010.

Smith, W.E. (1972). *We Must Run While They Walk: A Portrait of Africa's Julius Nyerere*. New York: Random House.

Snodgrass, D.R. and Sebstad, J. (2002). 'Clients in Context: The Impacts of Microfinance in Three Countries: Synthesis Report'. <http://www.cgap.org/gm/document-1.9.907> accessed 12 August 2008.

Sowell, S. (2008). 'A Comparative Study of Corporatism in Jamaica and Venezuela'. Georgia Political Science Association, Conference Proceedings.

Speth, J.G. (1997). 'Governance for Sustainable Human Development'. UN Management Development and Governance Report, January 1997.

Ssewanyana, S., Matovu, J.M. and Twimukye, E. (2010). 'Building on Growth in Uganda'. Working Paper prepared for The World Bank, Washington DC.

'State of Microcredit Summit Report'. (2005). *Microcredit Summit E-News*, December 2005.

Steffek, J. (2009). 'Who Compensates the Losers? Embedded Liberalism, Inequality and the Limits of Global Governance'. Technical University, Darmstadt, Germany.

Strom, S. (2010) 'A Marriage of Differing Missions: Joining Charity and Business: A Novel Idea, But Problematic'. *The New York Times Business Day*, 26 October 2010, B1, B8.

Taylor, I. (2002). 'Botswana's Developmental State and the Politics of Legitimacy'. Paper prepared for a conference co-sponsored by the Political Economy Research Centre, University of Sheffield and the Centre for the Study of Globalisation and Regionalisation, University of Warwick, United Kingdom, 4–6 July 2002.

Taylor, I. (2003). 'Ditiro Tsa Ditlhabololo: Botswana as a Developmental State'. *Botswana Journal of African Studies*, 17 (1), 37–50.

Terms of Contract Between the Norwegian Ministry of Foreign Affairs (MFA) and Tanzania Culture Trust Fund to Support the Strategic Plan for 2005–2007. (2004).

The 2010 Ibrahim Index of African Governance. <http://www.moibrahimfoundation.org/en/section/the-ibrahim-index/methodology> accessed 18 September 2010.

The African Capacity Building Foundation. (2011). 'Africa Capacity Indicators 2011'. Harare, Zimbabwe.

The Second Special Assembly for Africa of the Synod of Bishops. *The General Secretariat of the Synod of Bishops, Vatican City State* (2009).

Tisdell, C. and Zhunge, R. (1999). 'Sustainability Issues and Socioeconomic Change in the Jingdo Communities of China', *International Journal of Social Economics*, 26 (1), 21–45.

Todd, H. (ed) (2000). 'Poverty Reduced through Microfinance: the Impact of ASHI in the Philippines'. Cashpor. <http://www.microfinancegateway.org/gm/document-1.9.25891/19274_N_087.pdf> accessed 2 May 2010.

Tripp. A.M. (2000). *Women and Politics in Uganda.* Oxford: James Curry.

Tumukwasibwe, R. (2010). 'Parliament and the Politics of Poverty Reduction in Uganda: A Critical Appraisal', *The International Journal of Human Rights*, 14 (1), 51–74.

Tumusiime-Mutebile. (2010). 'Uganda's Experience in Regulating Microfinance Deposit-Taking Institutions'. Paper presented by the Governor, Bank of Uganda at a Conference on Microfinance Regulation, WHO Benefits, Dhaka, Bangladesh, 15–17 March 2010.

Tutu, D. (2010). 'Obama's Overdue AIDS Bill'. *The New York Times*, Op-Ed, 21 July 2010, A23.

Tvedt. T. (1998). *Angels of Mercy or Development Diplomats? NGOs and Foreign Aid.* Trenton: New Jersey: Africa World Press.

UCSD Secretariat (2007). 'Government Should Urgently Clear the Anxiety Around Bonna Bagaggawale (Prosperity for All)', *Uganda Sustainability Bulletin*, May–June 2007.

Uganda Investment Authority (UIA) (2007). 'Business Parks Implementation Manual'. Kampala, Uganda. 2007.

Uganda National Development Plan, 2010–2015. Government of Uganda, 2010.

Uganda National Farmer's Federation (2009). 'Farmers' Agriculture Sector Specific Growth Policy Concerns and Proposals to Government and Stakeholders for Action'.

UNDP (2009). 'Overcoming Barriers: Human Mobility and Development'. Human Development Report, New York.

UN Economic and Social Commission for Asia and the Pacific. (2001). 'The Emerging Role of the Private Sector in Delivering Social Services in the ESCAP Region'. Social Policy Paper, No. 4, 2001.

United Nations Capital Development Fund (2004). 'Microfinance Programme Impact Assessment 2003'. Based on case studies in Haiti, Kenya, Malawi and Nigeria. Enterprising Solutions Global Consulting LLC. <http://www.undp.org/exec-brd/pdf/main%20report.pdf> accessed 12 June 2010.

Uphoff, N., Esman, M.J., and Krishna, A. (eds) (1998). *Reasons for Success: Learning from Instructive Experiences in Rural Development.* West Hartford, Connecticut. Kumarian Press.

U.S. Department of State, Bureau of African Affairs. 'Background Note: Uganda' (2010). <http://www/state/gov> accessed 2 February 2010.

Van de Walle, N. (1999). 'Aid's Crisis of Legitimacy: Current Proposals and Future Prospects', *African Affairs*, 98 (392), 337–52.

Vanroose, A. (2007). 'Microfinance: Are its Promises Ethically Justified?'. A working paper.

Van Santen, R.M. (2010). 'Microfinance as a Poverty Reduction Policy'. A working paper.

Ver Hagen, K. (2001). 'Overview of Conventional and New Approaches Towards Impact Assessment'. Paper prepared for a European-based microfinance support organization, 30 May 2001.

Vision Reporter. (2011). 'Parties Boycott Dialogue with Government', *New Vision*, 2 May. <http://www.newvision.co.ug> accessed 3 May 2011.

Von Soest, C. (2009). 'Stagnation of a "Miracle": Botswana's Governance Record Revisited'. Working Papers No. 94, GIGA Research Papers, Hamburg, Germany.

Vor de Bruegge, E. (1994). 'Freedom from Hunger's *Credit with Education*: A Self-Help Strategy to Eliminate Chronic Hunger'. Testimony presented to the US Congress Subcommittee on Foreign Agriculture and Hunger, Sustainable Development Hearing, 1 March 1994.

Wakoko, F. (2010). *Microfinance and Women's Empowerment in Uganda: From Rhetoric to Empowerment*. Berlin: VDDM Verlag Publishers.

Wavamuno. C. (2007). 'Report on the Third African Microfinance Conference', 20–3 August 2007, Kampala, Uganda.

Weinformers (2010). 'Uganda Diaspora Remittances Increase to Two Billion According to World Bank Report on Africa Remittances'. <http://www.weinformers. net> accessed 21 April 2011.

Wellard, K. and Copestake, J. (eds) (1993). *NGOs and the State in Africa: Rethinking Roles in Sustainable Agricultural Development*. London: Routledge.

Westover, J. (2008). 'The Record of Microfinance: The Effectiveness/Ineffectiveness of Microfinance Programs as a Means of Alleviating Poverty'. *Electronic Journal of Sociology*, 5 (3), 1–8.

Westover, J. (2010). 'The Record of Microfinance: The Effectiveness/Ineffectiveness of Microfinance Programs as a Means of Alleviating Poverty', <http://www. abloggersuniverse.com> accessed 12 March 2010.

Wharton, A.S. (ed) (2007). *The Sociology of Organization*. Los Angeles, California: Roxbury Publishing Company.

Wines, M. (2010). 'China Fortifies State Business to Fuel Growth: Government is Taking a Larger Stake in the Economy'. *The New York Times*, 20 August, A1 and A6.

Wong, E. (2011). 'Two Schools, One Complicated Situation'. *The New York Times*, Philanthropy, 24 April, wk5.

World Bank. (1998). *Assessing Aid: What Works, What Doesn't, and Why*. Oxford: Oxford University Press.

World Bank. (2007). *The Global Citizen's Handbook: Facing Our World's Crises and Challenges*. New York: Harper Collins.

World Development Report (2004). 'Making Services Work for Poor People'. <http://ebooks.ebookmall.com/ebook/172351> accessed 10 June 2009.

World Development Report (2011). The World Bank, Washington, D.C.

Wrenn, E. (2005). 'Microfinance Literature Review for Trocaire'. <http://www.scribd.com/doc/48267761/MICRO> accessed 23 August 2008.

Yee, D. (2003). 'A Book Review of Amartya Sen's *Development as Freedom*'. <http://www.dannyreviews.com> accessed 10 May 2009.

Yildirim, A.K. (2008). 'Microfinance for the Poor: Burden or Blessing?' <http://www.fountainmagazine.com> accessed 29 August 2010.

Yu, W. (2003). 'Is the "Everything But Arms" Initiative All Good News and Everything the EU Can Do for the LDCs?' Policy Brief No. 8, Danish Research Institute of Food Economics, June 2003.

Zohir, S. and Matin, I. (2004). 'Wider Impacts of MFIs: Issues and Concepts', *Journal of International Development*, 16 (3), 301–30.

Index

Africa in Development

Series Editor: Jeggan C. Senghor
Institute of Commonwealth Studies, University of London

While African development remains a preoccupation, policy craftsmen and a multiplicity of domestic and international actors have been engaged in the quest for solutions to the myriad problems associated with poverty and underdevelopment. Academic and scholarly responses have built on traditional and non-traditional analytical frameworks and promoted a multidimensional discourse on, for example, conflict management, peace and security systems, HIV/AIDS, democratic governance, and the implications of globalization.

This series is designed to encourage innovative thinking on a broad range of development issues. Thus its remit extends to all fields of intellectual inquiry with the aim of highlighting the advantages of a synergistic interdisciplinary perspective on the challenges of and opportunities for development in the continent. Of particular interest are studies with a heavy empirical content which also have a bearing on policy debates and those that question theoretical orthodoxies while being grounded on concrete developmental concerns.

The series welcomes proposals for collected papers as well as monographs from recent PhDs no less than from established scholars.

Book proposals should be sent to oxford@peterlang.com.
